Praise for *Poor Workers' Unions*

"This is a wonderfully sunny history of recent ef[...]
commitments and tactical innovations of com[...]
movement, and especially to the ranks of low-wa[...]
—**Frances Fox Piven, coauthor of** *Poor People's* [...]
Why They Succeed, How they Fail

"This updated and revised edition of *Poor Workers' Unions* provides entry into a multiracial and multi-ethnic multitude of struggles inside and outside the union movement. It remains essential reading for students, scholars, and people who want to make their own history by organizing."
—**Michael Honey, author of** *Going Down Jericho Road: The Memphis Strike,*
Martin Luther King's Last Campaign

"*Poor Workers' Unions* is a much-needed reinterpretation of the labor movement since the 1960s. Vanessa Tait offers an expansive notion of both the meaning of labor and labor organizing—those who worked in traditional and nontraditional venues, for pay or not, nearly all of whom understood class as intimately bound up with race, gender, and ethnicity. This book offers hope and a vision for building a broad-based workers' movement. It is essential reading for anyone who cares about social justice or the future of the labor movement."
—**Premilla Nadasen, author of** *Household Workers Unite:*
The Untold Story of African American Women Who Built a Movement

"As working people seek to envision a new labor movement, they will find invaluable inspiration in the hidden history of social justice unionism revealed in Vanessa Tait's *Poor Workers' Unions*."
—**Jeremy Brecher, author of** *Strike!* **and**
Climate Insurgency: A Strategy for Survival

"This updated edition of *Poor Workers' Unions* more than provides a usable past for today's 'alt-labor' taxi drivers, domestic workers, freelancers, fast-food servers, retail clerks, and day laborers. Vanessa Tait shows that another labor movement is possible, one rooted in racial, gender, immigrant, and economic justice, that bridges community and workplace. In offering strategic lessons and inspiring stories, she envisions a brighter future for the people made by the people for all."
—**Eileen Boris, coauthor of** *Caring for America:*
Home Health Workers in the Shadow of the Welfare State

"Vanessa Tait's *Poor Workers' Unions*, upon its original publication a classic of incisive history and lucid interpretation, now reappears at a crucial moment, as the

demographic transformation of the working class accelerates. The threat of worsening conditions stands alongside the urgency and the possibility of new organizing. Tait's thorough revisions, Fletcher's foreword, and Tzintzún's afterword add vital updates and reminders. Buy this book and give it to your friends."
  —Paul Buhle, labor historian and editor of a dozen radical comic books

"With gripping tales of grassroots experiments in social justice unionism from the 1960s to the present, Vanessa Tait cracks wide open our concept of what a labor movement looks like, and shows how it can be part and parcel of movements for racial and gender justice. In the process, she does a stunning job of helping us imagine workers' movements that are creative, democratic, and, above all, build power from below—pointing the way to a vibrant future for labor."
  —Dana Frank, author of *Bananeras: Women Transforming the Banana Unions of Latin America*

"*Poor Workers' Unions* makes a critical contribution to the current debate about how unions can survive, in open-shop conditions, as voluntary membership organizations. Vanessa Tait emphasizes the importance of building workplace power through grassroots organization and rank-and-file control. This book reminds us that greater "participatory democracy"—a concept that animated progressive activism in the 1960s—should be the goal of labor and community organizing today."
  —Steve Early, former organizer for the Communications Workers of America and author of *Save Our Unions*

"While the AFL-CIO and its affiliated unions desperately try to figure out how to rebuild and energize the labor movement, Vanessa Tait reveals in this exceptional book that poor workers have been showing the way for the past forty years. Tait examines and analyzes in meticulous detail a wide range of movements organized by poor workers to improve their circumstances and build a more just society. She demonstrates that these movements were founded and developed upon principles of rank-and-file control, democracy, community involvement, and solidarity and aimed to improve all aspects of workers' lives. These are precisely the principles and aims upon which a new labor movement must be based but which the official labor movement has been slow to embrace. Both labor activists and labor historians will learn much from this book."
  —Michael Yates, author of *The Great Inequality* and *Why Unions Matter*

"As existing unions continue to bottom out and search fitfully for an answer to declining power and influence, Vanessa Tait's *Poor Workers' Unions* reveals the significance of successful labor organizational forms that demand our attention and understanding. Tait demonstrates that organizations with deep roots in communities are essential in paving the way for a more robust union movement in the United States. Bill Fletcher Jr. provides a compelling new foreword assessing challenges ahead as the US working class and trade unions seek to build a counterforce to the rapacious capitalist system. *Poor Workers' Unions* is essential reading for organizers and students of the American labor movement."

—Immanuel Ness, author of *Southern Insurgency: The Coming of the Global Working Class* and professor at City University of New York

Praise for the first edition:

"*Poor Workers' Unions* is an important and inspiring book about how workers of color and women workers are taking the lead in building democratic, grassroots labor and community movements even in today's hostile political climate."

—Karen Brodkin Sacks, professor of women's studies and anthropology, UCLA

"Vanessa Tait has made a critical contribution to broadening our understanding of who and what is the labor movement in the United States. With detail, analysis, and a compelling writing style, Tait captures the dynamism of alternative forms of working-class organization that have long been ignored. In formulating a new direction for organized labor in the United States, the history Tait addresses must become a recognized part of our foundation."

—Bill Fletcher, Jr., president, TransAfrica Forum and former assistant to AFL-CIO president John Sweeney

"At a time when the US labor movement is engaging in an unprecedented public debate over the course of its future—over what course will best assure that it has a future—one of the luckiest breaks we could hope for would be for an informed and talented labor communicator to publish a book that not only advocates a focus that has been missing from the discussion but also lays out the evidence of the past four decades for why this focus is critical to our success. *Poor Workers' Unions* does all that. This is the most important contribution yet to the current debate over the smartest direction for the labor movement's future."

—David Swanson, International Labor Communications Association, formerly communications coordinator for ACORN

"Rearranging the deck chairs on the *Titanic* won't revive the labor movement. *Poor Workers' Unions* examines some of the most exciting and impressive attempts to develop new forms to incorporate workers whom unions have largely neglected. Vanessa Tait makes a valuable contribution to the new impulse by showing us the struggles already under way."

—Dan Clawson, author of *The Next Upsurge: Labor and the New Social Movements*

"Vanessa Tait's insightful documentation of poor people's organizing and the labor movement over the last fifty years reminds us of this important history. *Poor Workers' Unions* is evidence that activism is not dead but has been rejuvenated under a broader justice agenda that addresses women and men's everyday lives."
—Mary Romero, author of *Maid in the U.S.A.*

"History has shown that periods of insurgence in the labor movement have been driven by workers who were formerly marginalized by the existing labor movement and that these workers have organized themselves and built institutions which differ markedly from existing unions. Tait's *Poor Workers' Unions* documents the contemporary recurrence of this historical pattern. The picture to which she gives us access offers hope to those of us who continue to anticipate a turnaround in the fortunes of the US labor movement."
—Peter Rachleff, author of *Hard-Pressed in the Heartland: The Hormel Strike and the Future of the Labor Movement*

"An impeccably researched book, *Poor Workers' Unions* will be of great interest to labor scholars, students, and activists. A strength of this book is that it disrupts the hegemony of whiteness and the (re)colonial mindset plaguing the labor movement."
—Dan Irving, *Review of Radical Political Economics*

"Stirred from sleep by its own near death and by relentless prodding from the activists whose work Tait chronicles, labor is rediscovering the shop-floor power and community magnetism of social justice unionism. Its most compelling vision now comes from veterans of poor workers' unions. Through their hard-won advances, those veterans have gained both the authority to reform unions from within and the resources to run bold organizing drives, such as Justice for Janitors and Hotel Workers Rising, among low-wage service workers, largely men of color and women."
—Nancy MacLean, professor of arts & sciences, Duke University and author of *The American Women's Movement: 1945–2000*

"Tait persuasively demonstrates that organized labor quickly strayed from its grassroots rank-and-file beginnings, becoming instead a conservative, class-based bureaucracy bent on the status quo and dismissive not only [of] poor workers but also of the real needs of workers everywhere—needs that stretch far beyond wages and benefits to encompass such social justice issues as welfare, childcare, housing, and immigrant rights as well as race and gender both in the workplace and community."
—*Altar Magazine*

Poor Workers' Unions

Rebuilding Labor from Below

Vanessa Tait

Haymarket Books
Chicago, Illinois

This edition published in 2016 by
Haymarket Books
P.O. Box 180165
Chicago, IL 60618
773-583-7884
www.haymarketbooks.org
info@haymarketbooks.org

ISBN: 978-1-60846-520-0

Trade distribution:
In the US, Consortium Book Sales and Distribution, www.cbsd.com
In Canada, Publishers Group Canada, www.pgcbooks.ca
In the UK, Turnaround Publisher Services, www.turnaround-uk.com
All other countries, Publishers Group Worldwide, www.pgw.com

This book was published with the generous support of Lannan
Foundation and Wallace Action Fund.

Cover design by Rachel Cohen. Cover photograph: Members of the
Coalition of Immokalee Workers, a human rights organization led by
Latino, Indigenous Mayan, and Haitian farmworkers, stand in front
of the workers' community center in Immokalee, Florida. © Laura
Emiko Soltis.

Library of Congress Cataloging-in-Publication data is available.

Entered into digital printing December, 2021.

To Tess, Craig, and Dana,
with love and gratitude

Contents

Members of SEIU Local 399, the janitors' union in Los Angeles, confront officials of their union who refuse to leave office after being defeated in an election, on the seventh day of a hunger strike in protest. Their headbands say "*huelgista*," which means "striker." At center, César Oliva Sanchez, who was elected as the local's executive vice president. *(Photo by David Bacon)*

Foreword

What makes *Poor Workers' Unions* so important is that it illuminates a struggle that has been under way for years over the soul of the labor movement. The original publication of *Poor Workers' Unions* helped to situate the rise of what has come to be known as "alt-labor," that is, a quasi-alternative labor movement that includes but is not limited to elements of the current trade union movement. Vanessa Tait was successful in both elaborating the history of alternative labor formations that have arisen since the 1960s and addressing changes that started to unfold within organized labor in the 1990s that appeared to be possible harbingers of a revitalized union movement—and quite possibly a new labor movement.

I

Poor Workers' Unions has played a critical role in helping many in the scholar and activist communities to appreciate several elements of a larger equation. The trade union movement is a subset of a larger labor movement. Today such a recognition may not appear to be particularly profound, but there was until recently (and I would argue still is) an assumption that trade union movement equals labor movement. Such an identification not only is historically wrong but has resulted in bad analysis and bad strategy.

Labor struggles and the labor movement in what is now the United States of America began during the colonial period, when

Europeans arrived on these shores, commenced the process of the attempted annihilation of Native Americans, and established a class structure that had a small wealthy ruling elite and a large laboring population that included workers and farmers. Among the workers, at least initially, were a mass of indentured servants and some slaves, with the indentured servant population including Africans, Europeans, and some Native Americans.

In North America, the Caribbean, and what we now know as Latin America, the rulers quickly encountered a problem: the workers did not like the situation in which they found themselves. Whether it was indigenous slaves in the mines of Peru, African slaves in St. Dominique (now Haiti and the Dominican Republic), or African and European indentured servants in the thirteen US colonies, these laboring populations continuously revolted against their horrendous conditions. *This* was the beginning of the labor movement. Whether in the form of slave conspiracies, secret societies, guilds, sabotage, or runaways, the laboring classes objected to the conditions under which they lived. It was only in the 1830s and 1840s that, in what was by that time the United States of America, organizations that could be described as "trade unions" came into existence as *one* manifestation of the resistance that workers undertook in the face of their oppression and exploitation.

The fact that workers continuously revolted against their conditions presented a major problem for the ruling elites. There were more laborers than there were wealthy. In most colonies throughout the hemisphere, there were moments when the colonial rulers wondered whether Judgment Day had arrived—for them. Bacon's Rebellion in Virginia in 1676 was a case in point. The African and Irish slave-servant conspiracy in New York in 1741 was another example. This meant that the colonial ruling classes had to put in place a mechanism to ensure the long-term stability of the system that we have come to know as capitalism. The solution was largely found in the concept and operationalizing of *race*.

With borrowings from both the English experience in colonizing Ireland and the Castilian Reconquista in Spain, "race" was constructed out of whole cloth—but not out of science—as an institution to divide humanity into superior and inferior beings. What is critical to grasp about this is that the construction of race, and specifically the mythical notion of a "white race," was not a guarantee that everyone declared to be "white"—a category, I might add, that has evolved over the years—would have a good life. Rather, it existed to ensure that a certain segment of the European population adopted a "racial uniform," was never enslaved, and offered the poorest of the so-called whites an opportunity to identify with and believe that their future was to be found with the richest of the so-called whites, a class that held the poor in complete and utter contempt. This was and is constantly reinforced through a differential in treatment along so-called racial lines.

Rather than seeing African and indigenous, and eventually Latino and Asian communities as allies situated in the same or a similar trench, the white laboring classes held on to an ambivalence, and frequently an absolute hatred of those of us of color, seeing in us a threat—a distorted mirror of their own existence.

The bulk of what came to be known as "organized labor" not only has failed to grasp this history—and its implications—but utterly fears any significant discussion of this matter. Contained in such a discussion is a clue to the confusion and misery of the US white working class; a clue to the myth that most have embraced; a clue to the betrayal to which they have been subjected and to which they have been accomplices. Official organized labor has also been divided along gender lines. Women were not an add-on to the trade union movement. They were organizing from the beginning, but they were generally segregated and held subordinate positions to men in trade unions. Unions did not see the struggles against male supremacy as central and in certain cases were quite willing to sacrifice the interests of women (for example, after World War II, when women were purged from much of the manufacturing workforce).

Yet contained in this discussion is also another clue: a clue to a path that could lead to power for working people rather than their existence as the doormat of capital.

||

Poor Workers' Unions draws the reader's attention to the emergence of economic movements that were extensions of larger social movements against particular forms of oppression that went beyond the worker-capitalist binary. This recognition is important in so many ways. Whether one is discussing the National Welfare Rights Organization, the Black and Latino caucuses in the building trades, or the ACORN-sponsored United Labor Unions, these efforts largely grew out of larger struggles for political, social, *and* economic justice—most specifically, struggles against racial/national oppression and gender oppression. In that sense they were quite distinct from traditional organized labor.

Through a reading of *Poor Workers' Unions* one comes to better appreciate an ongoing, and frequently bitter, struggle within the labor movement generally, and the trade union movement in particular, between forces that gravitated toward one or another variant of social justice unionism and those that have congealed around a more traditional (albeit sometimes militant) business unionism. Historically excluded by and from the official trade union movement, many of the groups that can be classified as "poor workers' unions" have either written off the official trade union movement as hopelessly racist, sexist, and archaic—quite understandably—or fought tooth and nail for recognition by and entrance into the ranks of the official movement.

It is important to be explicit, when speaking of poor workers' unions, regarding those forces that have embraced such efforts and the challenges that have been faced. Some contemporary trade unions have been allies of poor workers (such as progressive locals of the American Federation of State, County and Municipal Employees [AFSCME], the Communications Workers of America [CWA], and the Service Employees International Union [SEIU]), though their support has sometimes been inconsistent. Well prior to the period covered by Tait, efforts to organize workers frequently divided along class lines. The early American Federation of Labor, for instance, chose to organize primarily skilled craft workers, to the exclusion of unskilled and semiskilled manufacturing workers. Operating like an aristocracy, this union was very resistant to anything that would transform the demographics and content of organized labor.

With the formation of first the Committee on Industrial Organization and later the Congress of Industrial Organizations, segments of the working class that had previously been dismissed gained a new hearing. But not all segments. Agricultural and domestic workers, explicitly excluded by the National Labor Relations Act, were still not fully accepted within the so-called house of labor.

It was largely the political left that championed segments of the working class that were excluded from trade union organizing. If one looks at the history of the CIO, for instance, one sees in the work of the unemployed movement and efforts to organize agricultural workers (in the 1930s) and other important sectors the mind and hand of the left.

Much of the work done in the 1960s and 1970s in the building of the newer poor workers' unions was also carried out by committed leftists, though of different and differing political stripes. The work of building these organizations, whether of the unemployed, semi-employed, or economically marginalized, was frequently undertaken by individuals who were *politically committed to this work as a long-term transformational project*, whether in trade unions or in community organizations. In other words, while spontaneous initiatives certainly emerged, it is equally true—to borrow from Antonio Gramsci—that within those spontaneous efforts there were various forms of leadership. Some of these leaders were members of organizations of the left or were simply ideologically committed leftists. The extent to which they publicized their politics, however, was a separate matter that is worthy of another discussion beyond the framework of this essay.

It was also no coincidence that many of the efforts coming under the rubric of poor workers' unions came out of movements of people of color and of women. With the purging of much of the left from the ranks of organized labor following the passage of the Taft-Hartley Act and the initiation of the Cold War, the official unions' commitment to the fight against racist oppression, let alone gender oppression, weakened to the point of near collapse, though certain unions were exceptions to this rule. Poor workers' unions, in whatever variant, emerged outside of officialdom in part because they had to. In the absence of a strategic commitment by official organized labor to unite with the movements of women and people of color, and to work to transform its own ranks, efforts had to arise independently, and so they did. But nearly all such movements were underresourced yet plagued with immense demands whether with regard to organizing, maintaining their base, advocating, or engaging in coalition building.

III

As Tait notes, by the mid- to late 1980s a change became noticeable within segments of official organized labor. The SEIU, CWA, AFSCME, the Hotel and Restaurant Employees, and several other unions concluded that the old way of operating was failing. New approaches to organizing, and in some cases representing, workers appeared, sometimes with promising breakthroughs.

As Fernando Gapasin and I attempted to convey in *Solidarity Divided*, such efforts, while important, were limited by the framework within which they operated. And herein lies a problem for the movements associated with poor workers' unions. Whenever worker centers or independent unions among the poor sought a relationship with official organized labor, there was an inherent challenge: would official organized labor undergo a transformation, or would the poor workers' unions serve as air pumped into a slowly leaking tire?

Efforts undertaken by the official trade union movement to address this crisis—including the 2009 election of John Sweeney, Richard Trumka, and Linda Chavez-Thompson to head the AFL-CIO; progressive reforms introduced in the AFL-CIO and several other unions in organizing, immigration, and foreign policy; and the desperate and misguided 2005 split in the AFL-CIO resulting in the Change to Win Federation—have been unable to address the deeply rooted causes of the dilemmas facing labor generally and the trade union movement specifically. As Gapasin and I have noted, such reform efforts have not addressed the ideological parameters of the movement itself. To put it differently, the social justice orientation of the poor workers' unions has not been adopted by most of the reformers within officialdom. Instead, reformers have sought to retain the structure, function, and raison d'être of a movement based largely on a "business unionist" orientation inherited from Samuel Gompers and his cohorts in the late nineteenth and early twentieth centuries.

A realization of the limitations—and failures—of union reform efforts must link with a recognition of the changes that the US working class has been undergoing over recent decades. Not only have there been profound demographic changes, including the expansion of the number of women workers in the formal workforce and the increase of migrant workers from the global South, but there has also been a pauperization of the working class as living standards have stagnated or declined. Under such circumstances, a labor movement worthy of its name is essential if there is to be a progressive shift in society as a whole. Yet such a labor movement will need to rethink itself down to the very fundamentals. It is for this reason that *Poor Workers' Unions* remains a valuable instrument for the reformation of the US labor movement.

What *Poor Workers' Unions* identifies is a *social justice unionism* that may include but is not limited to collective bargaining. In many cases this unionism has its sights set beyond workers' relationship with a particular employer or set of employers. In some cases the workers are taking on the state, or in this age of global capitalism they find themselves engaged in struggles that cross nation-state borders and involve workers whose "citizenship" is economic, located within the boundaries of transnational capitalism.

IV

At the 2010 US Social Forum in Detroit, Michigan, organizations from the contemporary "poor workers' movement" united to form what was initially titled the Excluded Workers Congress. Later renamed the United Workers Congress, this collection of worker centers, independent worker organizations, associations, and alliances—alt-labor—sought to raise attention to the demands of segments of the working class that had been excluded from the National Labor Relations Act, the official trade union movement, or both. This effort exists as part of the legacy of the movements and organizations examined by Tait.

The United Workers Congress and other segments of alt-labor face significant challenges in this era. Many of these organizations function with a 501(c)(3) format and structure and are, as a result, staff-driven or led by self-perpetuating boards of directors. This contrasts such organizations not only with unions, which at least formally have democratic structures, but also with mass membership–led organizations that are ultimately dependent on membership involvement and control.

Alt-labor is also faced with challenges surrounding resources. Many such organizations have limited budgets and are dependent on foundation grants rather than membership dues. Often they lack capacity to undertake the extensive work needed to organize entire sectors or geographic regions. There is also the ongoing, and frequently subterranean, discussion regarding the relationship of alt-labor to the official trade union movement. This is something that can be managed but will never be ultimately resolved, given the tension that is present as official unionism faces the Gorgon of global capitalism and the contemporary political right, which sees no place and no role for any organizations of the working class.

Poor workers' unions and alt-labor must therefore clarify their own mission. Do they seek to serve as an "organizing committee" within the working class to envision and help to actualize a twenty-first-century labor movement? Do they seek to reform the existing official trade union movement, with the hope that this movement can reemerge?

Let me end by offering a metaphor. The film *The Flight of the Phoenix* (1965) chronicles the crash of a plane in the Libyan desert. Miles from any human habitation, the survivors survey the plane and conclude that it will never fly again. However, one of the survivors, an aircraft engineer, finds that there are sufficient parts in the existing plane to serve as the basis for an entirely new plane. The survivors have three choices: wait for help to arrive, which is unlikely (and if it does not, they will die); attempt to walk out of the desert; or embark on building a new plane, out of the remains of the old, with the hope—and only the hope—that it will fly them to safety. They choose the last of these options.

The question that you, the reader, should ponder is this: can the forces of alt-labor—the poor workers' unions—with a conscious left central to its rise, play the role of the aircraft engineer and help to bring into being a twenty-first-century labor movement that can fly the working class out of the desert of contemporary capitalism?

Bill Fletcher Jr.

Members of Mujeres Unidas y Activas (United and Active Women), an organization of immigrant women sponsored by the Northern California Coalition for Immigrant Rights, protest at the Mediacopy plant in San Leandro. Workers at the videotape copying factory started an organizing drive with ILWU Local 6 after an immigration raid on the plant resulted in the deportation of ninety-nine workers. *(Photo by David Bacon)*

Introduction

Organizing in the Margins

San Francisco, 1964. Fifteen hundred civil rights activists clog the elegant lobby of the Sheraton Palace Hotel around the clock, picketing by day and sleeping on the floor by night. The ritzy hotel hires few workers of color, and those who are on payroll work at the "back of the house" as maids and janitors. The multiracial group of picketers, most in their early twenties, has one goal: to confront employment discrimination using militant tactics of civil disobedience learned in the civil rights movement. In just two days, protesters emerge victorious with an agreement for fair hiring at the Sheraton and thirty-three other hotels. Other industry-wide hiring agreements follow, as civil rights organizations become de facto bargaining agents for job access and equity for communities of color.

Detroit, 1980. Amid deteriorating buildings and trash-strewn streets, a picket line of teenagers, mostly African American, marches. The target is a Burger King fast-food outlet in the Greyhound bus station. Holding signs that read "Union rights are human rights," they chant, "No more threats, no more lies, we want the right to organize." Although many are still in high school, they know that low-skilled service work may be their only legal option in the fast-declining inner-city industrial economy. Despite a high level of unionization in the city's auto plants, a wave of plant closings has already thrown many of their

1

family members out of work, and those who remain are faced with diminished job protections. Recognizing the need to fight for their own future, these teenagers organize the independent Detroit Fast Food Workers' Union at two of the largest corporations in the United States—McDonald's and Burger King—with the help of antipoverty activists turned union organizers.

Long Island, New York, 1997. A group of Latino day laborers treks to the state capitol in Albany and convinces legislators to support the "Unpaid Wages Prohibition Act," which they drafted themselves. Day laborers perform "casual" work, such as landscaping, construction, and house cleaning, getting paid by the day with no job security and few legal protections. The act dramatically increases penalties against employers who intentionally violate wage and hour laws by paying day laborers below-poverty wages or forcing them to work overtime without compensation. Though most of the day laborers are undocumented immigrants with no right to vote and do not speak English, they convince several conservative Republican senators to sponsor the bill. They are members of the Workplace Project, a workers' center that supports them in their battle for fairer employment.

These scenes of independent labor organizing among poor workers show us a side of the labor movement we rarely see. Rooted in struggles for racial, ethnic, and gender justice and existing largely outside the gates of conventional trade unions, poor workers' unions offer a different vision of what the labor movement can be: activist based, inventive, adventurous, and infused with ideals of social justice and equality. Taking different forms—economic justice organizing, community-based unions, workers' centers, and workfare unions—this movement is committed to racial and ethnic diversity, gender equality, participatory democracy, and community-based organizing strategies.

Although it emerged as early as the 1930s, poor workers' unionism started to take on its present shape in the movements of the '60s, spread nationally in the '70s and '80s, and by the end of the century had led to successful union organizing campaigns among tens of thousands of poor workers. Faced with the disinterest of most AFL-CIO (American Federation of Labor and Congress of

Industrial Organizations) trade unions in organizing low-wage workers in the 1960s and early '70s, as well as with entrenched racism, sexism, and bureaucracy, poor people invented their own organizations and pushed ahead with campaigns on a broad range of workers' issues. Organizing experiments emerging from that era's social movements included civil rights–based jobs campaigns, domestic workers' unions, feminist labor groups, and welfare rights organizations. By the late '70s, community-based workers' centers had taken up the fight for economic justice, an organizing concept that spread rapidly to cities across the nation over the next two and a half decades. Community organizing, also booming during that period, became another vehicle for poor workers' activism on a host of economic justice questions. Just like trade unions, these independent community-based groups won pay raises, improved conditions, and secured dignity for their members.

People of color and women constitute most of both the membership and leadership of these poor workers' unions, which became the voice for a wide variety of workers—including low-wage service sector employees (such as food service and home health care workers), and those with multiple places of employment (such as day laborers and domestic workers). Even "no-wage" workers, such as those receiving welfare benefits in exchange for work, have organized for their rights. From members of civil rights–era "freedom unions" who struck over poverty wages to contemporary immigrant day laborers who organize for better conditions, the struggle has been for dignity, social equality, and a living wage.

Working independently of AFL-CIO trade unions, as part of a larger labor movement fighting for workers' rights and social justice, poor workers' unions illustrate a way of organizing that values the direct action, flexibility, collaboration, and rank-and-file control common in social justice movements over the bureaucratic and legalistic methods on which traditional unions have often relied. While smaller in scale than traditional trade unions, they stand out because of their unusual approaches to organizing and their commitment to workers' empowerment—valuable lessons for today's labor movement as it struggles to survive amid shifting economic sands.

Unions matter for all workers, but particularly for those on the lowest rungs of the economic ladder. In recent decades, the owning class has mandated increasing poverty for these workers, as capital has found new ways to exploit the low-wage workforce and widen its profit margins. Between 1968 and 2012, the US minimum wage lost about 30 percent of its value while wage and income inequality have grown dramatically.[1] Disproportionately affected were workers in largely nonunionized sectors, such as clerical and service work, whose wages lagged far behind inflation. Globalization and deregulation, supported by neoliberal free-market ideologies, have adversely affected workers' lives—both in the United States and abroad—as older sectors of the economy decline and newer ones emerge, bringing labor-driven migrations across borders. Many undocumented immigrants work in the expanding "informal economy" without benefits or a living wage. They constitute a huge and mostly hidden second-tier labor market in cities (in restaurants, manufacturing, and service work) as well as rural areas (in agricultural work). Estimated at six to twelve million, undocumented workers make up 4–8 percent of the US labor force.[2]

Unions bring practical improvements such as higher wages and enhanced job security, health and safety protections, and dignity and respect, protecting workers against both the whims of individual bosses and the general climate of economic exploitation. The stronger the labor movement is, the more potential power it has to bring about policies benefiting workers. Perhaps most fundamentally, unions empower the individuals who build them, encouraging their sense of community and their ability to work for social change. They teach the basic democratic lesson that you can change the world around you as well as your working conditions. This empowerment can lead workers to advocate and act for broader social and economic justice, beyond their own lives.

At a time when US trade union strength has dropped to its lowest levels since the 1920s, questions about who and how to organize are again topping labor's agenda. While an independent poor workers' movement continues to blossom outside of the AFL-CIO, members inside the federation are also raising critical questions about how trade unions can reverse their precipitous decline. Which workers should organizers target? How should workers' institutions reorganize themselves? The AFL-CIO is undergoing its deepest reexamination in decades, with the debate ranging from those advancing plans for industry-focused campaigns to those who advocate greater democracy and intensified rank-and-file organizing. The outcome will affect millions of poor workers who urgently want to be part of a movement for social and economic justice.

Servicing the Status Quo

US trade unions have at various times served as vehicles for large-scale social change. For instance, the emergence of successful mass-scale industrial unionism by the Congress of Industrial Organizations (CIO) in the late 1930s, with its aim of organizing unskilled workers without regard to race or gender, was a major blow to the exclusionism of the long-dominant American Federation of Labor (AFL) craft-based unions. The half-million Black workers who joined CIO-affiliated unions, write historians Robert Korstad and Nelson Lichtenstein, were "in the vanguard of efforts to transform race relations" as they built the beginnings of a powerful "labor-based civil rights movement."[3] It is in such situations—when demands for democracy and equality come to inhabit trade union institutions and take them past immediate "bread-and-butter" issues—that the US labor movement is at its most inspiring. Radical trade unionists were often at the center of such social justice unionism. But the purging of leftists by union leadership from the late 1940s through the early '50s had a devastating effect, dividing institutionalized labor from other social movements. This separation has long made it difficult for trade unions to see themselves as part of a movement.

While trade unions have begun to put a priority on recruiting new members, until recently they were generally not a welcoming place for those wanting to organize. After World War II, most unions turned inward, to concentrate on "servicing" those who were already represented—employing paid representatives to resolve members' grievances through legal or contractual methods. Many trade unions swapped their former rank-and-file activism and militancy for "labor peace," an institutional stability that ensured regular wage and benefit gains and a process by which union officials cooperated with management to regulate and channel rank-and-file discontent. The containment of shop-floor activism that occurred during the '50s, as historian David Brody notes, became "a permanent brake on the self activity of US workers."[4] When organizing did happen, it usually consisted simply of signing up more members and establishing new locals on the same model, with little concern for developing an activist base to influence broader social and economic change. Movement energies of the kind unleashed by democratic rank-and-file participation were often the last thing leaders of such unions wanted to encourage in their own institutions.

These changes moved unions away from the social justice–oriented direct-action tactics the labor movement had once pioneered—strikes, boycotts, demonstrations, sit-ins—toward a contractual and legalistic framework of "labor relations." The increased hold of bureaucratic "business unionism"—running the union like a business, concerned with the economic bottom line—also took a major toll. Business unionism grew along with consumer capitalism in the 1950s and '60s, and while the improved labor relations brought better wages and benefits to millions of workers during times of economic expansion, it was at the cost of grassroots democracy and militancy. When the postwar boom ended in the '70s, business unionism was caught off guard with no viable strategy for strengthening its influence or broadening its reach.[5] Labor had become an institution protecting the interests of the organized few, instead of a broad social movement representing the interests of all workers.

Union membership fell dramatically between 1955 and 2003, from 35 percent to 12.9 percent of the total workforce.[6] From the mid-1950s to the mid-'90s, trade unions made few organizing forays into uncharted territory. The conservative leadership of AFL-CIO presidents George Meany and Lane Kirkland oversaw labor's devolution into a bureaucracy that promised little to workers outside its established walls.[7] Organizing was assigned a very low priority by the AFL-CIO as well as most of its member unions. In 1970, at the beginning of a period of dramatic economic changes, huge sections of the labor force, including low-wage service workers—predominantly women and people of color—were virtually unorganized.[8] Even up to the late '90s, most AFL-CIO unions still spent less than 3 percent of their budgets on organizing.[9]

The causes of trade unions' difficulties have been much debated. External forces largely outside of union control, such as global migrations of capital and technological advances, affected US workers at a frighteningly swift pace. By the 1970s, as corporations moved operations overseas and deindustrialization spread in the Northeast and Midwest, the low-wage service sector had expanded dramatically. In the wave of plant shutdowns that began in the late '70s, one of every three US manufacturing jobs disappeared, cutting out the heart of unions' traditional base.[10] The instability of employment that poor workers faced was exacerbated by the increasing expansion of contingent work in the US economy.[11] Demographic factors, too, played a role: with the sheer growth of the US workforce in the postwar period and unions' failure to recruit these new workers, the percentage of the total workforce that was unionized shrank rapidly, and without new organizing efforts, it would continue to decline. Trade unions also faced capital's increased ability to resist unionization efforts by employing sophisticated antiunion consultants whose job it was to intimidate and fire pro-union workers, and securing as many legal barriers as possible against organizers. Since the passage of the Taft-Hartley Act of 1947, labor had contended with severe legal restrictions on workers' rights to organize, strike, and bargain collectively. After 1980 the National Labor Relations Board's will to protect workers' and unions' rights evaporated as a result of then-president Ronald Reagan's conservative political appointments.[12]

Important as these factors were, they told only part of the story of union decline. While unions could not control external factors such as the shift from an industrial- to a service-based economy, demographic transformations, and management's predilection for union busting, they could determine their own tactical responses to these challenges. For much of its history the US labor movement had confronted a hostile economic, legal, and political climate, but despite fierce opposition it had won important concessions for those it represented, including substantial increases in wages and benefits, life-saving safety measures, and the eight-hour day. Making choices about where and how to organize was key to these victories. As trade union power stalled, then dwindled, and unions suffered setback after setback, progressives called for the labor movement to revisit these fundamental questions of inclusion, of who constituted the working class and how best to organize them.

Most trade unions were ill-prepared to do this, not only because of an internal culture of business unionism but because the very way trade unions had developed—craft by craft and industry by industry—limited their capacity to widen their constituencies. Many in the traditional labor movement did not believe poor workers could be organized, either because of their fluctuating job status or because of prejudices against their race, ethnicity, gender, or immigration status. It was in this climate that poor workers themselves began to organize for change.

Putting the Movement Back in Labor

As trade unions declined in strength, many poor workers were drawn into movements centered on race, ethnicity, gender, or community politics, struggles that occupied their imaginations and energies in a way the bureaucratized trade-union movement did not. Civil rights demonstrations incorporated economic justice demands for nondiscrimination in employment and fair wages. Feminist organizing articulated the "double shift" that women worked at their jobs and in their homes. Welfare organizing sought to convince the public that poor workers were entitled to a safety net of income and benefits. Protections from workplace abuse or police brutality, and for help in organizing for better housing, health care, and other working-class needs, came from concerted action among poor workers themselves, as they turned to labor organizing "in the movements," winning pay raises, benefits, contracts, and dignity. To provide an institutional framework for their struggles, they built social movement—and community-based organizations with working-class agendas demanding fair pay, affordable housing, adequate welfare benefits, and health care for all.

Their allies included progressive and left trade unionists who sought to revive aggressive organizing and rank-and-file democracy within the AFL-CIO. Together, they built an alternative labor movement that organized from the bottom up and raised questions about how the movement as a whole could represent all workers—especially how issues of gender, ethnic, and racial inequality would be addressed in its institutions. These questions were not new to the labor movement. Workers of color and women had long and complex histories of struggle within particular unions and parts of the labor movement. Left activists and progressive trade unionists had a history of community-based work—for instance, organizing the working poor alongside the unemployed in the 1930s.[13] But in the 1960s and '70s these questions took on a new urgency. Activism for equal rights and social justice blossomed in communities across the nation. Most trade unions appeared stale and routinized in comparison. Challenged by this efflorescence of organizing, the AFL-CIO and most of its affiliates remained paralyzed. Instead of riding the wave of innovation that could have brought substantial numbers of militant poor workers into the house of labor—and simultaneously brought trade unionism back to its roots as a social movement—the AFL-CIO closed its eyes and slumbered through the decades.

Progressive union activists knew that if the movement was to survive it needed to prioritize organizing and democratic change from within. As an alternative to "bread-and-butter" trade unionism, which minimizes social equity claims in favor of solely economic ones, progressive activists have long argued for social justice unionism—also known as social movement unionism—which rejects routinized bureaucracy in favor of rank-and-file control and activism, participatory democracy, broad alliances, innovative tactics, and a focus on far-reaching goals such as justice and equality. Social justice unionism takes the form of a multifaceted political movement, not limited to issues such as wages and benefits. In its ideology and practice, it acknowledges the need to radically restructure unionism to be consciously about race, ethnicity, and gender as well as class. It encourages community ties as it builds coalitions against entrenched power—whether in the workplace, in the neighborhood, or at the national political level. By relying on community mobilization as a strategy, this kind of unionism implicitly recognizes that workers' identities are not defined solely by their work lives. Philosophically at the heart of poor workers' unionism, social justice unionism has served as a bridge between progressive unionists, whether they worked within the AFL-CIO or outside of it.

Some of these activists formed unions independent of the AFL-CIO, such as the Distributive Workers of America, or caucuses inside unions, such as the Detroit-based Dodge Revolutionary Union Movement, or got involved in coalitions such as the Movement for Economic Justice or the National Welfare Rights Organization. These efforts showed that labor as a social movement was alive and well and living, in part, outside the AFL-CIO. Rejecting the narrow contractual focus and bureaucratic rigidity that had come to define much of mainstream trade unionism, the independents, caucases, and coalitions expressed the dynamism characteristic of movement organizing. By the late '80s, some in the mainstream trade-union movement began turning back toward direct action and community-based tactics, in part because of the influence of successful community-based poor workers' organizing. By the mid-'90s, tentative collaborations had begun between trade unions and poor workers' unions, primarily addressing issues of workfare and living-wage campaigns.

This history is at the heart of the ongoing debate about revitalizing the labor movement. It makes visible the histories of poor workers, who, although they have often been seen as "marginal" to the economy and to many trade unions, have transformed the labor movement. Indeed, the marginality of some poor workers' groups has been one of their most intriguing aspects, lending them a tactical, ideological, and legal freedom often lacking elsewhere in the labor movement. These working-class organizations reveal a whole universe of activity that can broaden the vision of trade unions and the arenas in which they operate, as well as offer possibilities for collaboration that could strengthen the entire labor movement.

Despite numerous barriers to organizing, poor workers built on the economic initiatives of the social justice movements by organizing and joining unions of their own making. Many of these organizing projects made progress under the same general economic conditions that led to decline for other parts of the labor movement. Why? Because their main purpose was, and nearly all of their energy went into, rank-and-file organizing and democratic movement building, relying more on direct action and worker solidarity than on legal maneuvers, and they targeted a population of workers hungry for organizing.

The Other Labor Movement

The labor movement is usually equated with trade unions, those workplace-based contractually oriented organizations usually affiliated with the AFL-CIO. Throughout this book I use "trade unions" to denote this more traditional part of the labor movement, which is organized mostly by industry or trade and is employment based. But there is another part of the labor movement composed of independent social justice– and community-based labor organizations, which are the subject here. I refer to these as "poor workers' unions" because they generally organize workers at or below the poverty level, and they primarily operate within communities rather than in specific trades or industries. These supposedly marginal workers are increasingly important in both the US and world economies. Both trade unions and poor workers' unions are, of course, participants in the "labor movement."

These categories, however, are not absolute. During the period covered by this book, some trade unions organized poor workers and exhibited some of the community-based characteristics of poor workers' unions, though usually within more bureaucratic institutions. For instance, the Hospital and Health Care Workers Union 1199, with its activist constituency of low-wage African American, Puerto Rican, and Filipina/Filipino hospital workers, carried out organizing campaigns that incorporated demands for social equity, particularly during the '60s and early '70s. Note historians Leon Fink and Brian Greenberg, "1199's members were precisely those the big unions had failed or neglected to organize."[14] The International Ladies' Garment Workers' Union (ILGWU, later to become UNITE) counted many Asian and Latina garment workers among its membership, who used community-based tactics in some of their local struggles. In the '80s the Service Employees International Union (SEIU) and the Hotel and Restaurant Employees (HERE) began large-scale organizing campaigns among low-wage workers.[15] The American Federation of State, County and Municipal Employees (AFSCME) and the SEIU also launched organizing drives in large public-sector bargaining units, resulting in tremendous growth—from some one million union members in 1958 to six million by 1978.[16] Large numbers of people of color and women worked in public sector employment, and as new members and activists, they brought increased diversity to some sectors of the trade union movement. But public sector organizing generally did not contain the great numbers of minimum- and sub-minimum-wage and informal economy jobs that largely defined the world of poor workers.

Poor agricultural workers were represented by the United Farm Workers (UFW), which had some stylistic parallels with urban poor workers' unions. Jointly formed in the early 1960s by Filipino and Chicano workers' associations, the UFW was originally an independent union that later joined the AFL-CIO. In its early days, it relied heavily on movement-style tactics like boycotts, demonstrations, and strikes.[17]

While these histories are admirable, this book's focus is a particular constellation of urban workers' activism that grew out of antipoverty, welfare rights, unemployment, and immigrant and contingent worker organizing, which has become increasingly important within the contemporary labor movement. This genealogy sharply distinguishes independent poor workers' unions from trade unions. The term *poor workers* includes low-wage workers as well as those who labor without wages— "no-wage" or unwaged workers—whether because of state regulations (as with workfare workers), social custom (as with unwaged household labor), or chance (as with unemployment). They are no less part of the labor force than the stereotypical manufacturing worker. In practice, welfare, unemployment, and unwaged and low-waged work form the real economic continuum along which poor people's livelihoods are found. Poor workers are used to moving from job to job, industry to industry, from welfare to work and back again. Almost half of those who receive public assistance—in the form of food stamps, welfare, or housing grants—have some sort of low-wage job at the same time.[18]

Poor workers' unions organize differently from most trade unions. Since poor people's livelihoods commonly fluctuate between earning wages and receiving welfare or unemployment benefits, their labor activism almost always concerns itself with more than just workplace-based issues. For members of this multiracial, urban working class, as historian Robin D. G. Kelley notes, class oppression is bound up with gender, race, and ethnicity, and battles fought on the job are also taken up in workers' communities when they go home.[19] Poor workers' unions therefore developed as small-scale, horizontally organized community-based organizations. While most trade unions tend to adhere to an employment-based organizing framework, poor workers' unions usually begin their organizing in the community, taking on multiple issues outside the usual scope of representation, such as affordable housing, health care, childcare, racial and gender discrimination, and police brutality.

The idea that the workplace and community divide and define workers has long been taken for granted among both trade union organizers and many academics. Often they have seen the workplace, rather than workers' communities, as the arena of action. This "productionist" perspective confined labor to the workplace or formal union institutions and failed to fully grasp the roles of movements in social change and community politics.[20] By definition it left out women who labored in the home, whether they worked in their own homes (raising children with or without welfare) or others' homes (doing domestic work). This type of work has often remained hidden economically, and women's class consciousness is often hidden with it. Contingent workers with multiple places of employment, or low-wage workers who bounced from job to job, were also less likely to be included in the thoughts of labor theoreticians. Because of this, the activities of poor workers who were not members of trade unions in the '60s, '70s, and '80s have remained largely obscured in academic labor studies. The activism and consciousness of workers who did not produce goods—who were, for instance, engaged in domestic work, childcare, clerical or janitorial work, or food service—were either generalized or rendered invisible.

But since the workplace is not the sole—or even most important—location of class-based mobilization, the division between labor

and community organizing is an artificial one.[21] Class-based movements exist on a continuum from productionist strikes to community-
based struggles for civil rights, housing, welfare, and other social
goods. In practice, women's and poor people's movements have often
challenged class oppression in all parts of everyday life. Their shared
experience of unwaged work has also created ties of solidarity at the
community and neighborhood levels that drew on broader understandings of class.

Along with deindustrialization, capital flight, and union decline,
the 1960s brought increasing suburbanization, which produced a
mostly white and propertied proletariat in the suburbs and a poor
inner-city working class of people of color.[22] This new geographic split
in the working class produced new forms of resistance that would expand even more dramatically during the following decades, such as
laying claim to local jobs, demanding capital disinvestment, organizing for tenants' rights, advocating for quality health care and educational services, and highlighting the economics of everyday life. Even
if a poor worker were represented at work by a trade union, improvements in publicly subsidized housing or food stamp allotments might
have a greater impact on his or her quality of life than a wage increase
won in a contract battle. A politics of place was inherent in much of
the class-based mobilization of poor workers during this period—
which focused on jobs, welfare, utility rates, neighborhood preserva-
tion, education, redlining and housing.[23] Trade unions by and large
were uninterested in these issues, but community-based groups ex-
celled at addressing them and easily expanded from them into labor-
oriented organizing projects.

Who Are Poor Workers?

Poor workers are not easily defined or counted, although scholars and
government agencies have counted them in myriad ways. In 1963,
around the time this organizing story begins, the Department of Labor
counted 8.5 million people—over half of them women—as "employed poor," consigned to low-wage work that brought in less than
$3,000 per year.[24]

The picture only got worse as time passed. In 1990 some 12 million Americans were classified as working poor (defined as working at least fifty weeks per year but not making sufficient income to lift a family of four out of poverty), an increase of more than 3 million since 1980.[25] Another 13.6 million people, mostly women, were enrolled in 1995 in AFDC (Aid to Families with Dependent Children, the largest welfare program), and nearly a million more received general welfare assistance.[26] Taken jointly, these three figures—of the working poor, AFDC recipients, and general assistance recipients during the '90s— equaled over 25 million people and give a very rough indication of the size and shape of the "class" of poor workers. However, this sum still left out those who worked for fewer than fifty weeks each year (the chronically underemployed), seasonal and farm workers, and those who labored in the informal economy.

In 2011 more than a quarter of all workers were earning poverty-level hourly wages—defined as $11.06 for a family of four—and workers of color and women were more likely to receive them than white men.

Share of workers earning poverty-level wages by gender, 1973–2011[27]

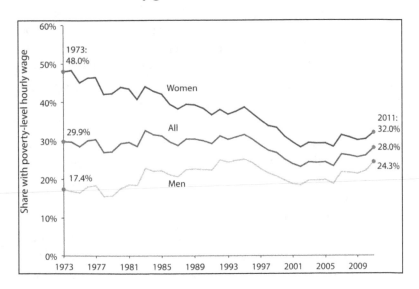

Share of workers earning poverty-level wages by race and ethnicity, 1973–2011[28]

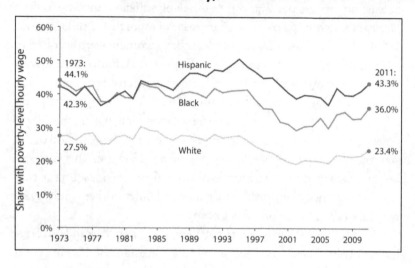

The occupations of nonagricultural poor workers are clustered in the service sector; among the top categories are private household services, child day care, garment manufacturing, restaurants, nursing and personal care facilities, building services or janitorial, and hotels.[29] Some economists use categories such as "core" versus "peripheral" or "primary" versus "secondary" labor markets to designate occupational divisions within the US working class. Census data for 1990 show that women, especially women of color, are overwhelmingly represented in the secondary/peripheral labor market, which includes service, household, unskilled labor, sales, and clerical work. Sixty percent of all white women labored in the secondary labor market, as did 70 percent of all African American women, 76 percent of all Chicanas, and 70 percent of all US Puerto Rican women. The statistics for men of color were similarly skewed toward the secondary labor market as well as the "lower primary" labor market, which included blue-collar occupations in transportation, security, and production.[30]

Workers in both the skilled and unskilled "core" economic sectors in 1970 constituted a much larger part of the unionized workforce than did those in the "nonskilled periphery and marginally employed strata."

These unionized workers were, during the '60s, '70s and '80s, more often white, male, and married.[31] Trade union representation raised the wages of this group, who make an average of 30 percent more than those workers not unionized.[32] This dichotomy was heightened in the 1950s, when most unions bought into the capitalist promise, leading to increasing segmentation of the labor market, dividing workers even while it offered some of them upward mobility and economic gains.[33]

Organized labor's demography has been changing: in 1996 overall trade union membership turned a corner and is no longer mostly white and male.[34] Still, both racism and sexism are deeply embedded in the institutional fabric of the labor movement. Trade unions have complex internal histories with regard to race, ethnicity, and gender— including AFL craft unions that systematically banned African American workers from membership and promoted violence against Asian workers; labor's historic support for the "family wage," which devalued women's work in relation to men's; and the AFL-CIO's long backing of anti-immigrant policies, finally reversed after much debate in February 2000.

Workers' organization in the United States in the twentieth century is not only a story of workers against bosses and labor against capital. It is also about laboring people's struggles within their own institutions for democracy, solidarity, and equality. Racism has shaped the consciousness and actions of the white working-class movement. "Working-class formation and the systematic development of a sense of whiteness went hand in hand for the US white working-class," writes historian David Roediger, becoming a "way in which white workers have come to look at the world" and at themselves.[35] The ideological baggage surrounding gender is just as heavy and has left similar scars on movements for class justice. Women's assignment to the "sphere" of home, and the devaluing of their work, has served to camouflage what women's labor means economically. The experiences of working women have usually been ignored unless they fall within the confines of factories or unions. As Susan Porter Benson puts it,

> Both women and people of color have been constructed as the "other" by a labor movement that, despite more inspiring moments,

has devoted most of its energy to enhancing the privileges of a constituency that was already in a position of privilege because of its race and gender. White men have historically dominated the movement in numbers and continue to do so in leadership positions.[36]

These "historical habits of thinking," Benson adds, continue to shape the labor movement, its organizing choices, and its ability to put forward an egalitarian social vision. In practical terms, increased union membership diversity has not translated into leadership diversity. People of color generally have a higher "union density" than white people—that is, a higher percentage of those who are employed are union members—yet they occupy leadership positions much less frequently, especially at the national level. For example, as late as 1984, there were only two unions headed by African Americans among the AFL-CIO's ninety-five affiliates.[37] Similarly, female membership in trade unions has skyrocketed over recent decades, but women remained seriously underrepresented in union leadership positions. For instance, in 1994, 85 percent of the ILGWU was female, but only 21 percent of its leaders were women, a pattern common across the trade union movement.[38] And even where racial and gender diversity had increased, the dominance of business unionism throughout the '70s and '80s—with the focus on production and contractual issues and with paid staff, rather than the workers they represented, setting the agenda—ensured that the new diversity did not often translate into new tactics.

Much of the tension between poor workers' unions and trade unions revolved around these issues. During the 1960s and '70s, most poor workers' unions had problematic relationships (if any at all) with trade unions. Connections were strong, however, between some poor workers' unions and rank-and-file movements for democracy within trade unions, which shared common concerns about racism, sexism, and poverty. By the '90s, both "parts" of the labor movement—poor workers' unions and trade unions—were redefining their tactics, and they were increasingly working together, giving hope to the idea that an enlarged labor movement could one day claim to represent the interests of the vast majority of workers rather than those of a labor elite.

Don't Mourn, Unionize!

As noted earlier, poor people's movements and organizations have often been the vehicles through which workers have pressed their economic claims. Frances Fox Piven and Richard A. Cloward, in their classic *Poor People's Movements: Why They Succeed, How They Fail*, wrote eloquently about the tradition of class-based organizing among the poor. They argued that the process of institutionalization could end up channeling effective organizing into routinized "normal politics," robbing movements of their power.[39] While this has sometimes been the case, it is not inevitable. Poor workers' unions show us a middle road where mobilization and institutionalization can coexist. Flexible, democratically controlled, nonbureaucratic organizations can provide a springboard and a framework for collective action, both in times of upheaval and in times of stasis.

Poor workers' unions belong squarely within the labor movement tradition, just as labor belongs historically to a social movement tradition of organizing, mobilization, and protest. While unionization efforts have often been initiated by paid organizers, rank-and-file poor workers themselves have built and run the most successful of these organizations, and thus they represent a distinctive force within a variety of social movements since the 1960s. Many poor workers' groups organized effectively without turning into bureaucracies or becoming controlled by elites, reinventing a bottom-up, democratic, and grassroots form of unionism. For instance, the National Welfare Rights Organization expressed, in the words of writer Guida West, the "social protest of poor women"—who knew themselves to be workers, even when unemployed and doing unwaged domestic work.[40] Welfare recipients forced to work for their benefits in the '70s and the '90s claimed their right to be called "workers" and to receive the real wages and benefits that accompanied that designation. Day laborers who organized the street corners of Long Island and elsewhere in the '90s did so not only to make a living wage but also to gain respect and dignity in an occupation that was accorded little of either.

These unions have certainly had their share of failures, including lost organizing campaigns, lack of resources, and internal organizational difficulties. In this they are no different from other people's organizations, including trade unions. Whether they are funded by dues from members, donations from progressives, or grants, most survive on a financial shoestring and money worries are common. This often means they have few financial resources for long fights against large employers, like some of the multinational corporations they have tried to take on. But their lack of sustained resources is a silver lining in at least one respect: it has forced them to rely more often on rank-and-file members than on paid staff. What they have lacked in finances they have often made up for in solidarity. When a thousand forest woodcutters who were paid by the piece won their 1973 strike against the paper corporations in the Deep South, they did it through widespread mobilization and solidarity. When Atlanta domestics organized to raise their wages in 1968, they did it by collectively refusing to work for below-minimum wages. During the early '80s, home care workers built solidarity among themselves and with their disabled and elder clients, as they organized for higher wages and better benefits in Boston and Chicago.

Are such poor workers' unions merely brief flare-ups in the history of independent labor? A few were, but most had remarkable longevity. It is the persistence of these organizations and the poor workers' movement as a whole over more than half a century that is so intriguing. While many of the economic organizing initiatives in the civil rights and women's movements in the '60s and early '70s were short-lived, some gave birth to organizations that exist to this day. For example, one independent workers' center, the Chinese Staff and Workers' Association, is over twenty years old; ACORN organized workers for nearly thirty years, before its untimely demise in 2010;[41] and the Distributive Workers, though it changed its name when it merged into the United Auto Workers, is still organizing many of the same workplaces thirty years later.

Still, success cannot be defined solely as a matter of institutionalization or permanence. And although some of these groups organized impressive numbers of workers, this story is not about quantitative wins either. What is more significant about these organizations, and what constitutes their greatest success, is that over the decades, their work has challenged the labor movement to broaden its conception of workers and unions, given collective voice to groups of workers who were not sufficiently represented, and broken down racial, ethnic, and gender barriers in organizing. While this kind of qualitative cultural change within labor isn't easily measured, it is nonetheless crucial in making the entire movement stronger and more diverse.

Poor workers' organizing efforts have much to teach the labor movement. The way they operate complicates traditional notions of union organizing—confined to the shop floor, oriented mainly toward economic issues, and based on simplistic conceptions of class identity separate from race, ethnicity, gender, and citizenship.[42] These notions were all hallmarks of trade union organizing during the '60s and '70s, which still remain dominant today. Poor workers' unions fight for justice in the workplace and, at the same time, consciously challenge the balance of economic and political power in local communities. The framework of community organizing widened their struggles from purely employment-based or job-centered concerns, laid the groundwork for useful alliances, and narrowed the gap between employed and unemployed workers, women and men, and workers of different racial or ethnic identities.

The labor movement is at a crossroads. It can respond effectively to the continuing political and economic challenges of capital only by creating new structures for collective action, or by dramatically transforming the ones it has, which are clearly failing. Weakened by its own internal structures and misplaced political priorities, and with membership at its lowest levels since the 1920s, the labor movement, according to the mainstream consensus, has been vanquished. If labor as a whole is to reverse its decline, it must build a broader, more democratic and progressive movement allied with other movements for social justice. Poor workers' unionism—with all its creativity, inventiveness, and historical variation over the last several decades—offers insights into that possibility.

Finding Poor Workers' Voices

Tracking down material about poor workers' organizing is difficult. Most of these organizations (with a few exceptions) have not been written about in either the mainstream or academic press. To bring poor people's voices into this project, I searched movement papers as well as old newsletters, strategy papers, and rally leaflets, which came from archives, and occasionally from activists' basements. Authorship and dating of such materials was, more frequently than not, unclear— these ephemeral materials were often handwritten notes, drafts of organizing materials, or mimeographed newsletters. Some were written by rank-and-file workers and some by staff organizers, while others were collaborative work.

Dozens of activists and organizers generously shared their knowledge and reflections with me. They are listed at the end of the book. Because of the transient nature of poor workers' lives, I had difficulty locating many rank-and-file activists from organizations in the '60s, '70s, and '80s. My interviews for these periods are primarily with the lead activists who maintained close ties to movement work over the years, rather than those who may have been active for a few months or a year and then moved on to another job or welfare or unemployment. This was not a significant problem for the '90s and beyond; activists in these movements were more easily located, and I was able to include their experiences directly.

I came to this project wearing several different hats. As both a rank-and-file labor activist and a paid staff member in a union, I have been in the trenches of organizing drives, contract battles, and fights over democracy. Having been involved in two different labor organizing projects that had built institutions from the ground up, it was clear to me that rank-and-file workers were among the most energetic and imaginative players in the labor movement. As a radio and print journalist, I have covered many independent organizing projects, interviewing activists who inspired me with their ability to confront the most trying circumstances and transform them into victories. A librarian by trade, I had frequently helped students researching the history of independent organizing, which was covered in the movement press but nearly invisible in scholarly work.

This story follows the historical patterns of development of poor workers' unions. The first chapter examines the economic organizing initiatives that emerged directly from the civil rights, New Left, and women's movements in the '60s and early '70s, including domestic workers' unions, civil rights job mobilizations, and welfare rights organizing. In chapter 2, the organizing efforts of mainstream trade unions are compared with more militant community-based initiatives. The early '70s brought an effort to combine welfare rights with working-class economic issues under the auspices of the Movement for Economic Justice, covered in chapter 3, as well as some early attempts to organize workfare workers. By the late '70s, covered in chapter 4, nationally coordinated campaigns to organize poor workers overtook the earlier, more fragmented projects. The independent workers' center model, with its focus on community-based organizing, is the subject of chapter 5. The workfare unionism of the '90s is covered in chapter 6, including a description of the problematic relationships that existed between most of these independent unions and AFL-CIO unions, as well as possibilities for future alliances. Chapter 7 looks at the debates within the AFL-CIO as the question of organizing reemerged on its agenda in the '90s. The conclusion considers the evolving intersection of poor workers' unions with AFL-CIO trade unions and the possibilities for a renewed labor movement.

Crowd outside of the Cadillac dealership on San Francisco's auto row, as Thomas Burbridge (NAACP) announces victory in the struggle for fair hiring. *(Photo by Jerry Stoll, Labor Archives and Research Center, San Francisco State University, PW 4/13 Fair Employment Practices Commission, San Francisco, April 18, 1964)*

1

Unionizing the Movements

Economic Initiatives in the Civil Rights, New Left, and Women's Movements

More than a quarter-million people turned out for the 1963 March on Washington for Jobs and Freedom. There Dr. Martin Luther King Jr. delivered his impassioned "I Have a Dream" speech, and Student Nonviolent Coordinating Committee chair John Lewis spoke about liberation from "economic slavery." "Hundreds of thousands of our brothers are not here," Lewis said. "They have no money for their transportation, for they are receiving starvation wages, or no wages, at all. . . . What is there . . . to ensure the equality of a maid who earns $5.00 a week in the home of a family whose income is $100,000 a year?" At the time, African Americans had twice the unemployment rate of whites, and those who had jobs took home on average 50 to 60 percent of white workers' pay.[1]

The march had been called by the Negro-American Labor Council, an organization founded in 1959 by A. Philip Randolph of the Brotherhood of Sleeping Car Porters in reaction to the AFL-CIO's refusal to adopt internal desegregation measures. The march was to focus on jobs and economic issues, but later organizers broadened it to include pending civil rights legislation. The nation's trade union leadership was unenthusiastic about the march: the executive council of the AFL-CIO, led by its president George Meany, refused to endorse it. However, some local, national, and international unions within the federation were active participants and endorsers. One such endorser was the United Auto Workers' Walter Reuther, the only white labor representative on the march's coordinating committee.[2]

This lack of enthusiasm for civil rights among white-led trade unions was hardly a surprise. Since the 1955 merger of the industrial union–based CIO with the trade union–based AFL, the AFL's conservatism had predominated, especially on issues of race, corroding whatever good relations existed between civil rights organizations and the more racially progressive CIO. Financial contributions from trade unions to civil rights organizations were insultingly small. In 1959, for instance, labor contributions to the Congress on Racial Equality (CORE), a major national civil rights organization, amounted to only $1,347, most of it from more progressive unions such as ILGWU and AFSCME.[3]

The scene at the Negro-American Labor Council's February 1961 meeting in Washington, DC, was typical: for the eight hundred unionists and community activists in attendance, reported the independent left newspaper the *Guardian*, "the AFL-CIO was the main target of attack. . . . Nearly every speaker criticized AFL-CIO leadership for 'dragging its feet'" on rooting out racism within the trade union movement.[4] Also in 1961, after years of skirmishes between Meany and pro–civil rights unionists led by Randolph, the National Association for the Advancement of Colored People (NAACP) released a scathing report on civil rights in the first five years of the AFL-CIO merger, detailing racist practices in trade unions, apprenticeship programs, and AFL-CIO bodies. "The basic status of workers in the labor movement who are non-white is that of second class citizenship," proclaimed Randolph, the sole African American on the twenty-member AFL-CIO executive council, to AFL-CIO convention delegates in 1961. But the AFL-CIO's executive council rejected the allegations, instead blaming pro–civil rights unionists for the "'gap that has developed' between organized labor and the Negro Community."[5]

All four major civil rights organizations—the NAACP, the Southern Christian Leadership Conference (SCLC), SNCC, and CORE—had protested union-backed racial discrimination and unfair hiring and had called on the AFL-CIO to organize unrepresented workers of color. Receiving no response, civil rights organizations launched nationwide protests in 1963 calling for jobs and fair employment. A few years later, in 1965, they began to try their hand at organizing "freedom unions" for poor workers unrepresented by trade unions.

In the late 1960s the women's movement faced a similar dilemma. Becoming aware of how gender relations structured economic oppression, feminist activists saw women workers making an average of fifty cents to each dollar paid to men, not including the unwaged "second shift" in the home. Women who were union members took part in widespread gender activism in the '60s and '70s—organizing against the sex-typing of jobs and winning major legal decisions against discriminatory employers.[6] But female membership in unions was abysmally low during the '60s—only about 12 percent of working women belonged to unions, even though women made up 40 percent of the American workforce.[7]

The male-dominated AFL-CIO's lack of interest, and in some cases lack of ability, in organizing primarily female workplaces drove women to create their own institutions outside existing trade unions. The solely economic focus of trade unions held little appeal for women workers, whose concerns—including day care, protection against sexual harassment, and respect and dignity on the job—often went unnoticed by trade union reps. Working a "double day" on the job and at home helped form a different consciousness about work—one that was not limited to economic issues in the waged workplace. This conception would become central to movement-based organizing efforts among women in clerical and service sector jobs. An emerging feminist consciousness influenced the formation of scores of organizations for domestics, welfare mothers, and clerical workers—all framing their demands in terms of workers' rights and civil rights, as well as class and gender solidarity.

Into this gulf of trade union inactivity a new generation of social movement activists launched a wave of economic organizing in which

class became central to movement building. While they didn't necessarily carry the label "labor," hundreds of campaigns for equal employment and workplace rights flourished amid the civil rights, New
Left, and women's movements of the '60s and early '70s. Some were
short-lived; others survived to establish a long-term presence in, and
an effect on, movements for social change. Most important, these organizations brought the voices of marginalized poor workers into the
struggle for economic justice, building consciousness about their experiences and expanding the labor movement in crucial ways. These
poor workers—day laborers, low-wage clerical and service workers,
welfare recipients, and the marginally employed—would play an increasingly important part in movements for labor and economic justice over the next decades.

Jim Crow Must Go

Following the 1963 March on Washington, civil rights organizations
impatient with trade union inaction put fair employment at the top
of their agendas from coast to coast. From 1963 to 1964, as CORE historians August Meier and Elliott Rudwick note, "campaigns against
job bias were the most common projects among the northern and
western chapters—and generally the most successful."[8] Activists in
San Francisco captured national attention when a coalition of civil
rights groups began organizing for equal employment in response to
high rates of joblessness in the Bay Area. Named the United Freedom
Movement, the coalition had the goal of confronting de facto employment segregation through confrontation, using militant civil disobedience. Sit-ins, pickets, and boycotts brought the Bay Area into the
forefront of the action and marked a new emphasis on economic oppression as a main focus of the growing movement.

The United Freedom Movement campaign harked back to earlier
"Don't Buy Where You Can't Work" campaigns of the 1930s, when
African Americans in several cities successfully boycotted exploitative
white-owned businesses located in their segregated communities.[9] But
the strategy also strongly borrowed from community-based labor organizing techniques. Activists presented employers with demands for

fair hiring and insisted that an agreement be signed directly with the United Freedom Movement. If an employer refused, they would commence civil disobedience. This bore striking similarities to union organizing drives—but in this case, a local civil rights coalition acted as the collective bargaining agent, and an employer's failure to sign a contract would be answered with civil disobedience by community members instead of a strike by workers.

San Francisco's United Freedom Movement first targeted Mel's Drive-In, a local restaurant chain that relegated African Americans to bottom-wage dishwashing and janitorial jobs. As historian Larry Saloman describes, daily picketers carried signs with messages such as "I'll have a freedomburger please," or entered the restaurant and placed orders for "freedom and jobs for Negroes." After nearly one hundred arrests and with the threat of more demonstrations to come, Mel's management signed a fair hiring agreement for all thirteen restaurants in the chain. Buoyed by the victory, San Francisco activists picked new targets. Merely the threat of a 1963 Christmas boycott of downtown department stores compelled the stores to sign hiring agreements. And the Lucky supermarket chain, with an atrocious record of minority hiring, became the testing ground for the "shop in." CORE picketers had found that shoppers in predominantly white neighborhoods crossed their lines, limiting their impact on the stores' business. So protesters entered the stores, filled their grocery carts, lined up to check out, then left saying, "I'll have more money to pay when you hire more Negroes." The Lucky action lasted nine days, and management finally signed an agreement with CORE guaranteeing that only people of color would be hired at Lucky stores for an entire year.[10]

In March 1964, the Bay Area civil rights struggle landed right in the middle of the San Francisco's elegant Sheraton Palace Hotel, glimpsed in this book's introduction. After a series of pickets and arrests, some fifteen hundred protesters surrounded the hotel, and according to historians Natalie Becker and Marjorie Myhill, "before long, the picketing turned into a walk-in, the walk-in into a moving, chanting serpentine, the serpentine into a sit-in, and the sit-in into a sleep-in," paralyzing the hotel's business. The spectacle of an interracial group of activists sleeping in the ritzy hotel lobby was splashed across San Francisco's newspapers. Demands included increasing the number of African American workers at the hotel; at the time there were only 19 Black workers out of 550 employees, and they worked in the "back of the house," out of sight of the hotel's wealthy clientele. After two days, activists emerged with a fair hiring agreement not just for the Sheraton Palace but also for thirty-three of the city's other hotels, many of whose owners feared they would be the activists' next targets.[11]

Civil rights activists also besieged San Francisco's auto row, lying in cars or on desks to press their demands for equal employment. "Young Negroes and whites slipped into shiny new Plymouths, Valiants and Furies," the *San Francisco Chronicle* reported, while "the showroom resounded almost continuously with chants, yells and songs."[12] Demonstrating crowds as large as five thousand virtually shut down business during March and April 1964, winning an industry-wide jobs agreement modeled on the Sheraton Palace victory. Activists moved on to the powerful Bank of America, which faced huge pickets in thirteen California cities and demands that it hire at least thirty-six hundred people of color within a year. In one demonstration, some ten thousand people surrounded a downtown San Francisco branch; in another, activists defied a court order by sitting in at a San Diego branch. Other tactics were smaller but effective: civil rights workers would ask a teller for pennies in exchange for bills, then circulate to a new teller to change the money back to bills. Months of such tactics, along with continual demonstrations and bad publicity, forced the bank to promise to increase its Black employment by nearly 40 percent.[13]

In all, the San Francisco jobs campaign produced over 375 equal employment agreements promising thousands of jobs to African Americans and other people of color.[14] This was classic grassroots labor organizing, and it was not limited to a single employer or even a single industry. Through direct confrontation, activists forced employers to bargain directly with civil rights groups and sign binding agreements with them. Civil rights groups became, in effect, bargaining agents for the Black community as a whole. In direct contrast, San Francisco's unions, for the most part, represented white workers in the industries targeted and did not participate in the demonstrations. One exception was the city's left-leaning ILWU local, which pressured the mayor to settle the Sheraton Palace dispute.

Young activists dominated San Francisco's multiracial CORE chapter, including eighteen-year-old Tracy Simms, an African American high school student who acted as spokesperson during the Sheraton protest. She'd gotten interested in civil rights at Berkeley's Woolworth's boycott at the age of fourteen. Writes historian Jo Freeman, "Newspaper accounts implied that it really stuck in the craw of the hotel association and the city leaders to have to negotiate with an 18-year-old girl."[15] Early on, some 70 to 80 percent of CORE's activists were young white college students, about half female. As the struggle wore on, participants were decidedly more racially diverse—over half were African American at the time of the auto row protests, with many more older nonstudents lying down to be arrested.[16]

CORE chapters across the nation attacked a wide range of discriminatory employers. Jobs campaigns in Seattle, Denver, Los Angeles, Boston, Columbus, East St. Louis, Berkeley, and Washington, DC, met with some success, though not as dramatic as San Francisco's. Such campaigns were notable for their emphasis on economic justice: in contrast to the South, segregation in northern cities was achieved through economic oppression, not laws.[17]

From the Freedom Movement to Freedom Unions

Civil rights activists also made the leap from organizing for jobs and fair hiring practices to encouraging the formation of independent community unions. In Mississippi, workers from SNCC helped residents of the Delta town of Shaw to organize the Mississippi Freedom Labor Union (MFLU). Shaw's main employer was a sewing plant that refused to hire Black people; most were relegated to poverty-wage day labor in the cotton fields. In 1965, angry residents decided to act and, an anonymous observer wrote, forty-five of them—"cotton day laborers, tractor drivers, haulers, domestic servants, part time carpenters, mechanics, handymen, former sharecroppers and renters"—met in a tiny church to form a union.[18]

Nineteen-year-old George Shelton was elected the union's chair. The group's draft constitution stated that its purpose was "to organize the poor people" and allowed any person over fourteen years old "who works, whether employed or not," to join. In a 1965 fundraising letter, Shelton told potential supporters that most farm workers in Mississippi made only thirty cents an hour, and "some workers, particularly the maids, don't even get this."[19] Even the highest-paid workers made only $3 for a ten-hour day at a time when the federal minimum wage was $1.25 an hour.

Demanding their right to that minimum wage for their work, as well as free health care, Social Security, and "equal employment practices in wages, hiring and working conditions," the MFLU spread to eight Mississippi counties and grew to over a thousand members, the majority of them cotton choppers or pickers, within just two weeks. The union's new members in three counties went on strike to end the "slave wages" of area cotton mills, such as the Delta Land and Pine Corporation, a former plantation that employed day laborers to chop, pick, and haul cotton. Members' dues provided a small strike fund, and community support was high. To raise funds, "women promised to sew aprons and bed quilts and some people planned to hold fish fries," wrote organizers, and to get by on less, "everyone agreed to enlarge the size of their garden plots, and plant one large plot in common."[20]

While ultimately the strike failed in its major goals—partly because higher-paid delivery drivers were not as willing to strike as the day laborers, partly because the young union lacked resources—it did succeed in raising wages in some areas from thirty to fifty cents an hour—constituting a 60 percent pay increase. Heartened by the partial success, strikers planned for another action in the fall, and sharecroppers in Tennessee, Arkansas, North Carolina, Alabama, and Louisiana formed their own Freedom Union locals.[21]

These southern Freedom Labor Unions had a northern urban sister, the Maryland Freedom Union (MFU), founded in January 1966 with the help of CORE's Baltimore chapter, to represent Black workers in small white-owned businesses located in segregated Black communities. CORE had backed AFL-CIO union campaigns since its inception but found that traditional organizing techniques—petitions, elections, and strikes—failed in poor communities where turnover was high and employer power was strong. Community support was needed to tip the balance in the workers' favor. "We saw the MFU as a combination of labor and community organization," wrote organizer Mike Flug in 1970, then chair of CORE's Columbia University chapter. It pursued a strategy similar to that of the United Farm Workers (UFW) in California. CORE activists had responded to UFW leader Cesar Chavez's call to help organize the boycott of table grapes and wines in urban Black and Puerto Rican communities in the north during the 1965 grape strike. The strike's success showed CORE that a community-based union might work in urban areas as it had for California's rural farm workers.[22] CORE proposed organizing low-wage workers in Baltimore.

Any worker, no matter his or her job or skill, was eligible to join the MFU. As soon as the union was announced, workers flocked to it—from workplaces throughout the city, including stores, laundries, hospitals, and nursing homes, they asked for help with organizing.[23] The new union's members were almost entirely African American women earning less than minimum wage. In February 1966, when one group of workers formed an organizing committee, only to be fired in retaliation a few days later by their employer, Lincoln Nursing Home, other nursing home workers walked out in support.

"Startled [CORE] organizers were told by the workers that Lincoln was 'on strike,' that the workers had named the union 'Maryland Freedom Union Local #1,' and that the CORE organizers had better come down . . . to show the workers how to 'run a proper picket line,'" recounts Flug. Workers compared their conditions to slavery, with wages of thirty-five cents an hour for up to seventy-two-hour work weeks. Many also cited, as a reason for striking, the undignified treatment of their elderly indigent patients, who suffered under terrible conditions in the understaffed nursing home. Less than two weeks later, after seeing the struggle covered in the city's Black newspaper, the *Baltimore Afro-American*, the staff from a second nursing home went on strike and called the CORE office to say they'd like to be "Freedom Local #2." Strikers' tactics included picketing the employer's home and breaking into one nursing home to show local journalists the conditions under which it operated. Though neither strike produced a contract, the high-profile tactics and the threat of more paid off: wages tripled from just 35 cents an hour to over $1 after the strikes.[24]

National CORE officials were proud of the union and in April 1966 announced that the Maryland Freedom Union would expand "to organize people in all areas not covered by the minimum-wage law as well as the marginal workers and the unemployed." The MFU began organizing retail store workers in downtown Baltimore, winning union recognition at a chain of clothing stores after a community boycott in support of the workers. The workers' wages more than doubled (from 70 cents to $1.50 an hour for full-time work), and they were guaranteed time-and-a-half for overtime, paid vacation, sick leave, and holidays. Recognition at two other stores followed.[25]

Trade unions suddenly began paying attention. Prior to organizing the retail workers, the MFU had approached the Retail Clerks' International Union to explore affiliating. The local's president responded that "he didn't organize 'those kinds of stores,' didn't want 'those kinds of workers.'"[26] As MFU's successes mounted, and as groups of workers already represented by AFL-CIO trade unions began asking the MFU if they could affiliate with it instead, Baltimore Central Labor Council officials accused the MFU of intentionally raiding the jurisdictions of AFL-CIO unions and of "dual unionism"—undercutting one union by forming another to compete with it. "So new were both CORE staff members and MFU officers to the disputes of the union movement," writes Flug, "that several weeks passed before they learned what the term meant." The UAW's Walter Reuther, a major contributor to CORE, complained "about CORE 'becoming a union'" and pressured CORE to stop the MFU. CORE complied, withdrawing the MFU's financial support.[27]

But this was not the end of the MFU. Cut off from CORE, MFU members elected rank-and-file officers in the five MFU-represented shops to oversee the union. With fewer than one hundred workers under contract and paying dues, the MFU began canvassing Baltimore's steel plants for donations from ordinary workers, who donated funds generously to keep the union afloat. However, by the end of the '60s, the continual financial crunch had weakened the local, and those workers still under MFU contract affiliated with a predominantly Black painters' union local in Baltimore.[28]

This became a recurring theme in economic organizing initiatives of the '60s and '70s: abundant energy and militant members willing to take direct action against their employers, but with few financial resources to draw on for the long haul. Organizers knew this was a weak point and often sought out wary trade unions with which to affiliate for financial support. But these small organizing projects, infused as they were with activist energy, frightened most trade union leaders, who were used to operating in a more legalistic and controlled framework. This dynamic would begin to change slowly over the next decades, as independent community-based organizing became stronger and trade unions began to rethink their organizing outlooks.

Sowing the Seeds of Resistance

The mostly student New Left also organized around economic grievances in the early '60s, trying to extend the reach of unionism into the ranks of the poor. Students for a Democratic Society launched its Economic Research and Action Project (ERAP) in the fall of 1963, two days after the March on Washington.[29] ERAP established what it called "community unions" in ten cities to organize around unemployment, welfare, housing, and other local issues. The first, Jobs or Income Now (JOIN) in Chicago, was "analogous to a trade union" according to its 1966 program, in that it brought community grievances against "policemen, educators, welfare caseworkers, landlords, loan sharks, day labor agencies and the like." Poor whites—factory workers and the unemployed—were JOIN's main constituency.[30]

Published theory to back up SDS's projects appeared, such as James O'Connor's "Toward a Theory of Community Unions," printed in *Studies on the Left* in 1964. Since the poor lacked steady jobs, argued O'Connor, the community rather than the workplace was the logical place to organize them. This theory would have supported CORE's activities as well, but unlike the Black-initiated CORE union projects, the mostly white-run ERAP enjoyed wide support from trade unions, churches, and foundations. An ERAP advisory committee formed with mostly left trade unionists, and a local of the United Packinghouse Workers Union opened an ERAP recruiting office near a South Side unemployment office. The AFL-CIO Industrial Union Department's executive director, Jack Conway, was "especially impressed" with ERAP's work, and Walter Reuther's UAW gave thousands of dollars to SDS for the program.[31] But ERAP was ultimately a failure, disbanding in 1967 amid conflicts over race, gender, and class—especially the last, as the mostly middle-class student organizers were charged with elitism by the workers they sought to organize.[32]

Activists in the South, too, were trying their hand at community-based labor organizing, with somewhat greater success. Initiated by former SNCC activists Bob and Dottie Zellner, Grass Roots Organizing Work (GROW) was started under the auspices of the Southern Conference Educational Fund (SCEF), one of the region's civil rights organizations. SNCC's Central Committee also provided a small amount of aid.[33] GROW lent its support to a variety of southern labor struggles, including AFL-CIO-affiliated union campaigns in some of New Orleans's plushest hotels.[34] But GROW became most widely known for its work in Laurel, Mississippi, in 1967.

A local of the International Woodworkers of America was engaged in a strike against the Masonite Corporation, the largest producer of hardboard in the world, as management tried to downsize the workforce and automate the plant.[35] The Woodworkers local, with roots in both Wobbly organizing and Klan racism, had struck without its national union's approval. Though the three-thousand-member local had been formally desegregated a few years earlier, the local, the largest in the state, had no Black officials, and a wide gulf remained between white and Black members.[36] For months, GROW used the strike to bring Black and white workers together to discuss democratic unionism and community support for the struggle. In December 1967, the national union put the local in trusteeship, removed its elected leadership, and signed a deal with the corporation. Nevertheless, GROW's underlying mission—undermining racism and laying the groundwork for a democratic and community-based union movement—was advancing. By late 1968, some eight hundred local unionists, who had not been allowed back to work and were still pursuing their jobs through a court case, had a racially integrated strike committee that included both men and women. They held weekly rallies at which "as many as 1,000 people assemble in a cow pasture and talk about how they can organize," according to one observer's report.[37]

At the same time, Black, white, and Cajun pulpwood workers who supplied raw materials to big companies such as Masonite, Scott Paper, Weyerhauser, and Georgia Pacific approached GROW for organizing help. The AFL-CIO-affiliated International Woodworkers Association had already denied their requests for organizing assistance.[38] These workers had formed their own nine-thousand-member independent Gulfcoast Pulpwood Association (GPA), which had twenty chapters across six states and was about 80 percent African American. These contingent workers labored for piece rates, hauling wood from the forests for the paper corporations.[39] A few years later, in September 1971, when Masonite's Laurel plant suddenly lowered the piece rate, forty GPA members refused to deliver wood. The strike spread across Mississippi, and Masonite backed down, offering a substantial raise in piece rates to the woodcutters. A second, partly victorious strike was carried out against the paper companies across the South in 1973. Civil rights groups, including the NAACP and the SCLC, organized support rallies and sent material aid to the strikers. At the same time, southern woodcutters discovered that their comrades in the Maine woods had created similar independent unions and traveled to meet with them.[40] In 1978, Mississippi woodcutters organized again to fight the timber multinationals, this time as the independent United Woodcutters Association. By 1982, UWA had grown into a statewide organization with forty-four locals and more than twelve hundred members.[41]

Meanwhile, the seeds of resistance that GROW had planted had taken root. Because of its high-profile work at Masonite, GROW was contacted by workers in other industries who wanted to unionize. It got involved in organizing poultry and catfish plant workers. "A man might have been a pulpwood cutter but his wife worked in the poultry plant," Bob Zellner recalls. In May 1972, tired of working conditions that they compared to slavery, some sixty Black women walked off their jobs at Poultry Packers, and, with GROW's help, the independent

Mississippi Poultry Workers Union was born. Six months later, the union won a collective bargaining election among the plant's two hundred workers. Eager for unionization, poultry workers at two other plants also voted in the new union, and organizing spread to plants in neighboring counties.[42]

GROW's development shows a striking array of organizing experiments in the antiunion South, across several industries, undertaken by former civil rights organizers in collaboration with poor workers. Like the freedom unions that had come before, these projects raised consciousness, made concrete gains, and laid the groundwork for future organizing. GROW's philosophy was to educate workers about labor solidarity but direct them as much as possible into the mainstream union movement, all the while helping them be independent and critical. For contingent forest workers battling multinational corporations, food-processing factory workers, and low-wage hotel employees in cities like New Orleans, these successful experiences raised hopes among both poor workers and their advocates that the trade union movement could, and eventually would, broaden its organizing strategies.

Equal Pay for Equal Work

While women were central participants in many of the civil rights–based worker-organizing drives during the '60s, by the end of the decade an emerging feminist movement was also interjecting gender explicitly into labor organizing. "Contrary to a popular ad . . . we have *not* 'come a long way, baby,'" wrote one movement activist in 1969. "We work in every job listed by the Bureau of the Census but as a rule we do mostly underpaid, menial labor, and are paid the lowest salaries with the lowest fringe benefits and the worst working conditions going." Women were often the last hired and first fired, and made about 50 cents to each dollar earned by men. Among the occupations held by women, the largest number of positions were in clerical, sales, service, and household work. Clerical and sales jobs accounted for 43 percent of employment for white women and 15 percent for women of color. Of service and household workers during this period, the majority were women of color, 54 percent to white women's 20 percent.[43]

From its beginning, the feminist movement had incorporated both waged and unwaged work in its conception of labor. Tens of thousands of women turned out for the first nationwide "strike for women's liberation" on August 26, 1970, some chained to housecleaning equipment or typewriters to make their point, others marching to a chant of "Scrub your own floors!" Socialist and Marxist feminists theorized that women were oppressed as a class through male supremacy or patriarchy, acting both as a reserve army of labor to bring down wages and as unpaid domestic workers in their own homes. "We're tired of getting the lowest wages and the crummiest work," declared the program of the Liberation Women's Union.[44]

Autonomous but like-minded groups sprouted up in cities around the country, calling themselves "women's liberation unions." They used direct action to make demands for equal pay, shared household work, and free childcare. The Chicago Women's Liberation Union, one of the largest, protested against corporations that oppressed women economically or socially. In March 1970, activists from the group sneaked into a business seminar in "straight" clothes to submit a list of demands including equal pay, paid parental leave, free childcare, and "an end to all hiring practices based on age, marital status, physical beauty, pregnancy or style of dress." When the businessmen refused, the women "hexed" them with a witches' curse.[45] Actions like these didn't bring contractual protections, but they did advance the cultural struggle for equality by raising the issue of women's rights in a highly visible and creative way.

Debates over housework, mothering, and women's "hidden work" in the home occupied page after page in the feminist press. Wages for Housework committees were organized in New York, Los Angeles, San Francisco, Chicago, Cleveland, and Boston.[46] In one nationwide contest, thousands of women submitted essays on "practical programs to achieve economic justice for homemakers." Essayists recommended remedies ranging from the individual ("have a special [compensation] contract made up as part of the marriage ceremony, and sign it before getting married") to the collective ("have an equal retirement and disability fund for the homemaker, paid by deducting a percentage from the wages of all working people"). "If all housewives went on strike," predicted journalist Cindy Felong in 1971, "the mess and filth would soon create a national crisis that would stop all production."[47]

Were women "the" working class, and was their unwaged domestic labor part of the capitalist commodity system? How did some women's economic status, race, and ability to find waged work enable them to at least partially buy their way out of this domestic division of labor by sex? Opinions ranged from unashamed biological determinism (like the often-quoted slogan "All women are housewives") to more nuanced analyses of how race and ethnicity structured both the economy and gender relations.

Many of these early feminist debates came from the point of view of middle-class white women and ignored divisions between women based on race, ethnicity, or class.[48] For instance, women of color had often performed domestic labor as paid workers as well as unpaid wives or mothers, and poor women in general had long worked outside the home. Household labor, whether paid or unpaid, was tied to the legacies of slavery and domestic servitude, continuing to affect the status and social worth of such occupations.[49]

The complexities of unwaged labor were nowhere more apparent than among welfare recipients, the majority of them women. Activism around welfare rights exploded in the late '60s, as poor people began organizing for the benefits due them in an economy that had marginalized their existence. Some of the feminist movement's consciousness about unwaged labor came from this struggle. Between 1960 and 1968, the number of public assistance recipients nearly doubled, from 745,000 families to 1.5 million, then doubled again by 1972, to 3 million.[50] Spurred by this burgeoning population of recipients, local welfare-rights groups sprang up across the country, demanding higher benefit levels, the right to earn additional income without penalty, childcare for working parents, and medical benefits. As a result of the lack of state-provided or state-subsidized childcare, combined with limited opportunities for living-wage jobs and society's relegation of parenting to mothers, it was women more often than men who drew welfare benefits, with white women making up the majority of recipients. However, proportionately more African American women were involved in the welfare rights movement as activists.

Representatives from seventy-five welfare-rights groups across the country founded the National Welfare Rights Organization (NWRO) in 1966. George Wiley, former associate national director of CORE, was elected executive director of NWRO, which sought to promote a multiracial movement of the poor around welfare rights. The group's blueprint came from an essay by activist-scholars Frances Fox Piven and Richard Cloward, "A Strategy to End Poverty," which argued that activists should inform poor people of their legal right to welfare and mobilize disruptive protests by which the poor could win the economic relief owed to them. During the late 1960s, tens of thousands of NWRO activists jammed into welfare offices and confronted authorities with demonstrations, picketing, and sit-ins, demanding a just welfare system and a guaranteed minimum national income. Thousands more benefited from NWRO assistance with their individual grievances, which often relied on direct action tactics similar to those being used by activists in the civil rights movement, and which had historically been used in the labor movement.[51]

While the focus of NWRO was on welfare benefits, the question of work always hovered in the background. But, noted Piven and Cloward in *Poor People's Movements*, "it was not clear how activists could, as a practical, day-to-day matter of organizing, mount an attack on poverty by attacking its main cause—underemployment and unemployment."[52] Instead, NWRO organized poor people around their moral right to a sufficient income, largely skirting the issue of employment.

Welfare serves as the ultimate safety net for all working people but is used most frequently by the lowest-wage workers—most often women and people of color—who shuttle back and forth from minimum-wage jobs, contingent work, or jobs in the informal economy to welfare grants, food stamps, and housing vouchers. Welfare is the unemployment insurance of last resort. In addition, welfare recipients often do the vital but unwaged and socially invisible work of raising children and other types of care.[53] Activists have long argued that welfare is compensation for this labor and point out that even if all recipients were offered jobs at living wages, a fair welfare system would still be necessary for those who can't work due to such responsibilities.

NWRO's strategists thought that benefits campaigns would bring greater numbers of recipients into a national network, leading to passage of a guaranteed national income in Congress. Such a measure, if passed, would have amounted to a pay raise for NWRO's members, the majority of whom were single mothers working in the home. Although framed by the language of welfare rights, the arguments of NWRO members could have come straight out of the labor movement. Johnnie Tillmon, a mother of six from Watts, California, and the first chair of NWRO, spoke of the productive, socially important work that welfare mothers performed. "If I were President," she said, "I would solve this so-called welfare crisis in a minute and go a long way toward liberating every woman. I'd just issue a proclamation that women's work is *real* work. . . . I'd start paying women a living wage for doing the work we are already doing—child raising and house-keeping. And the welfare crisis would be over. Just like that."[54] In voicing demands of this nature to the state, Tillmon and other welfare mothers reframed the debate about welfare around the value of their unwaged work. NWRO was, in effect, their union, though their work-places were scattered and they had no visible employer. By advocating for "motherwork," as historian Eileen Boris has called it, NWRO activists "defied the devaluation of caregiving."[55]

Indeed, NWRO's resemblance to a labor union was striking. Wiley, its director, envisioned a "national union of welfare recipients,"[56] and NWRO's structure closely mirrored that of a labor union. This union of the poor, like any other union, was run by its members and attempted to bargain collectively on behalf of all welfare recipients. NWRO usually required members to pay dues before its activists would assist with a grievance. As in a labor union, members elected their peers to national, state, and local policy-making bodies that set the movement's agenda. And as in progressive, democratically run unions, paid staff contributed their technical skills, but ultimate political control rested with the rank-and-file leadership. Although NWRO was not without internal organizational difficulties, it reflected the dynamism of movement organizing. NWRO and other social movement organizations didn't have binding contracts to enforce—as did most trade unions—so the parameters within which they operated were less formal, encouraging more experimentation and risk taking.

NWRO lasted nearly a decade, from 1966 until 1975, and obtained benefits for tens of thousands of recipients who wouldn't have received them otherwise. NWRO members demanded economic justice—in the form of more income, food, and shelter for themselves and their families—from a society that had stereotyped them as unemployable, morally unworthy, and undeserving. Because the welfare rights movement lacked legal protections, it had to mobilize in the welfare offices and on the streets to make gains. These direct action tactics would be taken up by welfare recipients in the '70s and then in the '90s, as they were again forced to work in exchange for benefits.

Wages for Housework

Waged domestic workers had a history of unionization attempts stretching back decades. In 1920 there were ten locals of domestic workers scattered across the South affiliated with the Hotel and Restaurant Employees, AFL.[57] In the mid-'30s, domestic worker unions started by CIO activists briefly sprang up in Washington, DC, and New York City. In 1968, activists in Atlanta formed the National Domestic Workers Union (NDWU), which they hoped would improve the wages and working conditions of the city's maids. Dorothy Bolden, a forty-one-year-old maid who had begun her paid work by washing diapers at the age of seven, organized support for the union by talking to other maids as they traveled on the bus to their employers' homes. The NDWU was initially more of a mutual aid group than a union, Bolden said in a 1985 interview, but "the word 'union' gave it clout, and working-class members understood the word."[58]

Membership grew rapidly. African American maids in Atlanta were earning only $3.50 to $5 for an entire twelve-hour day. The biggest challenge was the scattered nature of their work, which demanded new organizing tactics. "You can't negotiate with private employers, private homes," wrote Bolden. "You have to teach each maid how to negotiate" for herself, by refusing to work for low wages. This sort of "collective bargaining" relied not on industry-wide contracts but on pure solidarity. To be successful, most of the maids in a particular neighborhood would have to take part. They did, and the maids' wages increased in less than a year to $13.50–$15 a day with carfare.[59] This tactic, as we will see in chapter 5, is not unlike that of immigrant day laborers who use "streetcorner solidarity" to organize for higher wages in several US cities.

The NDWU and other domestic workers' groups joined an umbrella organization called the National Committee on Household Employment (NCHE). Founded in 1965, NCHE had its origins in the work of labor feminists, such as former Women's Bureau director Esther Peterson, who sought to infuse household labor with value. In 1971 NCHE formed the Household Technicians of America to organize women across the nation.[60] The group sponsored the first national conference of household employees that year and worked for the inclusion of domestics in the minimum-wage provisions of the federal Fair Labor Standards Act (a struggle it won, finally, in 1974). It also instituted a "model contract"—guaranteeing wages, hours, conditions and grievance procedures, much like a union contract—that employers signed when hiring domestic workers through NCHE's referral service.[61]

There was widespread support for domestic worker organizing in the Black community. Women's groups with predominantly white membership, such as the National Organization for Women, also supported organizing efforts by Black women, suggests Phyllis Palmer, "partially because white women's employment—and consequent need for household help—was rising as dramatically as the supply of domestic servants was dropping."[62] Yet Black, Latina, and white women's attitudes toward housework differed: while some white feminists, such as Betty Friedan, found housework degrading and would not do it even if paid, African American activists pointed out that such an attitude was what made organizing so difficult. "The sad part about domestic work," wrote Nikki Giovanni in 1975, "is neither the work nor the worker, but the attitude of those who hire the worker." Other types of domestic work that had moved from private homes into the market—food service, baking, childcare—benefited from increased respect, better working conditions, and sometimes higher wages. However, with a median income of about $1,800 a year, domestics were "still slaves, economically speaking," wrote Mary A. McClendon, president of the NCHE-sponsored Household Workers Organization (HWO), which had launched a drive to organize Detroit's twenty-nine thousand domestic workers. "That's $600.00 less than President Nixon's proposed minimum income for the unemployed."[63]

Household workers' unions focused on dignity and respect in addition to the more obvious wage issues. As well, domestic workers' organizations were confronted with a need for consciousness raising similar to that faced by other women's organizations. Domestic work was—pure and simple—work. But it was work particularly influenced by hierarchy, elitism, sexism, and racism. The contingency of the work placed it in the same category as other poor workers' livelihoods: employed one season, on welfare the next. "There is no grievance machinery to handle their complaints," wrote McClendon. "After a nine or ten hour day, spent cleaning two or three large suburban houses, the workers return to Detroit with often no more than nine dollars in their pocket, and no assurance that they will have a job tomorrow."[64]

In 1972 McClendon's Household Workers Organization launched a union drive at Dial-A-Maid, one of several domestic labor companies in Detroit providing maids to suburban employers. Though HWO eventually lost the bid to represent the employees, McClendon expressed hope that the effort was "only the beginning in bringing domestic workers within the mainstream of the labor movement."[65] That mainstream, however, showed no interest in the HWO, so McClendon turned instead toward affiliation with the Dodge Revolutionary Union Movement (DRUM), an independent rank-and-file caucus organized by the League of Revolutionary Black Workers.[66]

Organizing for Respect

In the '60s, public-sector union organizing had swept through federal, state, local, and university workplaces, but as it slowed by the early '70s, activists called on trade unions to begin organizing women in the private sector. "Unions must begin to make a greater effort to organize the 25 million working women," wrote activist Judy Edelman in 1970. "More than 1.7 million domestic workers, half a million farm workers, nearly one million retail sales workers, and millions of office workers throughout the country," many of whom were workers of color, remained unrepresented by unions.[67]

But trade unions launched few forays into the world of private-sector female workplaces. Like their sisters in domestic employment, clerical workers were obliged to organize themselves, drawing on their experiences in the civil rights, welfare rights, feminist, and labor movements. Nearly two dozen organizations for white-collar women workers formed outside of trade unions during the 1970s. Among the most prominent were 9to5 (Boston), Union WAGE (California), Women Employed (Chicago), and Women Organized for Employment (San Francisco). In some ways similar to earlier civil rights jobs mobilizations and construction trades protests, they focused on fair hiring, equal pay, and protections against discrimination and sexual harassment, and supported both race- and gender-based affirmative action programs. Reflecting the overall composition of the clerical workforce, most members were white, although women of color made up as much as one-third of the membership of some.[68]

Activists consciously set out to make the women's movement more responsive to working women, according to Karen Nussbaum, a 9to5 founder. "The women's movement," she said in a 1980 interview, "was not speaking to large numbers of women. We [needed] to broaden our base."[69] Starting in 1973 with a newsletter circulated in Boston subway stations, 9to5 went on to win many victories for office workers, often through publicity and policy debates rather than on-the-job organizing. In its 1975 campaign for equal wages in Boston's insurance industry, 9to5 activists dug up a little-known state law that forbade licensing of discriminatory companies. Demanding its implementation in public hearings before state licensing boards, 9to5 compelled the state's insurance commissioner to refuse licenses to companies that discriminated on the basis of gender or race. Other campaigns targeted the publishing industry and aimed at obtaining maternity benefits as a disability under company health plans. In 1983, ten years after its founding, 9to5 had grown to twenty-five chapters with more than twelve thousand members nationally. While it did not claim to be a labor union and did not engage in collective bargaining, it did establish a "sister" relationship in 1981 with SEIU District 925, under an agreement that gave it autonomy to pursue organizing plans of its choosing.[70]

Chicago's Women Employed operated similarly. In the first two years of its existence (1973–75), it took action against more than twenty employers, winning half a million dollars of back wages for women at a major Chicago insurance company and forcing public officials to enforce fair hiring and employment laws. In 1977 Women Employed joined civil rights organizations in a negligence lawsuit against the Chicago office of the Equal Employment Opportunity Commission, building a collaborative relationship with antiracist organizations while working for gender equity. This laid the groundwork for future coalition building. After ten years of organizing, Women Employed represented some three thousand women nationally.[71]

San Francisco's Women Organized for Employment (WOE) formed from a coalition of thirty women's groups in the Bay Area. It pressed California's Fair Employment Practices Commission for sweeping reforms and targeted employers such as savings and loan institutions, which discriminated against female job applicants. In "Tales of WOE," a column in the group's newsletter, women described their jobs as lacking dignity and a living wage. "We catered to our bosses in ways that went beyond simply doing our jobs well—we ran errands, handled personal matters, served lunches. Sometimes we were treated as though we were inanimate objects, like the machines we operated," wrote Margie Albert, in a 1974 piece intended to persuade her coworkers to join a union.[72]

Like domestic workers, activists organizing white-collar workers lamented the difficulty of convincing their colleagues of seeing themselves as workers deserving rights. Consciousness raising about class and gender oppression was necessary to assure them that collective action could make a difference. "Most of us had never been in a union," one worker reflected during a 1979 interview. "We considered ourselves 'professionals' who didn't need that kind of thing." Organizers maintained independence from trade unions, because they believed the organizing model used by trade unions was ineffective in reaching white-collar women workers. Instead these activists educated

women about exploitation at work, collectively creating workers'
power from the bottom up.[73]

These women were also fighting what Dorothy Sue Cobble has
called "gendered notions of unionism," based on the assumption that
women's workplace concerns were no different from men's and revolved solely around economic issues such as wages and benefits. But
in some cases they were distinctively different: demands for nonsexist
workplaces and respect and dignity on the job were central to women's
organizing. For instance, in 1972 "a group of tired stewardesses tried
to explain their concerns to the incredulous male transit union officials
who led their union. No, the primary issues were not wages and benefits, they insisted, but the particular cut of their uniforms and the sexual insinuations made about their occupation in the new airline
advertisements."[74]

Male union leaders often saw such demands as "not deserving of
serious attention, let alone concerted activity," Cobble wrote. These
stewardesses, like many female workers, experienced class differently
from their male counterparts. Their particular labor experience was
shaped by multifaceted gendered oppressions. They wanted not only
better wages but also control over definitions of their sexuality and
"personhood." When their union gave these demands cold reception,
they created their own national organization, Stewardesses for
Women's Rights, which successfully challenged many exploitive practices through lawsuits and media activism.[75]

Such independent labor-organizing efforts among women in the
late '60s and early '70s were, like the civil rights organizing of the period, strongly characterized by solidarity as an organizing principle.
Little else protected these poor workers from the employers who hired
them, although on occasion legal gains bolstered their rights. Unlike
in most trade unions, decision making in these groups remained in
the hands of rank-and-file workers—with new workers brought into
the struggle—enabling them to create and manage lightweight and
flexible organizational structures. This resulted in a dependence on
members, as opposed to paid staff, to do the organizing. The flexibility came along with a lack of the stable funding that trade unions typically enjoyed, which could make it difficult to win long battles against

wealthy employers. Still, the consciousness raising and on-the-ground organizing had a significant effect: by the end of the '80s, the level of office worker unionization (16 percent) nearly matched that of the workforce as a whole (17 percent at that time).[76]

The New Working Class?

Substantial differences clearly existed between the workers discussed here: they were waged and unwaged, blue collar or industrial as well as white collar, of different races, ethnicities, and genders. There were also differences in how their economic organizing initiatives took shape and what they aimed to achieve. Some were short-lived but ideologically influential on the left, such as SDS's Economic Research and Action Project and the Freedom Unions of SNCC and CORE. Others, such as Grass Roots Organizing Work, helped establish some of the first workplace unions for low-wage and contingent workers in the South. Still others, such as the civil rights jobs mobilizations, the National Welfare Rights Organization, and the clerical workers' organizations, influenced the formation of national, state, and local policy for years to come. A few, such as 9to5, continued to work for social and economic justice into the next decades.

But there were commonalities as well: each group was organized by poor workers who faced neglect, indifference, and even hostility from established trade unions. Many movement organizations made economic justice a priority and began engaging in their own labor-organizing initiatives. Working outside of trade unions, these groups formed a kind of "second front" within the labor movement, advancing concerns shared by the poor, whether welfare recipients, low-wage workers, contingent workers, or the unemployed. These early poor workers' groups supported each other's campaigns, built loose coalitions, and viewed themselves as separate from "mainstream" labor. By the end of the '70s, scores of small, local independent union organizing projects had sprung up—such as the aptly named Poor People's Union Local 1 in Atlanta, an organization of food service workers at the Georgia Institute of Technology. Movement activists formed independent unions representing workers in health care, manufacturing, and restaurant work, as well as Native American workers on reservations, gay, lesbian, bisexual, transgender, and queer workers, and prison laborers.[77]

Why did these groups develop outside the mainstream? Most poor workers' unions shared common disappointments vis-à-vis trade unions: queries on cooperative organizing were ignored, and if independent organizing did succeed, trade unions often responded with territorialism. Others asked for financial or organizing help and were turned away. Ultimately, trade unionism's record of racism, sexism, or simple disinterest in nontraditional workplaces spoke for itself. Race, ethnicity, gender, and sexuality often resonated more deeply as organizing motifs for poor workers than did the abstract class solidarity proffered by trade unions, especially when that solidarity was often more rhetoric than reality.

Perhaps more important, the organizing tactics of these independent initiatives differed dramatically from the ossified practices of most trade unions. They were light-years from the bureaucratic trade unionism of the day. AFL-CIO unions did little organizing in the '60s, and what organizing they did was centered in neat jurisdictions already close to their base and accomplished by routine methods like card counts, representation elections, and unfair labor practice charges. Trade union organizers, usually paid staff with no direct connection to the workers they were organizing, would collect signed "authorization cards" from workers supporting the union, and when at least 30 percent of the workforce had signed, they would turn them in to the National Labor Relations Board with a request to schedule an election. When employers launched antiunion campaigns or fired workers for supporting the union, often union officials' only response would be filing legal charges that could take years to decide.

Poor workers' organizations, by contrast, burst forth in a flurry of rank-and-file energy, using direct action techniques grounded in movement experiences. If card counts and elections were used, they were part of a larger, more militant and more visible campaign involving demonstrations, pickets, worker-to-worker organizing, coalitions with sister movements, and media coverage. They were well aware that labor had once been a movement and could be again. CORE activists in particular admired the CIO, and the first CORE sit-ins were actually called "sit downs" in homage to the CIO's direct action tactics.[78] Encouraging democratic decision making, these groups relied heavily on solidarity and community-wide participation rather than on legal strategies, and sought to organize horizontally rather than vertically.

Though many such efforts were experimental and fleeting, they were part of a historical strand that tied the civil rights and women's movements to later poor workers' unions. These organizing initiatives showed the complex interrelationship of the labor movement with other social movements, and simultaneously cast doubt on the usual view that "labor" was a single unified movement. Moreover, they made it clear that organizing the "unorganizable" ranks of poor workers—often scattered among various workplaces and performing different types of work—not only was possible but could be highly successful. Voting rights, political struggles, and cultural changes may have made more headlines during the '60s and early '70s, but the fight for economic justice was always present—sometimes behind the scenes, sometimes at the forefront. Bouncing from low-wage jobs to unemployment to welfare and back again, and diverse in terms of age, race, ethnicity, and gender, poor workers shared a desire to organize for justice. And organize they did, not only with independent unions of their own making but also against the trade union status quo.

Martin Luther King Jr., Cleveland Robinson, and Ralph Abernathy at District 65's Biennial Convention, September 1962. *(Robert F. Wagner Labor Archives, New York University, District 65's/UAW Photograph Collection, NP 63#20420 [cropped])*

2

The Fight Within

Trade Unions Respond to the Movements

The explosion of social movement-based organizing during the late 1960s and early 1970s also penetrated into the heart of trade unionism. Some workers inside mainstream unions launched a movement of their own, challenging ingrained ideologies and practices that had long crippled their organizations. The top leadership of most trade unions was substantially out of step with their membership's racial and gender composition as well as their concerns. Widespread sexism and racism within union institutions were everyday reminders that internal patterns of discrimination mirrored similar problems in the world outside. By the early '70s, as capital launched a full-scale attack on unions, abruptly ending the "labor peace" of previous decades, most unions were headed by highly paid officials not directly elected by their members. Contract bargaining often took place in inaccessible boardrooms, and rank-and-file workers rarely took part.[1]

On the organizing front, the trade union record increasingly resembled a dusty ledger of long-past victories. Established, complacent, not yet facing capital's more serious depredations of the later '70s and '80s, most AFL-CIO unions were largely uninterested in expanding into new groups of workers. George Meany's nearly three decades at the helm of the AFL-CIO, from 1952 to 1979, had induced a paralysis of both vision and action, and even a barely contained hostility toward workers who were not yet within the bounds of official trade unionism. Paul Buhle's critical study of AFL-CIO leadership, *Taking Care of Business*, recounts Meany's answer to a reporter's question in 1972 about why union membership was rapidly sinking as a percentage of the workforce: "'I don't know, I don't care.' When a reporter pressed the issue, 'Would you prefer to have a larger proportion?' Meany snapped, 'Not necessarily. We've done quite well without it. Why should we worry about organizing groups of people who do not appear to want to be organized?'"[2]

The few internal attempts made to break the spell of Meanyism came from the left-wing progressive sector of the trade union movement as it explored new ways of organizing during the late '60s and early '70s. For instance, Hospital Workers Local 1199, which organized private-sector hospital workers in New York City, tried to expand union demands from bread-and-butter issues like wage increases and contract provisions to broader social movement goals of democracy and equality. Local 1199's membership was diverse in race, gender, and skills, and the union's leadership consciously incorporated those differences into its organizing, even dubbing itself the "soul power" union. Moreover, Local 1199's organizers themselves often came from the ranks of social movement activists. In 1962 several Congress of Racial Equality chapters worked with Local 1199 to organize hospital workers. CORE organizer Sheila Michaels recalls that "the line between CORE/SNCC and 1199 organizing was porous. [1199] was sort of a halfway house for recovering community organizers," who brought community-based strategies into the union.[3]

Similarly, some public-sector unions such as AFSCME linked their organizing among workers of color to civil rights, as in the landmark February 1968 Memphis sanitation workers' strike. With pay as low as $1.80 per hour, some 40 percent of Memphis's thirteen hundred trash collectors were eligible for welfare. Their strike was about better wages, the right to form a union, and, most of all, dignity on the job. During pickets, workers carried signs that said simply "I am a

man." When the city council and the mayor's office refused to negotiate, African American ministers organized a community support
network and called a boycott of businesses and news outlets associated with the mayor, and later launched large-scale civil disobedience
activities, filling the city's jails. Two months after it began, the strike
was settled, with a raise for workers, a union contract, and an end to
racial discrimination in the sanitation department.[4]

Along with efforts like these, during the late 1960s interest in community-based tactics began to reemerge within a few trade unions for
the first time since the Depression, albeit often on a small, local scale.
The United Auto Workers was one such union, both targeted for reform by union dissidents and actively initiating reform programs of
its own. Two national and two local organizing projects were part of
these efforts: Alliance for Labor Action, the Distributive Workers of
America, the Detroit-based Dodge Revolutionary Union Movement
(DRUM), and the Watts Labor Community Action Committee
(WLCAC) in Los Angeles. WLCAC and Alliance for Labor Action—
both heavily subsidized by the UAW—worked within accepted parameters of liberal trade unionism and corporate capitalism, while
DRUM and the Distributive Workers presented more fundamental
challenges to the way unions operated. Taken together, these cases illustrate the complex relationship that existed between institutionalized labor and mass-based social movements. Social justice activism
emerged as a rebellious force within the house of labor, redefining
what unionism could mean for poor workers.

Rebellions in the Ranks

"Some black militants have come into the unions, but as sworn enemies, bent on destruction," wrote UAW education director Brendan
Sexton in the February 1971 issue of *Dissent*. Like many union staffers,
Sexton viewed with alarm the prospect that workers of color such as
those who founded DRUM might create what he called "centers of
black power" through either existing unions or organizations of "black
and brown workers at the margins of the economy."[5] Whether Sexton
feared such organizing because it might undermine what he saw as

class solidarity or because it would compete on an institutional basis with trade unions, he was commenting on a visible phenomenon within trade unions all over the country: the trend toward independent rank-and-file caucuses based on race. Steelworkers in Gary, Indiana; transit workers in Chicago and New York City; construction workers in Boston; auto workers in Fremont, California—union members of color were increasingly turning to an "internal caucus" strategy to oppose racism within their unions. In some cases these caucuses were founded or influenced by Black Panthers or other Black nationalist groups, bringing the rhetoric and tactics of movement activism directly onto the plant floor and into the union hall.[6] A few years later, radical women adopted a similar caucus strategy to combat sexism within trade unions.

DRUM was one of the best known of the caucuses, founded in 1967 by UAW rank-and-file activists impatient with decades of internal racism and bureaucratic control. It used critiques of racism and bureaucracy to mobilize a movement for change within the UAW. Charging both General Motors and the UAW with racism, it cited evidence that the best positions went to whites while African Americans had the dirtiest and most dangerous jobs. DRUM's leaders accused the nearly all-white union leadership of perpetuating this system by inadequately addressing African American workers' grievances and neglecting organizing. The UAW's membership was at least 30 percent Black, yet the union's twenty-six-member executive board had only two African American members; likewise, women made up 14 percent of the membership, but there was only one female board member. "Once considered the cutting edge of militant industrial unionism," write scholars Dan Georgakas and Marvin Surkin, "the UAW showed little interest in organizing the numerous non-union feeder shops in the industry, in moving for unionizing in the South, or in fighting for substantial gains such as 40 hours' pay for 30 hours' work."[7]

DRUM's theory was that racism was intentionally cultivated, by both management and the union, to divide workers and maintain better control. It countered by linking community and workplace issues as well as by consciously defining its organizing in multiethnic, multicultural terms, particularly in its outreach to Detroit's large Arab

American population. DRUM was not without its faults, including a deep-seated sexism, a reliance on inflammatory rhetoric, and what writer Herb Boyd calls an "'in-your-face' bravado," all too common in movement organizations of the time.[8] Still, DRUM helped transform the way Detroit's working class thought about itself, its culture, and its organizational power.

Auto workers at other plants formed sister "RUMs" (revolutionary union movements), including ELRUM at the Eldon Avenue plant, FRUM at the Ford plant, GRUM at the General Motors plant, all grouped by 1969 under the umbrella of the League of Revolutionary Black Workers. Later the group would launch a short-lived national organization called the Black Workers Congress. Relying on demonstrations and wildcat strikes, league members picketed the UAW International convention and ran against incumbents in union elections. The auto companies and the UAW alike were afraid of the RUMs, because they moved past rhetoric and organized actual shutdowns of plants. For instance, in July 1968, following a march to a UAW executive board meeting, DRUM members called for a wildcat strike the next morning at the Dodge main plant. Four thousand people walked out, surprising even the organizers themselves.[9]

UAW officials responded with red-baiting and called the league's publications "extremist hate sheets" and its members "racial separatists."[10] The UAW's secretary-treasurer Emil Mazey went so far as to imply, in a 1969 interview in the *Detroit News*, that this fearsome Black "peril" was more dangerous than the imagined red peril of 1950s anticommunism.[11] This response, from a union that prided itself on a nonracialist, politically progressive, industrially based unionism, showed that liberal trade union officials were not as different from conservative Meany as they might have liked to believe.

The radical left hoped the rank-and-file caucus phenomenon was a move toward democratic and egalitarian trade unionism. "A specter haunts Detroit that tomorrow will haunt the nation," wrote Robert Dudnick, the *Guardian*'s labor correspondent in 1969. For much of the left, rank-and-file rebellions signaled not only a rebellion against white male trade union leaders but also a long-overdue "internal revolution" against bureaucracy. Workers had begun questioning how unions "turned into their opposite," from worker advocates into "an independent power that imposes its discipline" over workers, wrote Detroit activist-scholar Martin Glaberman in 1966. The stagnation of the union movement became a common theme in activist circles. Some workers began questioning how seniority, that most basic of union principles, had been put in the service of racial and gender discrimination; or how automatic dues checkoff made unions more distant from, and less dependent upon, the rank and file.[12]

There was criticism too about a generational privilege that benefited older, already organized industrial workers and left out younger, poorer workers in the unorganized sectors of the economy. "Unions are fat and lazy," wrote Detroiter James Wilson to the editor of the Black magazine *Sepia* in 1969. "They've got it made and are more intent on enjoying what they have than preserving the rights for others coming along later. . . . Have men like [UAW president] Walter Reuther . . . forgotten how things were in the 1930s?" Indeed, for poor workers the 1960s looked like the 1930s. Unemployment among Black workers was more than twice what it was among white workers, and wages for both white women and people of color averaged around half what white men earned.[13]

For thousands of working-class activists who had experienced new modes of organization and political action in social movements during the '60s, the need for radical change within their workplace unions was obvious, necessary, and inevitable. Coming from civil rights, Black power, and later the women's and LGBTQ movements, they became the frontline troops who would push the limits of bureaucratic trade unionism from both the inside and the outside.

Trade union institutions, which owed their existence to prior social movement organizing, were clearly in a very odd and uncomfortable position. "Is a traditional instrument of protest action itself becoming a target of protest?" worried Peter Henle, chief economist of the Bureau of Labor Statistics in 1969. "Disruptive protest" for civil rights and equality had moved full force into trade unions, he warned, upsetting "normal collective bargaining procedures."[14] Rebellious workers angry at the failings of organized labor threatened its precious stability, the goal and byword of bureaucratic unionism.

Internal Dissent, External Funding

While some trade union leaders battled internal dissent, poor workers were pouring into the streets to call for social and economic justice via the civil rights movement. At times people's protests against racism came through the destructive force of a riot, as in New York City's Harlem in 1964 and the Watts neighborhood of Los Angeles in 1965, then escalating to twenty-one cities in 1966 and seventy-five in 1967.[15] Meanwhile, liberal labor leaders searched for ways to quell poor Black workers' anger through manageable "programs" for economic betterment, leading some unions to experiment with their own versions of community-based organizing.

One of the most ambitious efforts of this kind was the UAW's Citizens' Crusade Against Poverty, founded in June 1964 by Walter Reuther as an attempt to institutionalize the coalition of civil rights, religious, and labor organizations that had successfully lobbied on behalf of the 1964 Civil Rights Act.[16] One of its first programs was the Watts Labor Community Action Committee. In March 1965, borrowing the community union concept espoused by Students for a Democratic Society's Economic Research and Action Project, neighborhood residents founded WLCAC with the financial assistance of the UAW and fourteen other unions to address joblessness and poverty in Watts, an African American neighborhood in South Central Los Angeles. The UAW sought to use collective bargaining techniques to resolve the community's grievances, using what staffers in the AFL-CIO's Industrial Union Department called "prototypes of union forms to attack the problems of poverty."[17] UAW officials believed that union activists, many of whom had come from poor neighborhoods, could use their union-taught negotiating skills to improve neighborhood organization. Ted Watkins, a former auto worker turned UAW staff person, as well as an African American Watts resident, was appointed to lead WLCAC.[18]

In August 1965, only a few months after WLCAC's founding, Watts erupted into rebellion. WLCAC sought to channel the community's frustration into collective action around concrete needs. South Central Los Angeles's unemployment rate had been near 30 percent in some census tracts during the first half of the '60s, while the national rate hovered between 4.5 and 6.7 percent.[19] The group decided that employment and medical services were the neighborhood's greatest needs, and pushed for a hospital that would serve the community and offer jobs to residents.

Those South Central residents who did have jobs faced problems that more privileged workers seldom encountered. Watkins recounted in a 1968 interview that police frequently stopped Black workers as they drove to graveyard-shift jobs. Shortly after the Watts uprising, when a Los Angeles police officer fatally shot a Watts resident who had been driving his pregnant wife to a hospital twelve miles away, the incident became a rallying point for WLCAC in its demand for a hospital in the neighborhood as well as protections against police misconduct. The hospital became a reality a few years later, offering jobs to some two thousand residents.[20]

From the late '60s to the early '70s, WLCAC helped finance gas stations, supermarkets, a credit union, and a restaurant, as well as a training center designed to prepare youth and welfare recipients for jobs. In 1968 the organization started a 538-acre farm in Saugus, north of Los Angeles, raising thousands of chickens and five hundred cattle to provide poor residents with cheaper food than was available in chain supermarkets in the neighborhood. WLCAC built and rehabilitated hundreds of housing units, and it became a major property owner in Watts complete with its own management division to oversee rent collection, garbage, landscaping, and repairs.[21]

But WLCAC was far from a grassroots organization. It had a sizable staff, and its work was made possible by huge UAW donations and government grants. In 1971 the UAW loaned WLCAC $2 million to invest in vacant land to continue its neighborhood development projects. By the early '70s, WLCAC was receiving substantial funding not only from the UAW but also from the Ford Foundation (an $800,000 grant) and the US Department of Labor ($1.6 million). WLCAC was one of the largest employers in Watts, with a thousand workers on the payroll and assets totaling $4 million.[22]

Many of these projects were a boon to Watts residents, creating much-needed employment and physical improvements in the neighborhood and therefore in poor workers' lives. However, they came along with a conservative ideology, heavily colored by class hierarchies. WLCAC strongly emphasized Black business ownership and job training as the solution to urban underdevelopment. WLCAC's staff saw its community and business ventures as "beautifying" Watts and keeping middle-class residents in the neighborhood. Poorer residents who couldn't afford to start or own businesses were trained as workers. The Saugus Job Center's Orientation Manual aimed to instill "punctuality" and "discipline," along with good grooming, since "employers have little regard for that person whose dress brands him as different." Creating an obedient working class was high on the agenda, as was linking success in employment to individual attributes rather than structural issues.[23]

Job-placement arrangements were set up with governmental agencies and public hospitals, as well as with corporations such as Safeway, most of them for low-paying entry-level positions. In 1969 Mervyn Dymally, a Democrat from Los Angeles and the first African American elected to the California Senate, criticized WLCAC's programs as "a kind of 'Booker T. Washington program'" and a "dead end," resulting as they did in low-wage job growth.[24]

Building on the WLCAC model, in May 1968 UAW representative Schrade started another community organization in the largely Latino neighborhood of East Los Angeles. The East Los Angeles Community Union (TELACU) also developed into a multimillion-dollar community-development corporation focusing on housing and jobs. The UAW appointed Esteban Torres, an International Affairs Department staffer from East Los Angeles, to head it. The organization strongly emphasized "area entrepreneurs," and it boasted that it was "a force capable of serving . . . the interested investor, in terms of providing him with additional markets and manpower."[25] The UAW supported similar projects in Dayton, Ohio; Saint Louis, Missouri; and Newark, New Jersey.

That the UAW threw substantial resources behind these conservative models for job training and small business development, while opposing the more fundamental changes demanded by its own rank and file, indicates the limitations of vision within progressive union officialdom. Nationally, the civil rights movement had moved toward a focus on economic justice, as exemplified by the April 1968 national Poor People's Campaign organized by a diverse coalition of activists. Whether they made low wages or none at all, poor workers were increasingly at the center of movement activities. Radical union reformers sought to build a strong economic justice movement that could challenge the unbridled power of postwar capitalism. But for WLCAC and similar organizations, structural economic change was not on the agenda. While social movement activists and trade union radicals were agitating for the destruction of racial and gender barriers to employment and for collective empowerment, groups like WLCAC sought to reinforce those barriers by individualizing the complex societal issue of work.

The activities of WLCAC did not directly affect the UAW's membership, because few of the neighborhood's residents ended up in UAW-represented jobs. And to some extent, heavily funded neighborhood groups like WLCAC mirrored the UAW's own bureaucratic structure and organizational culture. It's little wonder that UAW officials gave millions of dollars to these kinds of projects. They were a safe bet that allowed liberal union reformers to profess a rhetoric of social change, while still defending the union's own fortressed internal politics.

Programming Change

By 1968 the UAW had turned its sights toward a new national effort to organize the unorganized, called the Alliance for Labor Action (ALA). UAW president Reuther was engaged in a long-running feud with AFL-CIO president George Meany, calling his administration undemocratic, complacent, and self-congratulatory, and long-simmering disagreements over the Vietnam War between progressive and conservative unions were coming to a head. In March 1968 Reuther challenged Meany to call a special convention so the UAW could present its program for "revitalizing" the labor movement. When the AFL-CIO refused, the UAW withheld its per capita payments, then disaffiliated in July 1968. Just three weeks later, the UAW and the Teamsters (which had left the AFL-CIO eleven years earlier following charges of corruption) announced the formation of the Alliance for Labor Action, inviting other unions to join them in organizing "millions" of unorganized workers and establishing community unions for the poor and unemployed.[26]

The UAW and Teamsters were the nation's two biggest unions, representing more than 3.5 million workers. Initially they provided the ALA with a budget of $4.5 million, funds previously paid to the AFL-CIO as per capita dues. This made the ALA far larger and wealthier than the CIO had been when it was founded to support industrial unionism in 1935. Reuther already had his eye on several unions he wanted to recruit to the ALA, notes historian Nelson Lichtenstein, a list that read like a who's who of the progressive labor movement: the United Farm Workers; the United Electrical Workers; Hospital Workers Local 1199; District 65 of the Retail, Wholesale, and Department Store Workers; the American Federation of State, County, and Municipal Employees; the International Longshoremen's and Warehousemen's Union; and a few others.[27] While the ALA initially offered to not "raid" the memberships of AFL-CIO unions—ensuring, in other words, that the ALA wouldn't organize in AFL-CIO jurisdictions—it later passed a resolution allowing raids when it judged that an AFL-CIO union was not doing enough to organize in a particular workplace or industry. In practice, the AFL-CIO treated the ALA as a competitor by threatening to suspend or expel any unions that joined it. In 1969 the International Chemical Workers Union joined the ALA and was promptly expelled from the AFL-CIO.[28] Of Reuther's wish list of joiners, only District 65 of the Retail, Wholesale, and Department Store Union, which would later split from its AFL-CIO parent union, eventually came over to the ALA.

The alliance's organizers were convinced that the new organization could not model itself on the AFL-CIO. The ALA "should be action-oriented and should never be allowed to become another labor bureaucracy," according to the proposal its organizers penned.[29] Its first and biggest campaign was launched in Atlanta, a largely nonunion city with strong connection to the civil rights movement. Success in Atlanta, organizers felt, would give them a springboard into other southern cities. In the fall of 1969, almost fifty ALA staffers converged on the city, home to a half-million nonunionized white- and blue-collar workers. All the organizers were male (though a staff of what the ALA called "girls" operated the phone lines at the union office), about half were African American and half were white, and some 40 percent were Atlanta residents.[30] Under the direction of Teamsters organizing director William Genoese, flown in from Washington, DC, organizers spread out across the city's business parks with an estimated two hundred rank-and-file volunteers. "Our jurisdiction is the yellow pages," the ALA leadership told local reporters.[31]

But the traditional shop visits the organizers made paled in comparison to the barrage of pro-union propaganda the ALA launched throughout Atlanta. The ALA's pricey public-relations campaign included wall-to-wall advertisements on television, radio, newspapers, and public transit. Billboards loomed over Atlanta with the messages "Earn more—join a union!" and "Let ALA help you." Anyone not already in a union was urged to contact the ALA to start a union campaign where they worked, with the goals of improved wages, benefits, job security, holiday pay, and medical insurance. Buses all over Atlanta carried the same invitation, and radio ads written by a public relations company filled the airwaves. "Write down this telephone number . . . it can help you earn more, worry less, and live better! It's 874-8675, the number of the Alliance for Labor Action. . . . ALA can improve your present job so it will pay you more money!" beseeched one radio ad. "There's no obligation! . . . But the first move is yours . . . call 874-8675."[32]

This kind of slick Madison Avenue–style campaign was novel: rarely had US unions cast such a wide net using public relations. But ultimately the strategy failed. Even though a survey commissioned by the ALA found that the ad blitz had made the ALA's name recognizable to 43 percent of Atlanta's citizens, few actually joined unions.[33] When the campaign ended in December 1971, after twenty-eight months of organizing, only 4,590 workers had voted for unions in representation elections (and with Georgia's "right to work" laws, even after a victory there was no guarantee the workers would join the union). The ALA balance sheet in Atlanta was negative: it had won 94 union elections but lost or withdrawn from 102. The first year's campaign costs alone came to some $4 million—or $1,200 spent for each potential member. Head organizer William Genoese admitted in a July 30, 1970, organizing report that expenditures were "high if compared with results" and that the campaign hadn't "really made the impact on Black workers," who constituted over half of those targeted.[34]

The campaign showed that simply throwing resources into organizing would not turn around trade unions' fortunes. While different from the AFL-CIO's staid methods, the ALA's campaign suffered from the worst in top-down organizing techniques. Most organizers didn't actually work in potential organizing sites, so they had no organic connection to those who did. Workers considered the high-pressure advertising too slick, and people expressed fears about risking their jobs to join an organization that had not yet proved it could deliver.[35]

Ultimately, the ALA's prime method, relying on people's individual responses to ads, was itself highly alienating. Rather than fostering a collective sense of solidarity and power by organizing from the ground up at the workplace or community level, this strategy made joining a union an individual and isolating process. The pitch enumerated "consumer" benefits a member would receive, almost like a department store advertising goods on sale (and, incidentally, not unlike the AFL-CIO's "union privilege" programs, which tout consumer items like special rates on credit cards and home loans as incentives to join). Workers considered the pitch but weren't buying.

The ALA's founders hoped to establish community unions to organize the poor, welfare recipients, and the under- and unemployed outside of traditional workplaces; they envisioned several pilot programs in communities of color and among poor whites. But these community unions never got off the ground; they were hampered by the ALA staff's lack of community organizing experience. The ALA became something of a "philanthropic committee," giving out large grants for job training and addressing community issues.[36] Nonetheless, close ties remained between the ALA and existing UAW-supported community projects, including those in Watts (where the ALA gave WLCAC a combined loan and gift of $200,000)[37] and in East Los Angeles.

The ALA's strategy was the antithesis of the approach embraced by movement activists in the plants and on the streets: bottom-up, highly political organizing. Some of those same activists had been critical of the ALA's formation, characterizing it as a "falling out among thieves," according to one observer in the *Guardian*. UAW militants in DRUM saw the ALA as a cynical and expensive ploy by liberals to deflect attention from the struggle over racism within the UAW. "Everyone in the shop is laughing at the Alliance for Labor Action," wrote Black rank-and-filer Charles Denby, "which they consider just some more of Reuther's power politics against George Meany." There would be no escape for Reuther and other union officials from the demands for change within their own unions, no matter how innovative their outside organizing efforts looked in the media. As historian Nelson Lichtenstein observes, "The radical cadre Reuther sought were already present in UAW-organized shops," but Reuther rejected them as too far left.[38]

This dynamic of turning outward to build a new structure while ignoring needed change within was clearly at work with the ALA, as liberal Reuther—isolated from AFL-CIO unions—climbed into bed with the mobster-ridden Teamsters. These same "allies" would shortly attack the United Farm Workers by signing sweetheart deals with California growers and would endorse Nixon in the 1972 presidential election. By mid-1972, crushed by expenses from a protracted General Motors strike and without a push from Reuther (who died in a 1970 plane crash) to keep ALA alive, the UAW cut its per capita payments to the alliance.[39] The ALA died shortly thereafter. But before the end, another union had joined the ALA fold. This newcomer brought an innovative agenda of its own that would carry it more successfully into the future.

The Workers' War on Poverty

The independent Distributive Workers of America was born on May 24, 1969, when members of the New York–based District 65 of the Retail, Wholesale, and Department Store International Union (RWDSU) disaffiliated from their national union after a lengthy internal battle for reform, and formed a new organization. Charging racism among the highest echelons of the RWDSU leadership, the thirty thousand members of District 65 walked out of the RWDSU, declaring that the goal of the new union would be to organize poor workers. Ten smaller RWDSU locals, representing some ten thousand workers—from Los Angeles and Phoenix in the west and Philadelphia and Tallahassee in the east—defected from the national union. Together they formed the independent Distributive Workers.[40]

RWDSU officials reacted to the Distributive Workers dissidents in much the same way as the UAW leadership had responded to internal criticism from DRUM: by turning the accusations of racism back on the dissidents themselves. Max Greenberg, president of RWDSU, told his executive board in October 1969 that Distributive Workers' organizing efforts consisted "in great measure of racist appeals to black workers."[41] The Distributive Workers received encouragement from ALA leaders, and, ironically, a $120,000 loan from the UAW, which would apparently extend a helping hand to change the racial topography of other unions, if not its own.[42]

About half of the new union's members were African American, and nearly all held low-wage service jobs. In sharp contrast to existing trade-union leadership, the Distributive Workers declared "as a fundamental American principle" the idea that a multiracial union could and should be led by people of color. At the founding convention in Suffolk, Virginia, delegates elected an eighteen-member executive board—nine of the members were Black, seven white, and two Latino; only three were women. Cleveland Robinson was elected head of the new organization unanimously, becoming the first Black president of a multiracial union in US history.[43]

Robinson had immigrated from Jamaica in 1944, at the age of thirty. Shocked at the existence of widespread discrimination in the US, of a kind he had not witnessed in the Caribbean, he became involved in the labor movement. A founder, and later president, of the Negro American Labor Council, he had long advocated a closer integration of civil rights and labor movements. "It is my belief that we ought to throw out a challenge to labor for the organization of workers," Robinson wrote in July 1967 to Martin Luther King Jr., "particularly in the service and light manufacturing sectors, with the objective of raising the lowest wage level to $100 a week within a very short time. On the other hand, if the mainstream of labor continues to ignore the plight of these workers, the overwhelming majority of whom are Negro and Puerto Rican, then we ought to take steps to encourage the formation of independent unions to carry out these objectives."[44]

Robinson and other Distributive Workers activists sought to link social movement energy with institutionalized labor-union strength. A few months before his letter to King, Robinson had rallied four hundred African American leaders to the cause of independent unions at a conference in Washington, DC, drafting detailed plans for a drive to organize nonunion low-wage workers and target unions that were not adequately representing their members of color.[45]

The union struck out on its own to organize poor workers outside what Robinson called the AFL-CIO's "rotten and dilapidated" walls. "There are 57 million unorganized workers in the United States, and the AFL-CIO is not relevant to their problems," Robinson told delegates at the Distributive Workers' founding convention. Government programs to fight poverty were "ineffectual," he said. "The only real war on poverty is the war of workers organizing for a living wage," one in which poor people themselves build the structures of their own liberation.[46]

With pledges to organize "the Mexican-Americans, the Black Americans, the poor whites and the American Indians," and with repeated criticism of the "lily-white" complexion of mainstream trade unions, the new union made plans to organize in fifty cities, opening its doors to any unorganized workers who asked for help.[47] The new name—Distributive Workers of America—was meant to include as many kinds of workers as possible, whether working in trades, industries, or services, in large workplaces or small. This was a conscious effort to move past the exclusionary trade focus of the many AFL-CIO unions, and even past the old CIO's focus of organizing along industry lines.

In its first year, the Distributive Workers brought more than two thousand previously unorganized low-wage workers into the union. Every new contract negotiated for those workers included what was at that time a unique clause: January 15 would be a paid holiday in honor of Martin Luther King Jr., with 40 percent of the day's pay going directly to a District 65 demonstration and rally fund. Moreover, the union insisted that rank-and-file workers be involved in organizing campaigns, because the "narrow objective of merely collecting dues would not . . . accomplish any useful purpose"; it would only replicate the mainstream trade-union movement's failures.[48] The Distributive Workers advocated "one-on-one" organizing instead, with connections made horizontally worker to worker, rather than vertically, paid union organizers or official to worker. With such practices, Distributive Workers activists successfully incorporated social movement-style organizing within an existing union institution, enabling them to organize across race, gender, and occupational lines in a way that was quite unusual at the time.

The Distributive Workers' organizing also extended into the community. The union sent teams of community organizers to dozens of neighborhoods to organize responses to abusive landlords, dangerous streets, and cuts in city services such as sanitation, bus services, and health care. "Just as other . . . organizers protect our workers in their respective locals, the community organizers . . . are dedicated to the task of aiding members in the communities where they live," wrote organizer Pete Gonzalez in a 1969 issue of the union's paper, *Distributive Worker*. Union members who became unemployed were encouraged to remain active and use the union to advocate for changes in policy and benefits. Welfare recipients found support in the Distributive Workers' opposition to the Nixon administration's 1969 plan to push recipients into jobs in exchange for their benefits, which the union called an attempt to "provide sweat-shop employers with a cheap labor pool."[49]

The Distributive Workers joined the ALA in May 1970. The same month, over six hundred people packed the Tabernacle Baptist Church in Atlanta, center of ALA organizing at the time, to hear civil rights activist Coretta Scott King speak in support of the new union, which she called "the conscience of the labor movement."[50]

Over the next decade, as it continued to organize low-wage workers of all types, the Distributive Workers took white-collar "women's work" especially seriously. Margie Albert, a Distributive Workers steward, wrote of a "new spirit" of unionism among clerical workers in a 1973 *New York Times* op-ed piece, which was read into the Congressional

Record by New York representative Bella Abzug the day it was published.[51] Incorporating demands for equal pay, childcare, and flexible schedules into their organizing plan, activists racked up victories in heavily female workplaces in both the public and private sector, including office workers at Barnard, Columbia, and Fisk Universities; editorial staff at several large New York publishing houses; workers at New York's Museum of Modern Art; and writers at the *Village Voice*. Even the workers at cruise line Club Med joined, along with sizable office staffs working in beauty salons.[52]

Affiliation talks with the UAW began in late 1978. The auto workers had announced their intention to organize workers outside their usual jurisdiction, particularly among white-collar women workers, and saw the Distributive Workers as key to those plans. Distributive Workers activists believed the UAW could lend greater resources to their organizing goals. In September 1979 the Distributive Workers affiliated with the UAW, becoming its "District 65," with a membership of fifty thousand in forty separate locals—a 20 percent increase in membership from a decade earlier and a nearly fourfold growth in the number of locals—at a time when union membership was generally in decline.[53] Its consciously multiracial, feminist, grassroots, social movement–style organizing strategy had paid off big time.

A Question of Change

Independent trade unions like the Distributive Workers, alternative federations like the ALA, and rank-and-file caucus movements like DRUM were critical developments within organized labor in the late 1960s and early '70s. Virtually ignored by mainstream news sources, they were covered intensively in the African American press, women's periodicals, and left publications, often with a sense of hope and excitement. Pressure inside trade unions combined with social justice activism on the outside to create a new opening for progressive unionism. Labor activists saw the possibility of a new stream of workers' activism emerging from the stagnant waters of the AFL-CIO.

But these attempts to raise awareness and organize poor workers were a small part of the postwar era's official labor movement—a mere blip on the radar screen of trade unionism. Successful independent initiatives were sometimes wooed back into mainstream trade unions and the AFL-CIO, as with the Distributive Workers' affiliation with the UAW in 1979, and as we will see in the next two chapters, the affiliations of several independent labor organizing projects with the Service Employees International Union in the late '70s and early '80s. In exchange for their independence, these unions usually received attractive financial support, vastly enhancing their ability to organize and expand. They did insist on maintaining the elements of their original structures that allowed a high degree of local autonomy and decision making. That some AFL-CIO trade unions absorbed a few of the more successful organizing projects was to those unions' credit and showed that they were beginning to acknowledge the need for alternative ways of organizing. These were not hostile takeovers but mutually agreeable collaborations between independent poor workers' unions and progressive-minded AFL-CIO trade unions.

Other dissident workers put their energies into organizations for internal reform. In September 1972, twelve hundred Black workers gathered in Chicago to form the Coalition of Black Trade Unionists. Led by the Distributive Workers' Cleveland Robinson and AFSCME's Bill Lucy, the coalition pledged to work within the framework of organized labor and rejected Black separatism.[54] Though its program included community-based organizing of poor workers, this work never materialized on a large scale. Such an investment in organizing would have taken substantial commitments from top trade union leaders, who not only determined organizing policy but also held the purse strings of major international unions. While those officials occasionally offered to affiliate successful independent unions, they were generally not yet convinced of the need for a broader expansion through large-scale organizing. The Coalition of Black Trade Unionists became heavily involved in lobbying for change within the AFL-CIO and working on local electoral politics.

Two years later, in March 1974, female unionists formed the Coalition of Labor Union Women (CLUW), which also stated that its goal was to "organize the unorganized" but then worked primarily on opening up union structures to female leadership. Indeed, CLUW

activist and historian Ann Withorn argued in 1976 that political conflicts between activists employed as trade union staffers and rank-and-
file activists led to CLUW's eventual devolution into what she
critically called "the official Women's Auxiliary of the trade-union bureaucracy."[55] Still, while not engaged in active organizing campaigns,
CLUW activists raised feminist consciousness within labor, advocating for issues such as the Equal Rights Amendment and women's re-
productive rights. Their more radical ideas slowly seeped into
AFL-CIO trade unionism in the later '70s and the '80s, helping to sow
the seeds for a broadening of the movement that would begin to
emerge in the 1990s.

Like the movement-based organizing highlighted in chapter 1,
these internal trade-union initiatives to steer the labor movement in a
broader direction were experimental, and some were transient. The
Distributive Workers, the ALA, and DRUM, like the civil rights–era
jobs demonstrations, freedom unions, welfare rights groups, and
women's liberation unions, grew out of a specific historical context and
its language of change. These efforts formed a continuum—from rev-
oluntary-influenced efforts like DRUM and the internal caucuses, to
the Distributive Workers' radical but practical trade unionism, to community-development corporations funded by unions like the UAW.

Neither the ALA nor the UAW projects rocked the boat of existing trade unionism. The ALA's support of organizing was refresh-
ing, but its generally top-down methods did not translate into
successful campaigns, as it sought to increase membership numbers
without any significant increase in member involvement. UAW-
funded neighborhood-based groups such as the Watts Labor Community Action Committee and the East Los Angeles Community
Union provided social welfare–type improvements but often at the
cost of reinforcing class and gender divisions within poor communities. They did little to challenge the root causes of poverty or empower working-class residents.

Activists in the Distributive Workers and the RUMs, on the other
hand, saw the need for grassroots empowerment and challenged established notions about organizing poor workers by insisting that they
needed a voice and a vote inside the unions—as members, organizers,

and elected leaders. Unionism had to be about more than paying dues, voting for an old-boys' network of leaders, and reaping a yearly pay increase. For them, union activism was a vehicle to pursue a deeper social transformation in which class, race, ethnicity, and gender oppressions were confronted by a membership that understood the value of participatory democracy and community-based activism. Continual organizing would lay the groundwork for an expanded membership base, and eventually a more diverse and capable movement. Collective power, not individual action, was the solution to movement decline. Over the next decades, both antipoverty activists and independent community-based workers' centers would take this lesson and run with it.

Welfare rights march. *(Labor Archives and Research Center, San Francisco State University, PW-P1)*

3

Economic Justice for All

A National Network of Low-Wage
and Unwaged Workers

I n the summer of 1971, in the midst of the worst attacks on welfare rights in a decade, National Welfare Rights Organization
(NWRO) activists gathered in Providence, Rhode Island, for
their fifth annual convention. Instead of the usual line of speakers
addressing welfare rights, the podium was crowded with representatives from every imaginable progressive organization—labor, ten-
ant, and consumer rights activists, radical feminists, and Black
nationalists. Delegates representing 125,000 members in eight hundred local chapters across the nation listened to keynote speeches
from two first-year congressional representatives: Bella Abzug, an
outspoken feminist from New York, and Ronald Dellums, a radical
young legislator from California. Both advocated a new coalition of
welfare recipients with the working poor, including low-wage workers, rank-and-file union caucus members, domestic workers, and
the unemployed.[1] Welfare rights activists hoped the convention
would launch a new effort to build a "majority strategy" on the left,
joining several disparate struggles under the umbrella of economic

justice and creating closer ties with trade unions, even engaging in joint organizing where possible.

Civil rights activist George Wiley had, in his earlier work as CORE director, organized a 1965 boycott of New York City liquor stores that carried wines made from nonunion grapes to aid striking United Farm Workers grape pickers in Delano, California. By the time he became executive director of NWRO in 1967, Wiley was contacting trade unions to ask for their support for welfare rights, a movement, he noted, that "in many ways parallels the early days of the labor movement." NWRO leaders frequently lent their support to high-profile trade union struggles, such as the two-month-long strike of service workers at Yale University, where Wiley and Al Evanoff of the Distributive Workers addressed strikers who disrupted the school's 1971 commencement exercises.[2]

But reciprocal support from trade unions for NWRO was not forthcoming. In response to a 1969 fundraising appeal, AFSCME's president Jerry Wurf gave NWRO a pittance—$500—and offered training programs for welfare rights organizers. The first substantial assistance NWRO received from trade unions was in April 1970, with the Alliance for Labor Action's one-time donation of $12,000. Churches, feminist groups, and civil rights organizations worked in coalition with NWRO, which was acknowledged as the main organization representing the poor—specifically welfare recipients and by extension, the unemployed and working poor. While some local unions allied with NWRO chapters, union support was conspicuously absent at the national level.[3]

Undeterred, antipoverty activists decided to create a coalition of the poor and other workers, building it from the ground up. The largest and most sustained efforts to organize poor workers in the '70s came from this loose coalition of former NWRO activists and other community organizers affiliated with two closely tied national organizations, the Association of Community Organizations for Reform Now (ACORN) and the Movement for Economic Justice (MEJ). Like most of the poor workers' organizations of the '60s, these groups were decidedly community-based. What distinguished them from previous groups was their attempt, ultimately successful, to form a viable national network between waged and unwaged workers, and their emphasis on organizing broadly across workplaces, industries, and diverse constituencies. While these organizations thought of themselves as similar to welfare rights organizing, drawing on its direct action methods and philosophy of grassroots empowerment, they also had aims in common with the trade union movement—decent jobs, workers' rights, and collective bargaining. They collaborated and sometimes affiliated with mainstream labor organizations, a track record that would become important as some trade unions moved into low-wage worker organizing in the '80s and '90s.

During the early '70s, what activists called "multi-issue, multi-constituency" organizing began in dozens of cities. Its ideological framework connected a critique of corporate welfare policies (tax breaks to the wealthy, probusiness legislation, antilabor legislation, etc.) to advocacy of a "guaranteed annual income" for the poor, including welfare recipients. Organizers increasingly pursued questions of workplace rights side by side with issues such as welfare and unemployment benefits, utility rates, the availability of community health care, and equal access to education. This multi-issue organizing style would emerge as the dominant template during the explosion of progressive coalition building in the '80s and would continue to serve grassroots movements well into the twenty-first century. Developing out of welfare rights and social movement work of the '60s and '70s, it opened up new and fruitful possibilities for organizing poor workers, whose lives seldom fit into neat packages of steady employment or narrowly defined economic concerns.

Organizing the Unemployed

The year 1970 marked the beginning of the end of the US postwar economic boom, as most key indicators of economic prosperity dropped, then took a dive in 1973 when the Organization of Petroleum Exporting Countries' oil embargo rippled through economies in the developed world. It was the deepest depression (or "recession," as some politicians euphemistically called it) since the 1930s. Throughout the late '60s, unemployment had remained level at about 4 percent for white people and 8 percent for Black. But 1970 brought a sharp upward spike.

By 1975 the rates had doubled to 8 percent for white people and nearly 15 percent for Black. The *New York Times* called the pace of this increase "a frightening momentum."[4] It was in these conditions that poor workers' organizations tried to organize unemployed, underemployed, and low-wage workers caught in an economy gone bust.

Some welfare rights advocates, including NWRO director Wiley, increasingly worried that the welfare rights movement was doomed to represent a small minority and to remain in a defensive posture because it had too narrow a base. Coalition building could help to broaden the movement, and workers on unemployment were a natural extension of unwaged workers on welfare.[5] In 1970 Wiley sent welfare rights organizer Wade Rathke to Little Rock, Arkansas, to see whether a broader antipoverty organization of unemployed and low-wage workers would be viable. Wiley consciously chose Arkansas as the launching pad for this new NWRO-affiliated organization, to be called ACORN—originally, Arkansas Community Organizations for Reform Now. The state's population was about a third African American, had a low median income of about $6,000, and was largely welfare eligible, factors that made it ripe for a successful NWRO-type organizing campaign. Within a few months a second organizer, Gary Delgado, was hired. ACORN's organizing focused on free school lunch programs and fairer leases and lower security deposits in public housing.[6]

By 1971 ACORN had branched out further, starting two workers' groups, the Unemployed Workers' Organizing Committee and the Vietnam Veterans' Organizing Committee. "The labor thing was a natural," Rathke later reflected. "As we did 'straight' community organizing on neighborhood issues, it was not uncommon for people to raise job-related concerns."[7] The Unemployed Workers' Organizing Committee developed a two-pronged strategy: pressure private and public employers for more jobs, and make the unemployment benefit system more equitable. The group organized "job demonstrations" at which unemployed workers displayed their willingness to work if the job offered a decent wage. Activists also demanded an extension of unemployment benefits from six months to one year, and an end to the waiting period for benefits.[8]

Their work was part of an upsurge of jobless worker activism across the nation. In October 1970 some 250 unemployed workers and their allies, under the banner of the Rochester Independent Workers, marched on city hall in Rochester, New York, to demand action on the problem of increasing unemployment. The following month, hundreds of Seattle's unemployed workers, many of them aircraft industry workers laid off from Boeing, marched with the Union of the Unemployed to demand that a closed Boeing plant be converted to produce mass-transit vehicles. About the same time, some fifty unemployed Black workers occupied the St. Louis city hall demanding jobs.[9]

The jobless rate among returning Vietnam vets was particularly high, nearly twice the rate of nonveterans. One Vietnam vet in Rhode Island used his anger to start a group that would evolve into one of the era's most successful poor workers' unions. Arthur Hazard had lost his job, and his weekly visits to the unemployment office left him feeling isolated and powerless. Hazard started the Unemployed Workers' Union (UWU) in August 1971, and within a month it had over a hundred members and five hundred supporters in the state's capital, Providence.[10]

The Unemployed Workers' Union's demands were similar to those of ACORN's Unemployed Workers' Organizing Committee—more jobs, an extension of benefits to one year, and respectful treatment at the unemployment office. Like NWRO, which focused welfare recipients' anger at the intrusive and abusive welfare department to organize resistance against its policies, the Unemployed Workers' Union (UWU) mobilized around individual frustrations that unemployed workers faced at the unemployment office. For instance, in response to state officials who pushed workers to take undesirable jobs under the threat of ending their benefits, the UWU successfully invoked a state law that gave the unemployed the right to refuse work if the position was vacant due to a strike or other labor dispute, or if the wages, hours, or other conditions were less favorable than those prevailing for similar work.[11] That law, combined with the proposed longer benefit period backed by UWU, would give unemployed workers much more control over their own working lives and deny Rhode Island's low-wage employers a ready source of cheap labor.

Funded primarily by the Catholic Inner City Center, the UWU

picked up broad support from Providence's antipoverty groups, as well as from religious and civil rights leaders. Trade union backing was missing, although some union leaders voiced their individual support.[12] Like their comrades in both the labor and welfare rights movements, the group's organizers advocated on behalf of individuals and sought to build activism through small individual victories. Supporters of the union gained collective visibility at the unemployment office (named the Department of Employment Security, or DES) by wearing bright orange and black buttons that read "MEMBER, UNEMPLOYED WORKERS UNION." Activists also recruited members by approaching people in line at the DES, and when bureaucrats locked the activists out of the building, the union took DES to federal court. In an important precedent-setting case, the organizers won the right to recruit members at the unemployment office.[13] The group's direct service work included appealing benefit denials and cutoffs, insisting on the right to free healthcare at state hospitals, and demanding translators for Spanish- and Portuguese-speaking workers in their interviews with the DES.[14]

The UWU's work on behalf of the jobless eventually led to its recognition by the DES as a bargaining agent for the unemployed, and the union elected a negotiating committee to represent unemployed workers in their grievances.[15] UWU activists won a meeting in early October 1973 with the state's governor, Frank Licht, to press for a special legislative session to increase unemployment benefits. After Licht failed to promise such a session, the union planned round-the-clock picketing of his reelection stops. The union also conducted several rallies at the state capitol in support of an unemployment extension bill, and it ultimately won thirteen additional weeks of benefits for thousands of Rhode Island's unemployed.[16]

Linking Unemployed, Welfare, and Low-Wage Workers

The Unemployed Workers' Union advocated for welfare recipients as well, as part of a conscious strategy to construct a multiconstituency movement of unemployed, low-wage, and welfare workers. Several factors made this strategy likely to suceed. The racial dynamics in

Rhode Island were different from those of many other urban areas: the state had very small African American and Latina/Latino populations but a large number of first- and second-generation ethnic Portuguese workers and poor white workers. This meant politicians lacked a significant stereotypical "minority" population to scapegoat as "welfare cheats." Further, these workers were no strangers to union organizing; most had exposure to the Portuguese trade union movement, one of the most militant in Europe, either directly or through friends and relatives. Many had been activists in prior workplaces, and they brought those experiences into the Unemployed Workers' Union.[17]

Observers were often skeptical that such a union could ever gain much power. But by 1973 it had grown tremendously, with local chapters in nine cities in Rhode Island. The group changed its name to the Rhode Island Workers Association (RIWA) and adopted a labor union–like structure, with geographically based "chapters" that elected officers to serve on a statewide executive board and an annual convention each year at which decisions on future activities were made democratically.[18]

Consciously borrowing from social movement organizing styles, the union's mode of operation was highly confrontational. After a state official refused to meet with RIWA about providing Portuguese interpreters at the unemployment office, recalls organizer George Nee,

> We got on a bus with about fifty Portuguese women, all in their fifties and dressed entirely in black, and we picketed her house for two hours. . . . We also did a lot of sit-ins in the unemployment office and got arrested occasionally. When we learned that workers had a right to free health care in the community, we forced the hospitals to start putting up signs in all languages saying that if people were poor or unemployed they had a right to health insurance free from that hospital. We had picket lines and sit-ins and demonstrations in many hospitals.[19]

This campaign resulted in the widespread use of available free health care by unemployed people.

RIWA's activists saw the problems with unemployment benefits as just the tip of the iceberg. The expansion of corporate power and the proliferation of low-wage jobs without health and other benefits were the real structural problems underlying individuals' experiences of unemployment. RIWA increasingly planned campaigns that sought to win expanded rights for poor workers as a class, rather than as individuals. In 1975, for instance, RIWA forced giant insurer Blue Cross to allow unemployed workers to continue their health coverage at the same low group rate their employers had paid, rather than forcing them to pay higher individual rates. Blue Cross initially protested, claiming such a program would cost it $5 million, but RIWA prevailed after a series of direct-action demonstrations at the workplaces of Blue Cross board members and officials.[20]

Nee, who had taken over from Hazard as lead organizer in 1972, had worked with the Hospital Workers Union 1199 and with Cesar Chavez in the United Farm Workers (and would later head Rhode Island's AFL-CIO). He was deeply influenced by Chavez's organizing philosophy of rank-and-file member involvement and worried that RIWA relied too heavily on a social service component and church and foundation grant funding. Just as the UFW had transformed itself from primarily a service-centered organization into a union, Nee thought, RIWA should move away from being a "do-gooder" organization that gave help "to anyone who walked in the door" and received most of its financial support "from well wishers on the outside."[21] As a service provider, RIWA would be unlikely to build a power base or increase poor people's capacity to work on their own behalf.

Despite its expanded focus, when RIWA eventually added low-wage workers to its mostly unemployed membership, it was almost by accident. In early 1976 Nee was representing a bus driver in his claim for unemployment. The driver said his coworkers were worried about wage cuts and sudden firings, so Nee asked whether they wanted to form a union. "'What union?' he says. 'Oh,' I said, 'how about the Rhode Island Workers Union?' We just made it up." The logic of joining unemployed with low-wage workers appealed to RIWA's elected leadership. While the group had always been democratically structured and run by the rank and file, like most small nonprofits, it relied heavily on grants. The newly formed RIWU would collect member dues. And instead of its chapters being organized geographically, they would be organized by workplace, as most unions were.[22]

The bus driver, along with his fellow dispatchers and mechanics in the state's largest private transportation firm, provided services to the area's elder residents. By building community support with the seniors they served, they pulled off a joint worker-consumer strike action and obtained their first union contract about six months later. Encouraged by the success, RIWU's board decided on an ambitious plan to organize the state's three largest nonunionized low-wage groups—office workers, healthcare and nursing home workers, and jewelry workers. RIWU decided to go it alone, without help from national unions. "Like the farm workers, we realized that we had to build up our own strength first, then we could talk to others," recalls Nee.

In May 1976 RIWU began organizing workers at the state's largest chain of nursing homes, and by December the union had signed contracts with three employers covering some 450 workers. Improvements in pay and leave policies, as well as the establishment of grievance procedures and elected committees on patient care, were part of the agreements.[23] Campaigns also began in Rhode Island's jewelry industry, which numbered some thirty thousand workers, mostly Portuguese immigrants who held low-income assembly-line jobs. Between 1976 and 1982, the Rhode Island Workers Union was involved in more organizing drives than any other union in Rhode Island—fifty-five campaigns at about twenty-five separate workplaces, about half of which ended in victory. By 1982 the union represented a fifth of the state's nursing-home workers, and its dues-paying membership had grown to eleven hundred.[24]

This was a remarkable achievement for a small independent organization operating in traditionally nonunion industries. RIWU and others like it launched vigorous campaigns in nonunion industries, flooding the state's labor movement with new footsoldiers. Some AFL-CIO unions took notice. The Service Employees International Union (SEIU), in particular, was becoming interested in expanded organizing and was on the lookout for promising independent unions of low-wage workers it could affiliate. In 1979 an internal SEIU memo noted RIWU's "substantial potential," and later that year RIWU affiliated with SEIU.[25]

Why was SEIU interested? First, the Rhode Island Workers Union was highly successful at organizing low-wage workers using a direct-action social movement style. Because trade unions saw themselves as workplace organizers, RIWU's decision to bring low-wage workers into the organization instead of remaining a group exclusively for unemployed workers was likely the key to opening mainstream union doors. By welcoming RIWU into the fold of "organized labor," SEIU tacitly acknowledged the strength of RIWU's broader organizing style, which included the unemployed.

For its part, RIWU gained a fast track to financial and organizational support for its campaigns, and with it the possibility of rapidly building a larger membership base. Union dues promised a higher degree of stability than foundation grants could provide. RIWU had made a good start: in 1976 its members paid a dues rate of two hours of salary per month, netting the union over twenty thousand dollars in its first year.[26] While RIWU leaders accepted SEIU's offer of affiliation and organizing help, they insisted on keeping control of key decisions—such as the right to go on strike or to disaffiliate if the members so chose—at the local level.[27]

As we will see in the next chapter, other successful independent community-based poor workers' unions were also wooed by trade unions in the late '70s and the '80s. With competition from rapidly expanding public-sector unions, some trade unions that operated in the private sector, such as SEIU, began to reach out to new constituencies to expand their base. As a result, activist unions like RIWU brought independent community-based organizing experiences into the mainstream trade union movement, helping to move it toward a more activist organizing philosophy.

Taking the Rich off Welfare

Although it emerged independently, the Rhode Island Workers Association was a key participant in the national network of similar groups called the Movement for Economic Justice (MEJ), launched in December 1972. Former NWRO director George Wiley told supporters that MEJ sought to develop a "majority strategy" by jointly organizing the nation's fifty million welfare poor with its seventy million working poor, many of them "very hostile" to welfare recipients.[28] The welfare rights movement had been successful "beyond any of our wildest imaginations," wrote Wiley, noting that payments to the poor in welfare grants had increased fourfold, from $1.7 billion in 1966 to over $6.8 billion in 1972.[29] But the movement that had transformed the social welfare system was growing isolated and coming under attack from conservatives in Congress. NWRO's 1972 national campaign for a $6,500 guaranteed annual income for welfare recipients had failed miserably. Workfare programs that required recipients to labor in exchange for their welfare benefits were being reintroduced in several municipalities, as the Nixon administration dismantled federal social welfare programs and turned responsibilities for them over to states. By late 1972, many activists believed they needed to broaden their base of support.[30]

MEJ would focus on that task—joining the poor, working poor, and middle classes in a common struggle around fair resource distribution. Well-known welfare rights scholars Richard Cloward and Frances Fox Piven, longtime friends of Wiley, agreed to serve on MEJ's board. Wiley hired Bert DeLeeuw, a young welfare rights organizer, to help plan MEJ's strategy. Convinced that MEJ should be driven by local actions at the grassroots, MEJ's founders sought to limit its national structure to coordinating and representational activities in Washington, DC.[31] Though they sought to make the organization self-sustaining through membership dues, during its first year nearly its entire budget of $165,000, supporting ten paid staff, came from progressive foundations and churches.[32]

MEJ's goal was to bring poor and working-class whites closer both ideologically and politically to an already radicalized population of poor workers, mostly people of color. To that end, MEJ staff developed several pilot organizing projects in early 1973 around the issues of tax reform, consumer action, and workplace organizing. Modeled on the NWRO strategy of providing assistance to individuals to draw them into supporting the movement's goals, MEJ's Tax Justice Project initiated tax clinics—125 of them in fourteen states in the fall of 1973—offering free tax-return preparation and education about the inequities of the tax system that favored the rich and corporations.[33]

Such a strategy had the potential to turn the popular understanding of welfare on its head by exposing corporate welfare and loopholes for the wealthy. Wiley hoped for a full-scale "taxpayers' revolt" against what he called "the real welfare program that takes care of the welfare of the corporations, of the corporate farmers, of the oil industry, of the millionaires and of the people who live off the public dole—who live at the public trough, who are the real chiselers and shiftless, lazy folk."[34]

Wiley produced pages of statistics in his testimony before the US House Committee on Ways and Means in March 1973, showing that tax burdens fell hardest on low- and middle-income workers, while corporations and the rich benefited from plentiful loopholes in the tax code, and that, moreover, government programs like social security were paid for disproportionately by workers with incomes under $15,000.[35] He demonstrated that runaway inflation, spiraling food prices, high unemployment, and sharply rising healthcare costs—all rife in the early '70s—were either directly or indirectly a boon to corporate stockholders. Tax breaks for property owners, Wiley noted, amounted to some $750 million annually, while funding for low-income housing came to only $23 million.[36]

This confrontation of corporate welfare showed that MEJ's critique of poverty was more structural than that of NWRO, which primarily helped individuals increase their welfare benefits. Rather than arguing for providing a solid floor for workers at the lowest end of the income spectrum, MEJ was proposing a national discussion about a redistribution of wealth. Such a discussion couldn't be conjured out of thin air, but MEJ was optimistic that it could be built from the work of existing grassroots organizations that were on the same ideological wavelength. MEJ organizers scoured the country looking for local efforts that could be included in their national network and found plenty. Wiley visited a community union project in Appalachia, as well as the expanding ACORN organization in Arkansas, which he had helped initiate three years earlier. MEJ supported former NWRO organizer Mark Splain in starting a model program in Chelsea, a working-class city next door to Boston, called Massachusetts Fair Share. Within two years it had become a network with more than thirty local branches working on tax, utility, and welfare issues.[37]

With Wiley's sudden death right before MEJ's launch in September 1973, however, the group's activists turned back from the ambitious project of creating a new national movement for economic justice. Perhaps more realistically, they hoped to support such a movement when it came into being.[38] The loss of George Wiley left a huge gap in the incipient organization's leadership, from which it was unable to recover. If MEJ had had the chance to develop its planned grassroots structure, it might have played a more central role in economic justice organizing. Instead, it threw itself into helping local groups design organizing strategies, recruiting and training organizers, providing seed money to new efforts, and publishing a journal, *Just Economics*.

Though MEJ gave up its grand vision of social and economic transformation, in its subsequent role as a clearinghouse for a new kind of community and labor organizing it provided a neutral ground for organizers from different groups to exchange ideas and develop common strategies (not unlike Kentucky's Highlander Center, Chicago's Midwest Academy, Oakland's Center for Third World Organizing, or Black Workers for Justice's Workers' Schools). Like the community-organizing tradition from which it emerged, MEJ activists stressed that a successful economic justice movement would be based on small, local, winnable victories rather than a call to revolution. Skeptical of notions of sweeping social change popular in the sectarian left during the '70s, MEJ's scattered constellation of activists chose instead a more grounded vision of local community-based social change. Their style of "one-on-one," member-to-member organizing resembled, more than anything else, the approach that labor organizers had used in their most successful drives of the past.

Fair Work, Not Workfare

Along with the unemployed, welfare recipients were an indispensable part of the "new majority" that economic justice activists sought to construct. Welfare recipients had been central to poor workers' organizing historically because most welfare recipients were caught in the same cycle that trapped other poor workers: low-wage employment, unemployment, welfare, and back again. The introduction of workfare programs in the '70s would present opportunities to build a movement of welfare recipients, this time as paid workers.

The Nixon administration's "Family Assistance Plan" of 1969 had included a new punitive mandatory workfare provision. Though the bill was defeated, in part through mobilization of welfare activists around the country, its forced work requirements were subsequently incorporated into the Aid to Families with Dependent Children (AFDC) program. Nixon's procorporate agenda tolerated high unemployment and controls on wages and prices (instituted in August 1971) but no controls on corporate profits. It even produced a new economic effect dubbed "stagflation"—spiraling inflation combined with economic stagnation. The economic downturn caused AFDC enrollment to increase dramatically throughout the '70s, as higher unemployment forced people to turn to welfare. Burgeoning welfare rolls were an excuse for conservative politicians to attack welfare recipients.

As early as 1970 the backlash was making itself felt, with conservatives, like New York's governor Nelson Rockefeller, accusing welfare recipients of being freeloaders in need of lessons in responsibility, and liberals such as Connecticut senator Abraham Ribicoff proposing that recipients work for their benefits by service to the cities and states that provided them.[39] Nineteen states actually cut welfare benefits in 1971, and nearly every state considered such action. The growing public hostility toward welfare recipients was evident in the popularity of songs like Guy Drake's "Welfare Cadillac," which stereotyped welfare recipients as generally making out like bandits—buying new luxury cars, eating free school lunches, and getting sacks of groceries without ever having to work.

New York's state legislature passed one of the nation's first mandatory work programs for welfare recipients in May 1971, requiring that those who could not find regular jobs be assigned to "work projects." Welfare rights activists immediately responded with a series of demonstrations that equated the mandatory work-for-benefits program with slavery: "WELFARE RECIPIENTS WANT TO WORK BUT AT DECENT JOBS WITH DECENT PAY. WE WILL NOT BE SLAVES!" screamed one rally leaflet.[40]

New York City's Work Relief Employment Project (WREP) began as a "national demonstration project" in June 1973. Within a few months, it numbered over ten thousand welfare recipients, laboring at eleven city agencies and more than four hundred separate worksites located in every borough. About three-fourths of the workers were African American or Latino, 60 percent were male, and half were over the age of thirty-five.[41] The WREP program sent recipients to work in city jobs that had previously been performed by unionized city work-ers—job titles such as office assistant, security aide, transcriber, painter, janitor, and "rodent control aide" predominated. The jobs were half-time with compensation of $2,600 a year—about equivalent to existing welfare benefits.[42] Workers were not entitled to medical in-surance, retirement benefits, or job security and lacked workplace pro-tections such as due process and grievance procedures. While welfare authorities promised that the program would lead to full-time, full-paying, secure jobs, only a tiny percentage of WREP participants were ever placed in permanent jobs. But under city law, WREP workers were permitted to organize for collective bargaining.[43]

Antipoverty activists decided to make New York City the testing ground for a new kind of welfare organizing—this time using the WREP program to illustrate the connections between welfare and jobs. It was clear to them that existing public-sector trade unions—the leadership of which was, at that time, mostly white—were not going to organize the WREP workers. Led by former ACORN organizer Gary Delgado, a multiracial WREP workers' organizing committee began investigating the possibility of conducting a union drive they hoped would not only win rights for WREP workers but also possibly bring poor workers on welfare and those in the city's powerful trade unions into common cause. "Because we believe that the separation between the unemployed and employed is fundamentally divisive, and that one of the major mis-takes of past organizing efforts was the failure to build bridges between organized and unorganized labor," wrote the committee members, "we are committed to the task of building those bridges."[44]

Organizing-committee members began seeking out WREP work-ers at their job sites to gauge their interest in unionizing—a difficult task since they often worked in inaccessible offices and the city refused to give organizers a list of WREP workers and their locations. "We did-n't know anything about putting together a union," recalled Delgado, a seasoned welfare rights organizer: "I knew how to put people together in a group, do actions, make demands, but I never saw unions do that . . . so I was very nervous about it."[45] Union leaders seemed to be guys in suits negotiating across big conference tables behind closed doors, each with the archetypal cigar dangling from the corner of his mouth—not people organizing in the streets.

With seed money from MEJ and help from the Harlem-based labor group Fightback and other community groups, the WREP organizing committee rented office space, hired staff, and bought a printing press. They hired a diverse group of eight organizers: five were Black, two Puerto Rican, one white; two were women, and six were men.[46] Later several WREP workers were added as paid organizers.

By February 1974, sixty-five WREP workers, representing dozens of worksites in Manhattan, the Bronx, and Brooklyn, met to officially inaugurate the organization, which came to be called United WREP Workers (UWW). Their objections included strengthening both workers' rights and welfare rights, and obtaining voluntary, full-time, adequately paying jobs and collective bargaining for WREP workers. Pledged to organize their coworkers "one by one," volunteer WREP organizers—alone or in the company of a paid staffer—combed the city signing up new members and inviting them to weekly citywide organizing meetings. "Remember," exhorted one flyer, "an organization of 10,000 workers begins with you and the worker next to you."[47]

Delgado recalled a worksite meeting early in the campaign, to which activists showed up armed with a small stack of union authorization cards for the expected few dozen workers but were greeted by four hundred clamoring to sign up. The new union was in hot demand: "When a WREP worker hears of the existence of the UWW, he *asks* to join," an internal WREP memo reported. Not only did workers want pay, benefits, and protections equal to those regular civil service workers received, but they complained of a lack of dignity and respect and resented their second-class status. "I want to be recognized as a public employee like other civil service workers. I want to cash a paycheck, not a welfare check," insisted Lena Jackson, a WREP worker in Brooklyn. Another, WREP worker Barbara Pruitt, added, "We do not have any kind of job security. More than 10,000 of us can be kicked out onto the streets at the simple whim of a WREP supervisor."[48]

Building the Union(s)

Activists' methods were straight out of labor movement annals: gather workers' signatures on authorization cards in support of the union, address individual grievances using direct-action methods such as demonstrations and pickets, and work toward a union election by the City Office of Collective Bargaining, which had legal jurisdiction over the workers. UWW's first direct action was to interrupt a conference of well-known trade union leaders, civil rights activists, and academics, which had gathered on June 14, 1974, at the New York City Hilton Hotel to form a "Committee for Full Employment."

The conference was convened by civil rights activist Coretta Scott King and chaired by UAW president Leonard Woodcock. The WREP workers believed that King, Woodcock, and others on the committee didn't understand that their push for "full employment" could be interpreted as supporting workfare programs like WREP. Some sixty WREP workers charged into the meeting to ask delegates to take a clear position *against* any "full employment" that did not pay a living wage—the punitive kind that New York City officials had made mandatory for welfare recipients. To their surprise, Woodcock yielded the podium, and after hearing the WREP workers' grievances, the conference voted unanimously to support UWW's demands.[49] It was quite a political coup for a brand-new independent organization.

UWW's relationships with local trade unions, though, were mixed. In 1973, before the new organization was off the ground, organizers contacted three unions within AFSCME District Council 37—the union federation representing most public-sector workers in the city— and one union outside of it. District Council 37 officials were skeptical about the feasibility of organizing WREP workers, but contacts with rank-and-file unionists were more encouraging. This was not the usual call to trade unions to "organize the unorganized" in some vast, nebulous, and abstract universe outside their jurisdictions. This time poor workers were right in the unions' backyard, in most cases performing their members' jobs at sharply reduced rates. It was not uncommon for laid-off city workers to be placed in WREP positions—sometimes doing the very same job they had done before being laid off. The city's own 1972 "productivity report" admitted that WREP had rung up $18 million in salary savings from its six thousand WREP placements, at the same time that a citywide freeze on hiring for entry-level positions was in effect. UWW argued that the program provided "fiscal relief to New York City by the direct exploitation of 10,000 Black and Hispanic workers."[50]

Alarmed by the large-scale replacement of unionized jobs and the substandard working conditions of WREP workers, the city's social workers' union was the first to lend support to the WREP workers' organizing campaign. Against the wishes of its parent organization, District Council 37, the Social Services Employees Union Local 371 endorsed the WREP workers' struggle in order to "help end the exploitation of our fellow workers and to put a stop to the City's attack on civil service."[51] Other locals within District Council 37, some not on record as supporting the WREP workers, provided under-the-table material aid, such as printing and mailing union literature at city expense—or, in the case of the social workers' local, surreptitiously providing United WREP Workers the entire eight-thousand-name list of WREP workers and their addresses, which the city had refused to provide to organizers.[52]

But this rank-and-file trade union support didn't extend upward into official ranks. Certainly District Council 37 officials were alarmed about WREP's effects on its members, and executive director Victor Gotbaum had sharply criticized the program. But they were also hostile to an independent organization like UWW organizing the workers. District Council 37 should have approved the organizing of WREP workers into a union—even someone else's—because then the WREP workers would be able to join in collective bargaining for decent wages and job protections, giving all workers more leverage in negotiations with the city. Instead, engaging in a turf battle that had become all too common between independents and trade unions, District Council 37 moved in to control the organizing. According to Delgado, Gotbaum sent spies to UWW's organizing meetings and initiated a campaign of red-baiting against the WREP organizers.[53]

By fall 1974, United WREP Workers had thirty-eight hundred members from all five boroughs of New York—well over the 30 percent required by the National Labor Relations Board to call a union election—and announced it would petition for such an election. Suddenly District Council 37 asked the state's public employment relations board to add (or in labor-speak, "accrete") the WREP workers into its jurisdiction before the election. "We were actually willing to let District Council 37 have them," recalls Delgado, "but we did not want people to be put into sections of DC 37 by their job titles because that would break them up," destroying the solidarity and power they had built while organizing. UWW wanted District Council 37 to keep the workers together in an "amalgamated local"—one big local covering all the job titles and worksites of WREP workers—because their problems often had more to do with their relationship to the welfare department than with their actual job title. Under this scenario they would have been members of a large, semiautonomous local within District Council 37. District Council 37 leaders, who may have been threatened by the prospect of a unit of ten thousand workers of color coming into their mostly white union with any concentrated power, refused. The United Electrical Workers, a non-AFL-CIO union, lent its lawyer to UWW to argue their case, but the state labor board sided with District Council 37 and ruled that the WREP workers would be merged into District Council 37's unit. "Once people were accreted into District Council 37, we were barred from worksites, and if we showed up to organize we were arrested," according to Delgado.[54]

A few months after District Council 37's victory, New York City's fiscal crisis deepened, and many WREP workers were laid off, ending up back on welfare. The WREP program was phased out, and UWW disbanded. But the United WREP Workers' high-profile campaign, regularly covered in the city's press, had succeeded in helping reframe the issue of welfare in terms of work, an impressive accomplishment given the tenor of the times. It may have also helped push some within the city's largest unions to take the connection between workfare and its own members more seriously. Nearly a decade later, in 1980, activists in District Council 37 briefly assisted workers organizing under a new workfare program called the Public Works Program Organizing

Committee.[55] For some trade unionists at least, welfare recipients could no longer be scapegoated as freeloading, Cadillac-driving loafers; instead, they had become coworkers and comrades in the struggle for fair employment and economic justice.

Creating an Organizing Culture

In their labor organizing work, the Movement for Economic Justice, ACORN, the Rhode Island Workers Union, and other poor workers' unions did much to change narrow assumptions about who could be considered a worker and to show what an enlarged labor movement could accomplish. Their record glowed with many local, and a few national, successes. By example, they showed trade unions mired in moribund notions of organization what an effective organizing culture looked like—it valued spontaneity, direct action, rank-and-file involvement, and small victories that laid the ground for larger ones.

Apprehension regarding new constituencies and sheer institutional weight kept most trade unions from adopting similar methods or organizing targets in the '70s. Like the poor workers' organizations covered in chapter 1, the Rhode Island Workers Association, Unemployed Workers' Organizing Committee, ACORN, United WREP Workers, and similar groups frequently went unnoticed by mainstream unions, organizing those workers in whom trade unions professed little interest. That would slowly change as these unions, worried about their plummeting numbers, started to reach out for new allies, new constituencies, and new models of organizing.

Union officials ignored this movement at their own peril. The ensuing decade would bring a repolarization of wealth that vastly increased the number of low-wage service sector jobs and simultaneously decreased high-wage manufacturing jobs as corporations turned to just-in-time production methods and relocated factories overseas or in nonunion states. New workfare requirements in the '90s would become a major force undercutting public employees' bargaining strength across the nation. An early foothold among these poor low-wage, unwaged, and unemployed workers could have strengthened trade unions' organizing experience and ability, as well as their negotiating position, in the new era of job flight, downsizing, and intensified worker exploitation.

By early 1975 the Movement for Economic Justice was assisting a variety of economic justice organizations, with a particular emphasis on organizing the unemployed. Some three dozen organizations—including Minneapolis's Workers' Rights Center, Massachusetts Fair Share, and Women Organized for Employment—had moved welfare or unemployed-worker issues to the top of their agendas. The successful work in which poor workers' unions were engaged earned the respect of trade unions, which sometimes joined them in local coalitions. The MEJ-funded Philadelphia Unemployment Project, for instance, worked closely throughout the late '70s with many of the city's established trade unions and led a delegation of over three hundred unemployed workers and dozens of trade union officials to Washington, DC, to lobby against cutbacks in jobless benefits.[56]

The Movement for Economic Justice, part of the glue holding disparate local campaigns together, faltered in 1976 when, due to lack of funds and energy, it suspended all activities except the publication of *Just Economics*. Nevertheless, by May 1978 MEJ had resurrected itself and went on to coordinate impressive protests against welfare cuts and unemployment in seventeen cities, which the *Washington Post* called a "rerun of the late 1960s." That year, in a kind of last hurrah, MEJ became the main backer for a new coalitional effort called Jobs and Justice, sponsored jointly with ACORN and Massachusetts Fair Share.[57]

The aim of Jobs and Justice was straightforward, if daunting: organize poor workers across the nation using a "high level of visible direct action."[58] This was brave talk in the waning days of the '70s, almost universally regarded by activists of all stripes as a terrible time for radical movement actions. As the nation was about to turn rightward with the 1980 election of Ronald Reagan to the presidency, antipoverty activists drew up ambitious plans for renewed organizing that would go to the heart of economic inequality in America, through perhaps the most unlikely of subjects: teenagers.

Home care members of SEIU 880 (formerly ULU) lobbying at the Illinois state capitol, mid-'80s. Irma Sherman (top row, left, fist raised) was the first ULU president. Helen Miller (front row, left, wearing dark pants) was then a board member and later served as president. *(Wisconsin Historical Society, SEIU 880-Collection, Whi-25340, 1987)*

4

Community Organizing Goes to Work

ACORN's United Labor Unions

They arrived in droves in downtown Philadelphia on May 23, 1978. Teenagers, row upon row, marching twenty wide and nearly fifteen hundred strong to the employment office to demand summer jobs for all low-income youth who wanted them. So many turned out from the city's outlying areas that there weren't enough rented buses to carry them downtown. Waving signs and chanting "Jobs now!" the kids were part of a multicity mobilization to address a troublesome problem of the recession-plagued 1970s: inadequate youth-employment programs.[1]

Teens on the march for jobs were part of a renewed community-based labor movement that took its own sustainability seriously. Organized by Jobs and Justice—a coalition of the Movement for Economic Justice, Massachusetts Fair Share, and ACORN—the outpouring of youthful energy was the first effort in the coalition's battle to organize poor workers from coast to coast. Jobs and Justice sought to "combine direct action organizing with the development of grassroots organizations," which would create pressure for better jobs, higher wages, and workers' rights.[2]

By the late '70s, the basic structural problem identified by welfare rights and economic justice activists—the "secondary labor market" of low-paid, short-term, dead-end employment—was growing worse. Moreover, the gulf between "regular" salaried workers and their less fortunate colleagues in this secondary labor market was as large as ever, marked by what organizers called a "welfare-unemployment-public service-low wage treadmill."[3] It was a revolving door that included not only welfare and low-wage jobs but also the Comprehensive Employment and Training Act (CETA) program, which, though potentially a useful public works program, had the effect of recycling participants back into dead-end minimum-wage jobs.

Although short-lived, the Jobs and Justice coalition bridged several community-based economic justice organizations and fueled development of ACORN's autonomous labor organizing projects, dubbed United Labor Unions (originally United Labor Organizations). While the Movement for Economic Justice had sponsored mass actions and facilitated networks among poor worker activists, United Labor Unions (ULU) went a step further by organizing union representation campaigns, bargaining for enforceable union contracts, and creating sustainable institutions. By the mid-'80s, ULU locals had used direct action methods to obtain the first fast-food industry contract in US history, unionized thousands of "invisible" poverty-wage home care workers, and made inroads into New Orleans's gigantic and nonunion tourist industry.

Drawing on both social movement organizing tactics and lessons from the industrial unionism of the CIO, the experiences of ULU activists belied the oft-repeated claim that dispersed low-wage workers were "unorganizable." Not every organizing battle was won, but many were, demonstrating that poor workers could indeed organize, as they had within the civil rights, welfare rights, and women's movements in the past. These organizations laid the groundwork for some of the largest and most successful organizing campaigns of the '80s and '90s and brought many new workers into the labor movement at a time when it desperately needed democratization, revitalization, and growth.

Mobilizing Discontent

Young workers had become such a central part of the low-wage employment and unemployment problem that the Congressional Budget

Office held a special conference in April 1976 on the "teenage unemployment problem." In 1978 the unemployment rate for sixteen-to-nineteen-year-olds was 16.4 percent overall, and 38.7 percent for Black teenagers.[4] For poor kids, summer jobs could make a real difference in family income. In the summer of 1978, Jobs and Justice organizers targeted seven cities—Boston, Baltimore, Denver, Detroit, Cincinnati, Philadelphia, and Seattle—that had received federal grants to initiate summer youth employment projects. In some locations there were many more applicants than jobs. Drawing on welfare rights strategies, Jobs and Justice argued that these jobs were "entitlements" and every young person who wanted a job should be provided with one.

One of the tactics Jobs and Justice used—mass convergences on employment offices to present job applications—was borrowed from welfare rights organizing and ACORN's Unemployed Workers' Organizing Committee, which had done the same in the early '70s. Four hundred Boston high school students marched on the city's youth employment agency in June 1978, with applications in hand, demanding that the jobs program be expanded. While the director of the program agreed with the students' demands and marched with them another six blocks to the Department of Labor regional headquarters, other city officials held a press conference that same day claiming that local government could not provide enough jobs and that the demonstrators should look to the private sector instead.[5]

The students took the advice. A week later, Boston's usually staid financial district became the scene of a rowdy march by hundreds of teens. Protesters targeted the city's largest corporations, including Travelers Insurance, First National Bank, and New England Telephone, with demands for jobs. By the time the students reached city hall, the deputy mayor announced that federal funding had been obtained for an additional five hundred jobs. Similar victories were won in other cities where teens were organizing, including Philadelphia, Denver, and New Orleans. In Philadelphia city officials added $2 million to the summer jobs program.[6]

Jobs and Justice also targeted CETA, the largest federal employment program since the Great Depression, accounting for up to 20 percent of the workforce in many large US urban areas. Private businesses received CETA funding to train unskilled workers, many of them young. CETA socialized the cost of maintaining a low-wage workforce and benefited employers, who used the federal funds to subsidize their own profits, at the same time that it cooled dissatisfaction among the unemployed by offering short-term jobs.

While CETA was supposed to train workers for permanent private-sector employment, many workers ended up being "recycled" back onto unemployment or welfare—as few as 15 percent of Boston's CETA employees found permanent jobs after their positions ended. Jobs and Justice helped a thousand Boston CETA workers due to be terminated get six-month extensions on the grounds that training and placement were substandard. A group of CETA workers in New Orleans received extensions amounting to $1 million in wages after they marched on city hall in July 1978.[7]

Jobs and Justice also organized domestic workers. In the summer of 1978 the Household Workers Organizing Committee, with some 250 dues-paying members, marched through the wealthy neighborhoods of New Orleans demanding fair wages and benefits. It sued individual employers and the US Department of Labor (responsible for enforcing wage and social security laws) over minimum-wage laws and even won back-pay awards in some cases.[8]

Jobs and Justice believed in the strength of grassroots mobilization and direct action. The group's early tactics focused on mobilizations to the exclusion of union building, reflecting an initial ideological predisposition against institutionalization.[9] On some levels these organizing experiments were a success. The summer campaign had shown that those who were thought of as marginal to the labor movement—such as young workers, domestic workers, and CETA participants—were quite ready to fight for their rights as workers. In New Orleans, Denver, Philadelphia, and Boston, Jobs and Justice had involved some five thousand people in direct job actions, winning about $9 million in jobs and benefits.[10]

Still, of all the projects undertaken in 1978 and 1979, none survived beyond their initial campaigns. In a year-end assessment, Jobs and Justice activists acknowledged "organizational difficulties," including lack of funding, setbacks in building membership, and collecting dues from an impoverished workforce, as well as "strategic problems" such as the need for a broader-based national campaign on behalf of poor workers. The former community organizers behind Jobs and Justice were well versed in the method of building from smaller, easier victories to larger ones but found that strategy less applicable to their new constituency. "Either you get a job or you do not get a job," they wrote. "The development of intermediate goals and campaigns is not easy."[11]

Once a member found a job, moreover, that person tended to drop out of the organizing campaign. Activists sometimes came and went so quickly that each decision-making meeting was peopled by different members. Workers' temporary and transient status made clear the need for a more stable structure within which to organize, a structure that would serve members before, during, and after they had permanent jobs. A union of poor workers was the model that seemed to make sense.

A McJobs Economy

At the same time, the trade union movement's long-standing neglect of organizing was about to come full circle. Public-sector unions met little opposition as they continued signing up workers in the expanding government workforce, but most private-sector trade unions did not do any appreciable amount of new organizing. They preferred to stay within the dues-rich areas they knew would yield the highest membership for the smallest amount of energy. A small circle within the AFL-CIO executive council (composed mostly of presidents of larger unions), including the UAW's Doug Fraser, AFSCME's Jerry Wurf, and International Association of Machinists' William Winpisinger, fought for a rededication to organizing. Other unions sympathetic to change and mindful of organizing included the Communications Workers of America and SEIU.[12]

By the close of the '70s, however, the trade union movement was in full retreat, the words "concessionary bargaining" on the lips of negotiators from coast to coast. While in 1979 auto giant Chrysler got $1.5 billion in government credits to rescue its profits, the UAW, which represented Chrysler's workers, agreed to a wage freeze and a $1.15-an-hour wage cut a year later.[13] By 1982 unemployment had climbed to its highest level in a decade.[14] The concept of solidarity suffered as well, as the drive for concessions pitted unionized workers against their nonunionized counterparts. Labor costs and union-free pastures elsewhere tempted corporations to close unionized plants and relocate to the US South and Southwest as well as overseas.[15] During this period the professional "union-buster" reappeared on the scene, hired by corporations to conduct customized antiunion campaigns that relied on intimidation, bribery, and spying as well as a thorough knowledge of how to use US labor law to kill representation drives.[16]

Even to labor's partisans, the '80s seemed to sound the death knell for a once-great movement. "Labor gives off now an almost animal sense of weakness," wrote union lawyer Thomas Geoghegan in 1991. "Concessions, de-certs, shutdowns. It's like the Italian army in 1918: cars breaking down, baggage getting lost, officers getting fired on by their own troops."[17] Though the political landscape was undoubtedly hard for trade unions, structural divisions within the movement, which had been allowed to deepen over the preceding decades, had weakened its ability to fight. Moreover, for decades trade unions had primarily concentrated their energies on winning legal rights and influencing political parties rather than on the basic task of organizing workers. It was not surprising that when the legal and political climate changed in the '80s, employers and government wreaked havoc on workers and their institutions.

While employees in the auto, steel, and manufacturing industries had faced corporate layoffs and cutbacks in the late '70s, the low-wage service sector was skyrocketing. In early 1982, when service-sector jobs surpassed those in manufacturing for the first time, the low-wage burger empire McDonald's, it was estimated, employed more than twice as many people as US Steel.[18] Fast-food chains accounted for $24 billion in annual sales, more than a third of the entire restaurant industry.[19] Other rapidly expanding low-wage sectors included home care, janitorial, and hotel and restaurant (or "hospitality"). Within geographic regions, these occupations collectively constituted industries peopled by poor workers. Why not organize them using the lessons of the CIO in the 1930s—across job titles, encompassing the whole industry?

If trade unions would not take up the challenge, community or-

ganizers would. "In the best of worlds, low-paid workers would organize into [AFL-CIO] labor unions," wrote one ACORN organizer.
"There are no indications, however, that this is about to happen."[20] In
response, ACORN's United Labor Unions adopted key structures of
trade unionism. A formal union constitution laid out rules for membership, dues, and a democratic structure that included workplace
chapters, local unions, councils, and districts, and a national executive
board, and declared it an independent organization "run by our members." Though formally separate from ACORN, the constitution
noted, the union shared ACORN's broad goal of "economic justice
for low and moderate income people in the neighborhoods and in the
workplace. [The two groups would] work together in any way that will
benefit our members and all low and moderate income people."[21]

Along with continuing the organizing of the unemployed and welfare recipients pioneered by earlier groups, this new union would embrace a "new style and new models of organizing low wage workers,
focusing more on direct action and worker-community linkages and
less on the legalistic framework of National Labor Relations Board
(NLRB) procedures."[22] This lack of interest in, or concern with, the
traditional instruments of labor relations would allow United Labor
Unions to maintain a fluid movement style, as opposed to a legalistic
or bureaucratic style. The ULU's constituency was a multiracial and
multilingual mix of African American, Latina and Latino, Caribbean,
Asian American, and white workers. Its organizing staff of twenty-
three were racially diverse and nearly equally male and female.[23]
United Labor Unions started organizing in cities where Jobs and Justice activities had been particularly effective—Philadelphia, Detroit,
New Orleans and Boston. It surveyed each city's economy for likely
organizing targets, choosing whole industries if possible.

In Detroit, where plant doors were slamming shut and low-wage
service work was expanding, organizers picked the fast-food industry.
Workers at Detroit's two big national franchises, McDonald's and Burger
King, were mostly African American teens paid minimum wage with no
benefits. In December 1979 four ULU organizers, two Black and two
white, began walking into local fast-food franchises, ordering burgers and
sodas, and talking up the need for a union with the cashiers.[24]

Contrary to the organizers' expectations, organizing proceeded at a lightning pace. By February 1980 Detroit's ULU was hosting citywide meetings with workers from nine separate outlets. In some locations, organizers signed up the majority of the workforce in a day.[25] In others it was impossible to speak to workers on the job, so organizers made home visits. In all cases ULU staffers set up organizing committees of rank-and-file employees, helping them to run their own campaigns and set up pickets and demonstrations.[26] On February 22, 1980, two months into the organizing drive, the fifty-three employees of the Burger King in the Greyhound terminal in downtown Detroit voted for representation in an NLRB-sponsored election, making it the first unionized fast-food franchise in the United States. Workers in three McDonald's and two other Burger King franchises also filed for NLRB elections.[27]

The *Detroit Free Press* characterized the organizing campaign as a "classical, old-style union battle," with wealthy corporate employers facing off against "a neophyte union led by four young men who have backgrounds in community organization, a large amount of enthusiasm and drive, staffed by a growing population of workers who can't find much good to say about their employers."[28] Indeed, the young workers soon threw themselves into the fight to sign up their fellow workers and run the campaign. They published a newsletter in which columns like "Your Boss and the Law" informed coworkers about the right to organize. Employees at McDonald's challenged a manager to a debate in one issue of the newsletter and ridiculed him later when he declined the invitation.[29] Nearly every issue included hand-drawn satirical cartoons, such as bosses standing over employees with whips, or company mascot Ronald McDonald stuffing his pockets with money, singing the praises of a nonunion workplace.

Thanks to Detroit's prolabor culture, community support was strong. Sympathizers joined pickets outside stores, asking customers to boycott the franchise until management signed a pledge acknowledging the right to unionize. At one Burger King franchise, workers confronted a manager with a demand that she sign an agreement recognizing the union. When she refused, picketers—both off-duty workers and community supporters—turned away 90 percent of the store's business.[30] Prominent religious, community, and labor leaders signed an open letter supporting the organizing campaign. The United Auto Workers as well as locals of the Hotel Employees and Restaurant Employees lent their support, though other unions were notably absent from endorsement lists, presumably because the ULU local was not affiliated with the AFL-CIO. The autoworkers' support was "a bright spot" in a difficult campaign, wrote organizer Daniel Cantor, noting an important connection: "The sons and daughters of UAW members who led the McDonald's drives were merely continuing the family tradition."[31]

Detroit's ULU was contacted by workers interested in organizing at other fast-food outlets, such as Church's and Kentucky Fried Chicken.[32] But the initial victories were followed by the realization that workers faced an uphill battle, with multinational corporations taking the offensive and sparing no expense to fight union drives. The ULUs were a "headache," industry spokespeople told the *Washington Post* in 1981, due to their role in a successful lobbying campaign to defeat a subminimum-wage proposal in Congress that year. Republican senator Orrin Hatch's bill would have allowed employers to pay teenagers 75 percent of minimum wage for the first six months of employment. Dubbed "the McDonald's amendment," it would have been a financial boon to the industry, whose own trade association calculated that 16 percent of the nation's 1.5 million working teenagers were fast-food workers.[33]

Fast-food franchise owners opposed the union campaign, holding "captive audience" meetings with their employees to argue against the union on work time, offering workers perks and small pay raises to undercut support for the union, and firing union activists. "They fired all our key leaders, who were just sixteen or seventeen years old," recalls Cantor.[34] Challenging a termination in the legal system took time and was received coldly by the conservative, Reagan-appointed NLRB. It almost always meant the loss of a member/activist, who moved on to another low-wage job somewhere else while waiting months—or years—for a verdict. When one Burger King supervisor harassed an employee in May 1981 for wearing a union button, it took two and a half years to settle the case.[35]

The fast-food industry's exceptionally high turnover rates—conservatively estimated at 100 percent per year—meant that new activists came and went at an astonishingly fast pace. Even wide employee and community support was not enough to prevail against such turnover combined with management's antiunion assault. Detroit's fast-food workers ended up voting in several more union elections—three at McDonald's franchises in April 1980 and one at a Burger King in June 1980—but all failed. At the end of the campaign, only a single unionized outlet remained—the Burger King at the Detroit Greyhound station. Even there, employer challenges to the election process delayed bargaining for over three years.[36]

Confronting the Boss

In hindsight, Detroit's ULU organizers admitted they were outgunned, having taken on a difficult opponent in their first industry-wide organizing attempt.[37] These experiences with the traditional machinery of labor relations reinforced ULU activists' initial instincts that operating outside the NLRB election process could yield faster and better results—not simply in terms of winning a job back or organizing an election but in building strong bonds of solidarity. The Detroit ULU turned its attention to smaller local employers, which were less likely to have the unlimited resources of a multinational corporation and more likely to be affected by worker and community pressure.

ULU organizing committees had been using demonstrations or confrontations with company managers instead of, or in addition to, the usual request for an NLRB-sponsored election. Recognition actions, where workers would "'come out of the closet' in front of the boss," wrote organizer Keith Kelleher, gave them their first taste of collective power, and a chance to "intimidate the boss for a change, and . . . [put] management on notice that the workers are well organized."[38] For instance, workers at Goldman Manufacturing in Detroit won their ULU representation election in October 1980. Frustrated with a month of company stonewalling in bargaining, a large group of employees stormed into a negotiating session to confront the boss and his lawyer. "We're sick of hearing all this legal bull!" said worker Larry Picket, pointing at Goldman's lawyer. Another employee, Carl Hobson, said, "We want to see some more money, you aren't offering us nothing!" By the end of the encounter, management conceded to several demands and agreed to allow employees to negotiate on work time.[39]

Such "recognition actions" would serve as the glue uniting workers in their campaigns for union representation and later for fair contracts. The ULUs increasingly made a point of relying on this kind of direct action. In New Orleans, Tulane University's cafeteria workers joined ULU Local 100 in the spring of 1981 to win back the holidays, vacations, and sick pay that had been axed several months earlier when Tulane contracted out the food service to a private corporation. The workers, nearly all female and African American, also complained of poor pay and a lack of dignity and respect on the job. Tired of the company's stalling, one day some two dozen women stopped work in the middle of the morning and surrounded a manager. The manager said he had to consult with his boss before recognizing the union. After nearly a week of waiting, the women gathered again, trapping a manager in one of the cafeteria turnstiles and chanting, "Students can't eat, 'cause Gailey won't meet." According to the union newsletter, "With over half the workers standing right up in his face, Mr. Gailey didn't have much choice. He met." The cafeteria workers won an NLRB-supervised election a few months later and negotiated a contract that restored their benefits and provided for substantial pay raises.[40]

Few recognition actions yielded prompt and voluntary union recognition or agreement on a contract, but these actions were vitally important to organizing because they brought workers together to act for themselves and allowed rank-and-file leaders to gain confidence in their roles. The collective, public nature of the actions built solidarity between workers and their allies (in the case of the Tulane cafeteria workers, students and other staffers). But it was a risky business. Walking off the job to confront the boss was prohibited under labor law because it was an unauthorized work stoppage. "I don't think we knew it was illegal until after the fact," recalls New Orleans organizer and ACORN cofounder Wade Rathke about the Tulane action. "All of [the workers] could have been fired."[41] But it was this experimentation that differentiated the ULU's organizing from that of many trade unions. Relying first on direct

action and only later on legal procedures built a more effective and engaging union, one to which workers wanted to lend their energies.

When the Neighborhood Is the Workplace

In New Orleans, ULU organizers set their sights on tourism, the quin-
tessential low-wage service industry. It had long been one of the city's
largest industries and was an extremely profitable one, with millions
visiting the city for the annual Mardi Gras celebration and jazz festival.
There was a special advantage here from which organizers could
profit. Unlike other industries in which corporations could pick up
shop and leave when challenged by a union, the New Orleans "hospitality" industry was anchored by the specificity of place, which gave
employers one less weapon with which to fight unionization. These
jobs couldn't go overseas—not when the tourist draw was the unique
French Quarter or the historic St. Charles streetcar line.

In the late '70s most of the city's hotels were nonunion, and few,
if any, of the city's seventy-five hundred hotel workers—maids,
porters, dishwashers, laundry workers, garage attendants, and others—made more than minimum wage no matter how long their
tenure. Most jumped from one job to the next, doing private household work during the tourist hotels' seasonal layoffs.[42] By organizing
among domestic workers in the spring of 1978, New Orleans's ULU
local had developed numerous contacts among hotel workers, who
had often gotten their jobs in the industry after leaving private household work. ULU organizers held a series of citywide meetings in late
1979, at which workers from different hotels gathered to exchange
ideas and strategize. Through these meetings, workers decided on a
campaign to secure partial unemployment benefits during the slack
tourist period and to gain union representation.[43] With the support of
religious and community leaders, the union won a certification election in June 1981 at the huge Hyatt Regency Hotel, the first union victory in New Orleans's hotel industry in twenty years.

In Philadelphia, ULU organizers could find no single industry to
organize, so they targeted sweatshops in the neighborhoods where most
of the city's poor workers lived and worked. Among the first efforts was

a rag recycling plant called DuMont Export, which employed over two hundred workers, mostly African American, to collect and sort rags, which were then sent to Bangladesh for use in its textile industry. Du-Mont's workers were part of a global chain of production that began with the castoffs of poor communities in the United States, which were remanufactured into clothing and rugs by poor workers in Bangladesh and subsequently sold in South Asia or exported back to the United States by multinational corporations. The union overwhelmingly won an NLRB-sponsored election in the fall of 1979, and workers elected a bargaining team and began negotiating. When management suddenly fired several union leaders, the entire workforce walked out on strike.[44]

While neighborhood supporters gathered daily at the plant gates to reinforce the picket lines, and local churches organized delegations, union members "jumped on buses and went on a tour of the three local employment agencies to urge them not to send scabs," according to organizer Mike Gallagher. Confronted by dozens of boisterous striking workers from their own neighborhood, the owners of all three employment agencies quickly signed agreements pledging not to cooperate with the company, and they held to that pledge throughout the six-week strike. "What we were doing was an unfair labor practice," said Gallagher. It was an illegal "'hot cargo' agreement which induces a non-party to cease doing business with the employer."[45] ULU organizers, who claimed they didn't know at the time that they were breaking labor laws, admit that they were naive and inexperienced. But such inexperience also brought with it open minds and creative organizing.

The DuMont strike was eventually lost—again, the victor was a wealthy corporation with the resources for a protracted antiunion campaign. But the short ULU balance sheet in Philadelphia was positive. It had won two other union elections: one at a microfilming company that employed hundreds of African American women in substandard conditions; another at a furniture-manufacturing shop where a multiracial workforce won its first contract after a one-month strike.[46]

In addition to maintaining community support, a top priority for the ULU was to retain the contractual right to strike, instead of trading it off at the negotiating table for binding arbitration, as was the usual practice. One ULU shop of some three dozen packaging workers in

Detroit successfully negotiated the right to strike over grievances in November 1980. The union's newsletter announced that this was something "other locals will want to copy," informing members that "after the last step in the plant [grievance] procedure, the union has the choice of going to arbitration or *going on strike!* Keeping the right to strike over a grievance means that you can avoid getting bogged down in a lot of expensive arbitrations."[47]

The ULU's contracts didn't bargain away workers' ability to undertake rank-and-file actions. They aimed instead to protect and facilitate such actions, which were seen as long-term strategic assets in the toolbox of union building. This kind of contract was not favored by most trade unions, which usually sought to restrain the ability of workers to perform shop floor actions and preferred engaging in legal procedures or negotiations between union officials and management.

Insurance Salespeople We Are Not

Like RIWA and ACORN before it, United Labor Unions modeled its organizing strategies on the work of community-based labor organizers like the United Farm Workers' Cesar Chavez and Fred Ross of the Community Service Organization, as well as trade union traditions of rank-and-file membership organizing. "We do not approach workers as 'salespeople' for the union trying to sell the union's benefits as if we were selling insurance or vacuum cleaners," wrote organizer Keith Kelleher.[48] Rather, ULU organizers sought to build strong member-run organizations that would be difficult for management to undermine.

Activities such as targeting, list building, and house visits helped gather information about a particular group of workers and identify possible activists and leaders. Visiting workers at home meant the boss wasn't looking over their shoulders, and they could discuss their grievances freely. It gave ULU organizers the opportunity to make workers aware that "the union" was them, the workers. By coming into their homes on nonwork hours and asking for their commitment to workplace action, organizers made clear that rank-and-file members would not only do the work of organizing but have the power to decide how it was done. ULU organizers weren't shy about asking for dues ($5 to join and 1 percent of gross salary after that), because financial commitment reinforced the awareness that workers owned the union and it would succeed or fail based on their own actions.

The rest of the model—leadership development, organizing committee meetings, recognition actions, and elections campaign— aimed to create a democratic structure run by the workers themselves. Workers were quickly asked to chair committee meetings, sign up members, and make decisions. The organizer's role was to make sure no one monopolized discussion and to explain technical details about the union drive. Members elected their own representatives. By the time of the election campaign, workers were electing stewards, collecting dues, conducting house visits, making phone calls along with organizers, producing their own newsletters, and interacting with the media. On a practical level, member involvement made the ULU's larger campaigns possible, despite limited monetary resources. But perhaps more important, this horizontal rank-and-file campaign was harder for employers to undermine and provided infrastructure for a lasting organization.

These were classic tactics of labor organizing, which the ULUs had added to the community-organizing repertoire they inherited from ACORN. Community organizing had grown exponentially in the '70s and '80s. Hundreds of grassroots organizations formed across the country to work on issues such as jobs, housing, utilities, health, and education. ACORN's expansion around the nation was one part of this growth.[49] Neighborhood organizing flourished, having grown from the teachings of community organizer Saul Alinsky, including groups affiliated with the Industrial Areas Foundation (IAF), begun in 1940, which based its organizing in church congregations and other community institutions. Alinsky's model emphasized a geographically based, non-ideological, replicable organizing model focused on concrete goals.[50]

ACORN was heavily influenced by the IAF tradition, but its structure was quite different. While the IAF groups were usually local and autonomous, ACORN aimed to build a nationwide network of affiliates supported not by institutional grants but by dues-paying members. Its constituency was also poorer and more racially diverse.

Like members of democratic trade unions, ACORN members worked as activists in their organization, ran their own meetings, acted as press spokespersons and leaders, and elected their own governing board, to which paid staff were accountable.

But, as with many trade unions and community organizations, ACORN's model didn't always live up to its ideals. In its early years ACORN suffered from what cofounder Gary Delgado calls a "staff oligarchy," limiting the ability of rank-and-file members to challenge organizational policies. While members were often the decision makers on the day-to-day level, hired organizing staff turned out pages of research and strategizing before members were even recruited. This gave the staff power over the agenda, even if subsequent discussions allowed members input into the details. Most of ACORN's earliest paid staff were white—only about 10 percent were organizers of color; the organization eventually reached 64 percent staff of color in 2003. Ideologically, many of the senior staff minimized race and gender while emphasizing class, creating what Delgado calls a "white" staff organizing culture within most ACORN offices.[51] A 2003 decision of the National Labor Relations Board concluded that ACORN management tried to prevent union organizing among its staff by laying off two workers who had begun such a campaign with the Industrial Workers of the World.[52]

ACORN also had its share of external conflicts, particularly during its first two decades. It often avoided working in coalitions with other progressive groups, and friction with other community-based organizations in various localities was not uncommon.[53] For instance, in 1986 activists with Boston's already-established Dudley Street Neighborhood Initiative complained that ACORN set up organizing shop across the street and began undermining their work.[54]

But the internal and external dynamics in ACORN's autonomous labor-organizing projects—United Labor Unions—were different. Staffing in the ULUs was among the most diverse within ACORN. Rank-and-file members—overwhelmingly people of color—were commonly hired on as paid staff, breaking down the dichotomy between members and organizing staff. In the mid-'80s the ULU staff was approximately 60 percent African American, and about half female, and, notes Delgado, the organization encouraged democratic decision making.[55]

The larger culture within ACORN itself began to change by the late '80s. An affirmative-action hiring program was mandated by ACORN's elected governing board, and the organization began hiring staff from its existing membership. The staff became more diverse (in 2003 the staff was 38 percent African American, 36 percent white, 24 percent Latina or Latino, and 2 percent Asian or "other"). Coalitional work with unions and other organizations became more a part of ACORN's organizing style, as is evident in its role in "living wage" coalitions in dozens of cities.[56]

Scattered Workplaces, Dispersed Workers

The ULUs followed their grassroots organizing philosophy closely, including during what would become the group's most successful campaigns in numerical terms, organizing the almost exclusively female home care workers in Boston and Chicago from 1981 to 1984. Since most home healthcare workers did not share a common workplace, direct action and rank-and-file-centered organizing methods became especially useful, holding scattered employees together in a way little else could. Workers who ordinarily would not have known their colleagues developed relationships of mutual support and solidarity while attending union meetings, participating in legislative campaigns, or organizing strikes and other workplace actions.

The usual work of the home healthcare worker (or "homemaker," as she was sometimes called) involved cleaning house, running errands, cooking meals, and providing for the personal hygiene, diet, and exercise needs of her client. Home health care developed as an alternative to nursing homes, as a high-quality and humane way to provide for elders' and disabled people's needs. In 1970 it was a $500 million industry, but by 1981 it had grown exponentially, raking in some $2.5 billion a year. Highly profitable, the industry included corporate giants like Kelly Health Care (a subsidiary of the Kelly Girl temp service) and Upjohn, a Fortune 500 drug company. "Once considered economically marginal," write Eileen Boris and

Jennifer Klein, "home care has moved to the center of the economy," becoming one of the fastest growing occupations by the end of the twentieth century.[57]

Unlike the hotel workers in New Orleans, who labored together in small and large workplaces in tourist neighborhoods, home care workers in Boston and Chicago were individually dispersed among private homes. Some had never even met a fellow home care worker. And although they numbered in the tens of thousands in US cities, most union organizers didn't know they existed. The US government did not begin tracking the industry until 1987. By then the workforce was reported to number 291,000 nationally (a figure that increased to 680,000 by 1997).[58] Boston's ULU organizers only stumbled across some of the city's five thousand home healthcare workers while circulating a petition outside subway stations to raise the minimum wage. Organizers got a tip from a worker to come on any Friday afternoon to a building in the suburb of Brookline, where they'd find hundreds of women arriving to pick up paychecks. "We went out there, and sure enough, hundreds of people are walking in and out of this office called Suburban Homemaking," recalled Mike Gallagher.[59]

Soon ULU organizers tracked down some seventeen thousand such workers in Massachusetts—almost exclusively African American, Caribbean, and Latina women—all employed by private corporations that received state funding to provide in-home services to elders and the infirm.[60] Simply locating the workers was a task in itself. To make contact with home care workers, organizers waited at bus stops, in laundries of senior housing projects, and in grocery stores that elders frequented. Once asked, most workers immediately joined the union, and a rank-and-file organizing committee for each home care employer began meeting.[61]

Many home healthcare workers enjoyed helping clients cope with everyday living but were aware of being exploited. "I like what I do, but I've been working two years without a break and I'm too tired to keep it up," one worker told union organizers. "The homemakers have to work together to get the rights that other workers have."[62] Chief among those rights were a living wage and basic benefits. Most home care workers were so poorly paid that they were eligible for welfare,

Medicaid, and food stamps. The home care corporations typically received at least twice as much from the state as they paid to the workers hired for the job. For instance, in 1981 the reimbursement rate from Massachusetts social service agencies to a home healthcare corporation could be as high as $12 per hour, while the home healthcare worker herself was rarely paid more than $4 per hour. (The federal minimum wage at the time was $3.35.) Ironically, these women who were providing basic health care to others did not themselves receive medical insurance, sick leave, or vacation.[63]

Home care corporations boasted of the supposed benefits they offered to compensate for the low pay. "Flexible hours and work in your neighborhood" was one company's motto. As organizers pointed out, this revealed the industry's stereotype of its workforce—"housewives, women with children, who want to pick up a few dollars," instead of working women whose paychecks would support themselves and their families. The work mirrored the unpaid domestic chores of the housewife and the paid domestic chores of the maid, but with a twist: companies appealed to workers' sense of social responsibility for helping others, while they exploited the workers themselves. Employment ads for home care workers played up the self-sacrificing ideal of home care as "women's work." One declared, "You are special because you CARE!" while another revealed that workers would be chosen for their experience attending to children and parents in the home. Home care workers acknowledged this dilemma. "If my little lady calls me on a Saturday to say that she's out of bread and orange juice," one worker told organizers, "I know I'll be there, even though I'm not on the time clock." ULU organizers concluded that, "in effect, the homemaker subsidizes the social service system out of her own pocket."[64]

Workers learned to use these contradictions as powerful organizing tools during their first union campaign at Suburban Homemaking. In July 1981 dozens of Suburban workers began meeting weekly at the ULU offices to plot a strategy to win a union-representation election. A key element was the support of "clients"—elders who generally had more than a business relationship with their home care worker. Workers delivered politely worded letters to clients explaining the union campaign and asking them to call Suburban's CEO, Emma Birnbaum, at home and "let her know that you think your Homemaker deserves better. . . . Tell her to recognize the union and start bargaining for better wages and benefits."[65] A flood of calls had Birnbaum's phone ringing off the hook. About the same time, home healthcare workers twice traveled en masse to Birnbaum's suburban neighborhood—television and radio reporters in tow—to picket her home and lobby her neighbors to demand that she voluntarily recognize the union. Before city officials and seniors' organizations, workers made a case for wage improvements, pointing out that they were doing socially important work for impossibly low pay.[66]

Tired of waiting, Suburban home healthcare workers voted to strike rather than hold out for an NLRB-sponsored union vote, then altered their plans when management agreed to stop stalling the election process.[67] On November 18, 1981, when the union won the election by a two-to-one ratio, Suburban became the first home care agency in Boston to unionize.[68] But the company threw more obstacles in the union's path. Management hired an antiunion law firm and dug in its heels during bargaining, refusing to offer any benefits and putting a dismal wage offer on the table: a raise of two cents an hour over three years.[69] After nearly a year of bargaining, and after building support among their clients, Suburban home healthcare workers struck on November 1, 1982. The company tried to break the strike by hiring replacements, but many clients refused to let the scabs into their homes, while some of the workers visited their clients on the sly to tend to their needs. Within three weeks, Suburban management settled.[70] Activists had used a strategy that united low-income social service clients with the workers who served them, a model that would prove highly useful in future public-sector organizing.

During that fruitless year of bargaining, workers at several other home healthcare corporations had unionized with Boston's ULU local by overwhelming votes, bringing roughly one thousand of the city's five thousand homecare workers under collective bargaining by late 1982. Meanwhile, in Chicago another ULU local opened shop in May 1983 to target the large home care workforce in that urban area.[71] "If anything," wrote organizers, "wages and other conditions are even *worse* in Chicago than those encountered in Boston two years ago. . . . It is a shame and a scandal that people who are doing some of the most sensitive work of society are rewarded so poorly, but it is not hard to figure out why. Jobs are hard to find and options are limited, particularly if you are Black, middle-aged and a woman."[72]

The Chicago organizing drive faced an uphill battle. State appropriations for home care were extremely low, keeping home healthcare workers' pay at "bargain basement levels." Difficult as the conditions were, however, Chicago organizers observed that home healthcare workers "do not seem at all shy about getting into the fight."[73]

In the summer of 1983, the ULU's Chicago organizing committee found its first target: McMaid, a for-profit agency employing over two hundred home healthcare workers, was among the most exploitative of the home healthcare corporations. Union activists organized pickets of managers' homes, marches to legislators' offices, and regular public events to keep their struggle visible, and six months later, they won the election. A string of election victories at other home care companies followed. By 1985 the Chicago ULU local represented nearly one thousand workers and had a contract with one of the largest home healthcare companies in the state.[74] In Boston the union represented two thousand workers, and pay had risen from subminimum wage to $6 plus an hour. In both cities, workers won vacation and sick leaves, grievance procedures, and other benefits. Encouraged by success, the Chicago local began discussing ambitious plans to branch out into other low-wage occupations, such as fast food and cafeteria work.[75]

Home healthcare workers also carried their fight to the state legislatures charged with appropriating funds to pay the home care companies. Along with exposing poor conditions for workers, ULU members highlighted the limited services clients received in order to argue for better benefits overall. Former Boston-area state representative Mel King helped lobby on the workers' behalf, describing the home healthcare system as "gross exploitation" and "workfare in disguise."[76] Such connections between low-wage work and forced work welfare programs emphasized to the public as well as to poor workers themselves the class they occupied. They were relegated to an underclass of the poor and unemployed, facing welfare bureaucracies as often as employer exploitation. Their organizing efforts were not only fostering an increasingly cohesive sense of class identity—which emerged with full force during campaigns in the '90s around low-wage work and workfare—but also creating a new framework for the labor movement as a whole, one that recognized the individual and collective agency of the poor.

Crossing the Threshold

These organizing stories illustrate a conundrum that all movements face: what balance of mobilization and institutionalization will produce the best possibility for lasting social change? The flexibility and spontaneity of movement organizing are its greatest strengths, but often they come at the expense of stability. The majority of trade unions in the mid-twentieth century illustrated the hazards of the opposite approach: institutionalization to the point of bureaucratization. But can there be institutionalization *and* rank-and-file involvement and control? Institutionalization without bureaucratization?

United Labor Unions provided an example of how a nonbureaucratized institution could benefit low-wage workers. And new organizing efforts from trade unions such as Hospital Workers 1199 and Service Employees International Union (SEIU) showed that the same impulse was alive within the mainstream. For example, the large organizing drive at Beverly Nursing Homes, conducted jointly by SEIU and the United Food and Commercial Workers in 1983–84, successfully used worker-to-worker organizing and community support to win thirty-five out of fifty elections representing some six thousand low-wage workers.[77]

ULU's years of independence had given it freedom to experiment, but the lack of funding had had serious consequences. In an assessment of their progress three years into their nationally coordinated campaign, ULU organizers noted a recurrent obstacle: "understaffing and under financing."[78] Even though the ULUs represented thousands of home care workers in Boston and Chicago, as well as hotel workers at the giant Hyatt chain in New Orleans, financial difficulties were taking a toll. In Detroit the ULU had contracts with several small employers, as well as a contract with a single franchise of a multinational corporation (Burger King), but realized that without a broader national campaign against the whole corporation it would not mean much.

While these new "external" organizing campaigns would need a solid base of funding, there was also "internal" organizing to be done among the locals already affiliated with United Labor Unions. Winning contracts in dozens of workplaces meant that the ULUs needed a permanent and adequately funded framework for yearly bargaining, grievance handling, and other activities that they were now legally required to perform. They generally relied on rank-and-file leadership for most of these activities, but the ULU locals still needed money for office rent, occasional arbitrations and legal fees, and some paid staff. It is clear from the ULU experience that institutions were important to facilitate grassroots organizing and create a capacity for movement building. It was equally important to keep those institutions democratic and flexible.

The innovative style ULU employed among the large and scattered workforce of home care workers caught the eye of SEIU, one of the first AFL-CIO trade unions to begin to seriously expand its organizing efforts among low-wage private-sector employers and those that were quasi-private, like the home care sector. In the early '80s it had already affiliated the San Diego–based United Domestic Workers of America, whose work in some respects paralleled that of ULU.[79]

In early 1984 SEIU offered to affiliate the ULU locals, giving all five a collective organizing subsidy worth $216,000 in the first three years, and allow the locals to keep most of their dues; ULU leaders bargained the subsidy up to $360,000 a year.[80] The offer signaled the willingness of a mainstream trade union to incorporate combative and movement-style tactics into its national organizing strategy.

For the ULUs the SEIU affiliation offer was an astonishing amount of money. After years of collecting union dues by hand and scrambling for grants or "street money" collected by sidewalk canvassers, the thought of affiliating with a mainstream union was surprisingly welcome. SEIU had "put its money where its mouth is" in helping to organize the poor, ULU Boston organizer Mike Gallagher told the *Christian Science Monitor* in 1981, adding that the previous week the union had raised all of $130 by selling hot dogs in the city's

South End neighborhood. Organizer Keith Kelleher recalls that for union financing "you didn't have to suck up to foundations. These people just wanted to know, how many are you organizing. They spoke our language."[81]

Under the affiliation deal, United Labor Unions' existing constitution and by-laws remained essentially the same, allowing it to retain local control over organizing decisions and continue its confrontational direct-action tactics. Each ULU local held citywide membership meetings to discuss the proposal, followed by a secret ballot membership vote. The proposal to affiliate passed in mid-1984. Chicago, Boston, and New Orleans ULU locals became separate SEIU locals, while the two smallest ULU locals—Detroit and Philadelphia—merged with existing SEIU locals. The two biggest locals, New Orleans SEIU 100 and Chicago SEIU 800, grew rapidly during the next two decades, signing up over 17,000 new members and contributing to the recruitment of some 150,000 home healthcare, hotel, and janitorial workers into SEIU.[82]

For SEIU, the affiliation was part of its rebirth. Two years later, in 1986, SEIU launched a national campaign to organize janitors, which a few years later brought thousands to the streets of Los Angeles, Atlanta, Washington, DC, and other cities under the "Justice for Janitors" banner.[83] In 1988 SEIU began a campaign among forty thousand home healthcare aides in Los Angeles.[84] The fact that SEIU was beginning to organize low-wage private-sector workers in large numbers was greeted with approval by progressives both inside and outside of trade unions.

Few ULU activists had a favorable view of the AFL-CIO—or the AFL-CIA, as some of them jokingly called it, alluding to the federation's history of working closely with the US government to suppress leftist labor movements abroad. But affiliation with a union belonging to the federation—as long as it was on the ULU's terms—offered enticing benefits. ULU activists put into writing their right to keep a special relationship with ACORN as a "sister" organization, which meant working jointly on issues that affected poor workers, such as preserving the Community Reinvestment Act, affordable housing, welfare, and banking reform. "Those are labor issues," notes ULU cofounder

Keith Kelleher; "it's just that labor didn't know it yet."[85] The United Labor Unions gained a stronger national network to support their organizing as well as entree into a union movement which they hoped to influence in a progressive direction.

ACORN was the nation's largest and most radical community-organizing network, winning living-wage laws across the nation, undermining the financial industry's predatory lending practices, and helping poor people get voting rights, educational benefits and tax refunds. Between 1995 and 2005, ACORN had won $15 billion in benefits for its members, according to one report commissioned by the group,[86] and it became a favorite target of conservatives. "Critics are appalled by both ACORN's size and breadth," former ACORN organizer Gary Delgado reflected admiringly in 2006. "Detractors point to the organization's 'presence in more than 100 cities with a national budget of $37 million' [as well as] 'two radio stations, a housing corporation, a law office, and affiliate relationships with a host of trade-union locals.'"[87]

Nevertheless, in the fall of 2009, after thirty-eight years of activism, ACORN collapsed, undermined by sustained right-wing attacks, an embezzlement scandal, and internal difficulties. "Most foundations decided to stop funding the organization," wrote Fred Brooks, "and dozens of government bodies (city, state, national) voted to stop funding any ACORN-affiliated organization. Although ACORN fired staff and made numerous internal reforms, it was unable to win the public relations battle."[88] A few of ACORN's larger chapters reconstituted themselves under new names, but most disappeared, and in November 2010 ACORN declared bankruptcy.

But some of the organization's staff and activists who had been spending time at subway stops and laundromats waiting for home care workers over the previous decades had made their way into the ranks of AFL-CIO reformers, bringing with them a new appreciation for creative community-based organizing tactics. They were but one stream of social justice unionists who increasingly pushed a hesitant trade union movement toward a renewed commitment to act for all workers, organized or not.

Left to right, Garment Worker Center activists Lucy Chavac, Cliseria Piñeda, and Esperanza Hernandez lead a protest directed against both Forever 21—for selling clothes made in sweatshops—and Assi Market, a Koreatown supermarket—for violating grocery workers' rights to form an independent union. The center, sponsored by Sweatshop Watch, organizes Chinese, Latina, and other workers in Los Angeles, where less than 1 percent of garment workers are unionized. *(Photo courtesy of Garment Worker Center)*

5

"Organizing Where We Live and Work"

The Independent Workers' Center Movement

I n the spring of 1978, the same year teenagers were marching for summer jobs in Boston and a year before ACORN's United Labor Unions began organizing fast-food workers in Detroit, another front had opened in the campaign to unionize poor workers. This time the opening salvo was fired by waiters in New York City's Chinatown, who began organizing what would, a year later, become the independent Chinese Staff and Workers' Association, one of the first among many community-based organizations calling themselves "independent workers' centers."

Operating mostly within communities of color and the immigrant workforce, workers' centers are profoundly local organizations, arising in response to specific conditions in particular locations. They build explicitly on linguistic, ethnic, racial, and gender solidarities as they attempt to combat multilayered forms of oppression in both the workplace and the community. Like earlier civil rights and feminist labor activism, workers' center organizing often starts in the community, then broadens to the workplace. Workers' centers don't limit themselves to grouping workers by their industrial affiliations.

Instead they bring together those workers who labor in diverse low-wage occupations. Usually they organize the most exploited and invisible workers—those consigned to temporary or contingent work in the informal economy. Workers' centers have played a leading role in the antisweatshop movement and as advocates for immigrant workers, winning concrete victories as well as developing grassroots organizers and leaders.

Activists have founded dozens of community-based workers' centers across the nation in recent decades. Immigrant workers are the focus of many of these centers, such as the Chinese Staff and Workers' Association, the Latino Workers' Center, the Workplace Project, Workers' Awaaz, and the Taxi Workers' Alliance, all in New York City; the Workers Defense Project in Houston and La Mujer Obrera in El Paso; the Latino Union of Chicago; Asian Immigrant Women's Advocates in Oakland and Korean Immigrant Workers Advocates in Los Angeles; and the Miami Workers' Center and the Coalition of Immokalee Workers in Florida. Others, such as the Worker Organizing Committee in Portland, Oregon, join immigrant and native workers under one umbrella. A few serve mostly nonimmigrant workers, such as North Carolina's Black Workers for Justice and Virginia's Appalachian Women Empowered.

Some workers' centers build alliances with trade unions, but many do not, seeking instead to open space for poor workers to organize themselves on an independent basis. Workers' centers have usually developed in response to two conditions. First, when existing trade unions frequently failed to organize adequately—or didn't organize at all—among workers who wanted representation, those workers or their advocates began to build from the ground up the organizations they believed would empower them. Given the increasing prevalence of temporary and contingent work, the broad-based multioccupational composition of the resulting workers' centers has been an appropriate organizational focus. Second, sometimes the circumstances of employment made traditional trade-union organizing techniques (card counts, union representation elections, and contract bargaining) difficult or ineffective. The broader strategies of workers' centers answered the need for innovative tactics.

Workers' centers are active across a wide variety of industries, including day labor / construction (25 percent), hotel/restaurant/casino (19 percent), agricultural (16 percent), domestic work (13 percent), health care (6 percent), manufacturing (6 percent), poultry work (6 percent), temporary work (6 percent) and workfare (3 percent).[1]

The concept of a "workers' center" is not new. The United Farm Workers has used a similar idea—the "service center"—since the 1960s. In organizing migrant agricultural workers who traveled from one job to another, the UFW found it more practical to reach potential members away from worksites, in community-based centers that provided social services and other activities. In the '80s and '90s the nationwide emergence of independent urban workers' centers was in part a response to the increasing exploitation of immigrant labor and the growth of contingent temporary work among nonagricultural laborers. While many trade unions were built by an earlier wave of immigrant workers during the late nineteenth and first half of the twentieth centuries, the low level of new organizing by trade unions more recently has left many contemporary immigrants to invent their own institutions.

Out of the multitude of workers' centers that exist, this chapter focuses mainly on three. The Chinese Staff and Workers' Association, based in New York City, is the earliest example of a contemporary workers' center founded as an alternative to mainstream unions. It has had widespread influence on later workers' centers. Long Island's Workplace Project focuses particularly on empowering immigrant workers to act collectively. Last, the North Carolina–based Black Workers for Justice has a somewhat unusual coalitional relationship with mainstream trade unions, which illustrates possibilities for increasing collaboration between these two distinct parts of the labor movement.

Waiting for the Union

While poor immigrant workers have much in common with other poor workers in the US, their situation differs in several respects. Often immigrants face language-based discrimination, both on the job and within established trade unions, which sometimes don't have staff with the language skills necessary to communicate with rank-and-file workers. Anti-immigrant discrimination can also adversely affect these workers' access to adequate housing, education, and healthcare services. A significant number labor within the informal economy, specifically in the restaurant, service, or garment industries, or in day labor as domestics, landscapers, or construction workers. In occupations with large numbers of undocumented workers, employers use their "illegal" status to drag down the wages of all the workers. Employers' threats to report these workers to the INS, with the implied result of deportation, add another layer of difficulty to organizing for undocumented workers.

The Chinese restaurant waiters who eventually formed the Chinese Staff and Workers' Association in New York City had asked the Hotel and Restaurant and Bartenders Union, Local 69 (affiliated with HERE, the Hotel Employees and Restaurant Employees), for help in unionizing several large, profitable restaurants owned by Chinatown's business elites. The waiters, most of them older men who had been in the United States for many years, were paid low wages for long hours, with no benefits or job security. There were some 450 restaurants in Chinatown, and another thousand in the greater New York City area, but as Peter Kwong explains in *The New Chinatown*, Local 69 was not interested in launching such an organizing campaign, preferring to concentrate on proven venues such as expensive restaurants and hospital dining rooms. Local 69 was a typical business union, dominated by white leaders. Those leaders believed the Chinese restaurant workers were too dispersed to organize efficiently. Yet New York's large Chinese restaurants were no smaller or more dispersed than many other shops that Local 69 had previously organized. Likely a measure of racism was at work as well.[2]

Despite union leaders' doubts, the waiters joined Local 69 and in May 1978 succeeded in organizing Uncle Tai's, on the Upper East Side, without much assistance from the union. Within a year, staff at four other Chinese restaurants in the city had joined Local 69 and begun to organize. They soon became disillusioned as union officials neglected to enforce contracts, refused to hire Chinese-speaking organizers, and even sided with management in several disputes. Union activists formed the Chinese Staff and Workers' Association (CSWA) in 1979 to put pressure on Local 69 to better respond to the community's needs.[3] CSWA cofounder Wing Lam, who had worked in factories represented by the International Ladies' Garment Workers' Union in the '80s, recalls, "We had seen the limits of the unions. Each time we sent a worker to the union, and they got a contract, the worker would sit back and wait for the contract to expire."[4] CSWA would be a different sort of organization, one that relied on direct action, concentrated on solidarity actions among workers, and involved itself in community issues.

In February 1980 management at Chinatown's largest restaurant, the Silver Palace, fired fifteen of its one hundred waiters for refusing to give a greater portion of their tips to the management. CSWA began a direct-action campaign, widely supported by Chinatown residents, of nearly continuous picketing outside the restaurant's doors. Meanwhile, waiters visited other restaurants to spread the word and collect strike fund donations. With its business severely affected by the picketing, management soon agreed to settle with the workers.

At this point the workers knew they needed a union. CSWA had acted as their advocate while Local 69 had stood silently by. After several heated debates, workers voted overwhelmingly to form their own independent union. After months of contract negotiations, the Silver Palace workers got a contract other Chinese restaurant workers only dreamed of: a forty-hour week, minimum wage, overtime pay, health benefits, paid holidays, and job security. Other restaurant managers, fearing union drives at their establishments, slowly improved wages and conditions. Within two years, several other groups of Chinese restaurant workers had organized independent unions as well.[5]

Organizing Sweatshops

A different dynamic was at work in Chinatown's numerous garment factories, where thousands of immigrants—mostly Chinese women—worked. Unlike HERE, the International Ladies' Garment Workers' Union in New York had been recruiting Chinese workers since 1957.

Chinese women workers became a majority of the ILGWU's New York City membership by 1974, after it obtained industry-wide agreements with the area's contractors and manufacturers. In 1982 some twenty thousand of these workers turned out in a successful strike against the city's garment industry contractors. Still, writes historian Xiaolan Bao in *Holding Up More Than Half the Sky*, Chinese women—and many Chinese men—were long excluded from the local's top leadership. It was not until 1996 that the ILGWU even had a permanent office in New York's Chinatown. Many members turned instead to CSWA for advice on workplace problems.[6]

Globalization hit the garment industry hard, and workers faced the problem of increasing imports and overseas production, including the threat of plant closings to drive down workers' wages and protect corporate profit margins. Throughout the '80s and much of the '90s, most union-represented garment factories in Chinatown were only marginally better than unorganized shops, where workers were still fighting for the eight-hour day. Wages averaging as low as $1 per hour for an eighty-plus-hour week were typical.[7] One ILGWU researcher admitted to the *New York Times* in 1981 that out of fear of factory closings, "sometimes the union doesn't enforce the contract as rigidly as it should."[8] It was not uncommon for contractors to close shop and leave town without paying workers thousands of dollars for labor they'd already completed, all without significant protest by the union.

Indeed there was not much in the ILGWU's contracts that prevented shop closings. In an era of highly mobile capital and fragmentation of the production process, union contracts in any industry were weak weapons against the problems of globalization, because they could rarely compel a factory to remain open. Trade unions' usual reliance on contracts inherently assumed the continuation of a stable capital-labor relationship, which had long ceased to be. Workers' centers haven't been able to stop runaway shops either, but with persistent organizing and community-based fightbacks, they have obtained court actions leading to large monetary settlements for the affected workers.[9]

The ILGWU's difficulties were partially caused by changes in the global economy and the union's inability to adapt its organizing strategies to the new economic realities. During much of the '80s the ILGWU's energy was directed at lobbying in Washington against imports and conducting a "buy American" campaign. ILGWU leadership was more concerned with "cutting complex deals with the smaller and smaller circle of manufacturers that would deal with the union at all," writes historian Dana Frank, "than with empowering garment workers to fight for themselves."[10] Organizing once again had taken a backseat to contractual agreements, still seen by some trade unions as a panacea for workplace problems.

Organizing had also become more complicated, although not impossible. In an era of capital fragmentation and labor outsourcing, workers and their unions now had multiple targets in organizing campaigns: local labor contractors *and* the domestic or international corporations to which those contractors sold their goods. In the face of organizing, local contractors chose not to move their shops because money to be made exploiting workers was too good. For instance, a single garment worker, on average, produced $100,000 worth of goods a year but got paid less than 2 percent of that. For a $100 dress, $50 went to the brand-name manufacturer, $15 to the contractor, and only $1.72 to the worker.[11]

This type of extreme exploitation existed in several cities across the nation, though the ethnic and racial makeup of the workforce differed by location. For instance, Los Angeles was bursting at the seams with some five thousand garment industry "contract shops," which by 1994 had displaced aerospace as the area's leading employer.[12] Los Angeles's garment industry workforce was 67 percent Latina, 14 percent Asian, 8 percent European American, 2 percent African American, and 9 percent unidentified, and average yearly wages ranged from $5,000 to $8,000. Some workers turned to the garment industry after losing their jobs through plant closings in other industries. Others came from regions where US military or economic aggression caused increased migration of workers, such as Central America and the Caribbean. In any case, immigrant workers often bring with them experiences as members of unions or community-based organizations back home. These "sweatshop warriors," as Miriam Ching Yoon Louie calls them, are practiced at standing up for themselves.[13]

New York City garment workers increasingly turned to CSWA for help in obtaining lost wages or better conditions, whether or not they had union representation through the ILGWU. In 1990 CSWA began using high-profile direct-action public campaigns against individual shop owners who oppressed workers on the job or cheated them out of their wages. Activists launched publicity campaigns and recurrent demonstrations to successfully force several contractors to pay hundreds of thousands of dollars of back wages. In one case in 1991, a group of seamstresses occupied a contractor's factory until he paid them $20,000 in owed wages.[14] In another case in 1995, even after the US Department of Labor penalized Street Beat Sportswear, a subcontractor of Sears, Roebuck, for violations of overtime requirements and nonpayment of wages, seamstresses were working over one hundred hours a week for less than $2 an hour. The workers turned to CSWA, and after a two-year campaign—which included facing down death threats from their bosses—finally won close to $300,000 in overtime and damages.[15]

In the San Francisco Bay Area, the Oakland-based Asian Immigrant Women Advocates (AIWA) used similar direct-action methods successfully against big fashion companies—famous labels such as Jessica McClintock, the Gap, Liz Claiborne, and Guess Jeans—that routinely subcontracted their work to sweatshops, then accepted no responsibility for making sure the workers who manufactured their clothes were treated fairly. By the mid-'90s the ILGWU (which merged in 1995 with the Amalgamated Clothing and Textile Workers and was renamed UNITE) began to adopt some of the same organizing and public pressure techniques that workers' centers like AIWA and CSWA had pioneered, including instituting "justice centers" to assist nonunionized workers and their families at the community level.[16]

Though the industries in which these poor workers labor (garment, restaurant, service, etc.) vary widely in important respects, the workers share a crucial organizing question: how can they fight back against the unchecked power of employers and corporations that brutally undercut their wages or force them to work virtually around the clock? Workers' center activists believe the solution is to rejuvenate direct action and solidarity among poor workers so they can build collective power and confront oppressive employers even if those employers relocate, and regardless of whether the workers are covered by collective-bargaining agreements. Whether this power will be used to build new, independent organizations or work within existing AFL-CIO unions is a decision for workers themselves to make. Either way, activists aim to strengthen the basic scaffolding of the labor movement by nurturing the roots of solidarity.

Community Power, Workers' Power

Tackling the global economy, many workers' center activists say, begins by organizing locally. One way workers' centers like the Chinese Staff and Workers' Association differ strikingly in orientation from contemporary trade unions is that they establish a solid base in the community in addition to, and sometimes even before, engaging in employment-based activism. Unlike traditional trade unionism, the workers' center model doesn't privilege the paid workplace. Its organizing is more holistic, treating workers as more than the sum of their economic parts. Workers' centers offer classes not just in labor rights but in English-language skills and political lobbying—what they term "liberation through communication." In the words of CSWA organizer Kwong Hui, "By 'organize' we don't just mean joining the union. We see the union as a means to organize something greater. We have to transform how people . . . see the world, where they fit in, and how they can fight for their own interests. We organize where we live and work."[17]

Poorer residents of Chinatown needed affordable housing, medical care, childcare, and public transportation—all issues taken up by CSWA along with its labor-organizing activities. For instance, in 1986 on Manhattan's Lower East Side, where housing was rapidly becoming unaffordable for most of its constituents, CSWA launched a program to build housing, which resulted in a dozen low-income co-op apartments and two storefronts opening up for community organizations.[18]

CSWA's work frequently brought it into direct confrontation not only with local Chinese, Japanese, and Hong Kong business elites but also with the Chinese American Planning Council, a nonprofit organization that played a major part in Chinatown's economic development. Although the council was a publicly funded organization, the majority of its board were bankers, landlords, lawyers, and appointed government officials. Its political decisions reflected that makeup, especially on housing issues, where it usually supported gentrification.[19]

Wages were a battleground as well. During the late '80s, for example, the council ignored legal requirements that its federally funded projects pay prevailing wage rates. Instead it hired poor workers at bargain basement rates of $4 to $8 per hour to do the dirtiest and most dangerous jobs, echoing the situation of Comprehensive Employment and Training Act workers during the '70s and presaging the even more widespread abuse of workfare programs in the '90s (which triggered, as we will see in chapter 6, another wave of union organizing). Using poor workers' labor at over one hundred demolition and construction sites allowed the council to avoid hiring union carpenters, painters, and construction workers who would have made from $12 per hour for an apprentice to $30 per hour for a skilled craftsperson. The workers hired were supposed to acquire housing-renovation skills, but they were kept in "training" positions for years on end, received no benefits, and worked in unsafe conditions. While such practices were technically illegal under federal guidelines, enforcement was lax, and workers had to organize to bring their case before the public and the courts. Under these conditions, one worker pointed out, they couldn't even afford to live in the federally funded low-income housing they were building. CSWA director Wing Lam argued that the council's treatment of poor workers was itself racist—it reinforced a two-tiered workforce, with people of color at the bottom.[20]

In 1988, when one worker had been reinstated by the National Labor Relations Board after being fired for complaining of safety violations, the entire workforce employed in Chinese American Planning Council rehabilitation jobs decided to form an independent union with CSWA's help. After an NLRB-sponsored election in which the workers voted unanimously for union representation, the council not only refused to recognize the union but shut down the program and fired all the workers. Some six months later it reopened the program, offering newcomers $5 an hour for jobs lasting only six months.[21]

Workers took their case to the streets, demonstrating outside the Chinese American Planning Council's 1990 New Year's banquet at the Silver Palace and sitting in at the city's housing office in Manhattan. That year CSWA also filed suit against both the Chinese American Planning Council and the city of New York, arguing that thirty-five workers had been paid substandard wages and exposed to cancer-causing asbestos between 1986 and 1989.[22] Activists kept the story in the public eye through demonstrations and media coverage as the legal case proceeded. A year later they won big. The US Labor Department ruled in 1991 that more than two hundred of the workers in the program should have been paid prevailing wages and ordered the Chinese American Planning Council to pay them over $2 million. Moreover, in 1992 the National Labor Relations Board ordered the council to pay the workers a year's wages—over $1 million—for having fired them in retaliation for forming a union.[23] This time, with egregious violations abundantly evident, poor workers won using legal means, even though they had to wait three years for the results.

Another confrontation with the neighborhood's elites came from Chinese and Puerto Rican workers who served as "senior aides"—federally funded home healthcare workers—at a large Chinatown housing project run by the Chinese American Planning Council. They organized a union with CSWA's help in 1991, becoming the first of the more than sixty-four thousand federally funded senior aides nationwide to have union representation.[24]

In another dispute, workers at Jing Fong, which had become Chinatown's largest restaurant, went on strike in 1995. Students from area colleges supported them by launching a hunger strike on the steps of the restaurant, which, along with frequent demonstrations, kept customers away. The conflict quickly escalated into an open battle that pitched restaurant workers and their supporters against the neighborhood's wealthiest residents and investors. In a display of class solidarity, fifteen hundred business leaders crossed the picket line to attend a restaurant industry fundraising dinner in April 1995 and condemned the organizing efforts. Again, the workers eventually won—in 1997 the waiters settled for $1.1 million in back wages after filing a lawsuit in US district court accusing Jing Fong of profiting from "slave labor."[25] Indeed, the history of New York City's immigrant workers reveals this constantly replayed dilemma: while some immigrants within each community have made it to the top, most are left with unstable, exploitative jobs that keep them in poverty.

But the community's business elites were only part of the problem. The exclusionary practices of New York City's building trades unions were another. CSWA's organizing work highlighted the sharp class differences that existed within the Chinese immigrant community and pointed toward class solidarity among not only Chinese immigrant workers but all poor workers as the solution. CSWA developed close relationships with other independent workers' groups in New York City fighting racial and gender discrimination in the building trades. White officials ran most of the city's building trades unions, and the apprentice system still served as a hurdle to people of color and women who wanted to enter the trades. At one worksite protest in August 1992, some thirty members of the CSWA-sponsored Chinese Construction Workers' Association joined with the African American activist group Harlem Fightback to disrupt construction. They took control of the freight elevator and crane, displaying posters that accused the contractor of racism. A half-dozen CSWA and Fightback members were hired at the site.[26]

CSWA activists also targeted a multimillion-dollar federal building project in Manhattan's Foley Square in the fall of 1992, demanding, as they put it, "a real end to the Chinese Exclusion Act of 1882." They argued that the building trades unions kept workers of color out of their ranks, allowing employers to exploit the "atmosphere of scarcity in which workers of different races are pitted against one another in the fight for 'limited' resources." Chinese workers lucky enough to obtain off-the-books construction work were paid an average of $5 to $10 an hour—slightly more than restaurant or garment work, but much less than union construction workers, who made $20–30 an hour.[27]

Chinese workers had built their own union in an attempt to counteract both histories—that of internal community exploitation and that of white domination of building and other trades. In the process, they had reached out to other poor workers as well. Their battle-grounds were as frequently the communities in which they lived as the workplaces in which they labored. Bringing the community into union organizing did more than facilitate a voice at work. It trans-formed union struggles into broad political ones that went to the heart of inequalities based on race, ethnicity, gender, and citizenship.

Street Corner Solidarity

The Long Island Railroad carries passengers from the urban ferment of New York City to a world of suburban quiet. After pulling out of midtown Manhattan, the train whisks passengers through Queens and toward Long Island's rolling lawns, manicured gardens, and luxury mansions. Here lives much of New York City's upper and upper-mid-dle class, close enough to commute to the city's high-end businesses.

These wealthy suburbanites have attracted an informal economy of huge proportions. About an hour's train ride from New York City is Hempstead, the center of Long Island's community of more than one hundred thousand Central American immigrants.[28] During the '80s and '90s, people fleeing civil wars, poverty, or human rights vio-lations in their home countries came to urban areas in the United States, finding work in suburban informal economies like those on Long Island. They often came from countries with strong labor move-ments but where the difficulties of struggle were much greater than in the United States. For instance, through the mid-'90s in El Salvador and Guatemala, reprisals against trade unionists commonly included jailings, beatings, death threats, kidnappings, and assassinations. Hav-ing fought for years or witnessed social or economic revolution in their home countries, many such workers knew how to organize a collective response and were unlikely to back down when confronted with an abusive boss.

The primary employment available to these new immigrants to sub-urbia was (and is) in low-wage restaurant, construction, landscaping, and domestic work. Most of these workers were undocumented and faced harassment from employers and the Department of Homeland

Security (formerly the US Immigration and Naturalization Service) over their citizenship status. Employers often took advantage of undocumented workers by not paying the legal minimum wage, or any wage at all, at the end of a day's or week's work. Seventy-hour weeks at $2 or $3 per hour in restaurants or food service work were common. Bosses sometimes abused workers sexually, and otherwise dangerous work, often with hazardous chemicals, was prevalent.[29]

The Workplace Project was founded in 1992 to respond to such mistreatment. With initial funding from a public-interest law group, founder Jennifer Gordon set up a weekly legal clinic as a way to draw workers into the organization. She soon learned that far from promoting collective rights, providing legal aid to undocumented workers was more like being a social worker ministering to individuals' problems. The situation was strangely analogous to the bureaucratic unions' focus on grievances and "servicing" to the detriment of organizing. Winning legal cases for individual aggrieved workers directly undercut possibilities for collective organization. "By 'paying off' the bravest and most determined workers with a settlement or an award," Gordon wrote later, "the Workplace Project's legal program plays the role of the employer who decapitates an organizing effort by making a deal with its leaders."[30]

Workers empowered to act collectively stood a better chance of challenging the exploitative labor relations prevalent in Long Island's informal economy. In 1993, the project's second year, it hired Omar Henriquez, a local Salvadoran resident, as lead organizer and, in consultation with a board of directors made up entirely of immigrant workers, set a new course, paying careful attention to the strategies of already-existing workers' centers such as CSWA in New York and La Mujer Obrera in Texas. Workers coming to visit the Workplace Project's legal clinic would now first meet with an organizer to discuss collective responses—demonstrations, publicity, solidarity among workers—that might prove more effective methods of correcting workplace problems.[31]

One of the Workplace Project's earliest campaigns was for higher wages for day laborers. Landscaping and construction work provided quick employment for immigrant men without green cards. Like many towns across the nation, Hempstead and other Long Island communities had developed a thriving "informal labor market" operating on street corners where day laborers waited for employers to pick them up and transport them to worksites. Labor activists in some cities have tried to institute hiring halls for such workers, to give them a dignified place to contract with employers—a strategy that keeps workers out of the rain and cold but doesn't necessarily help them win better wages or benefits. The Workplace Project had a more ambitious plan: organize the street corner workers to collectively demand more for their labor.[32]

In the spring of 1994, several Workplace Project activists began organizing their coworkers on each of three Long Island street corners. Over a period of three years, the average wage rose from $40 per day to $60–70 per day as day laborers agreed to refuse work with employers who offered low wages.[33] The day labor committees also organized direct actions against employers who violated day laborers' rights. In the case of one worker who was not paid for several days of landscaping work, Workplace Project members arranged a noisy protest in front of the employer's subsequent project, at a private home on Long Island. Embarrassed, the employer agreed to pay the worker what was owed.[34] This scenario was repeated many times by day labor activists, usually with success.

Such achievements do have to be continually defended. Victories that come from street corner solidarity take more energy to enforce than a union contract. Yet as any trade union activist knows, even a contract is strong only if workers are prepared to actively defend it.

Domestic workers also organized under the auspices of the Workplace Project. In 1997 a group of immigrant women developed a campaign to force the six largest domestic worker placement agencies on Long Island to end their practice of hiring out workers for subminimum wages and then requiring these workers to pay double the agency "placement fee" allowable for a minimum-wage job. The women wanted agencies to require each individual employer to sign an employment contract called the Domestic Worker Bill of Rights, which set standards for fair pay and treatment with their individual employers, much like that used by household workers in the '70s.

After organizing with community allies and launching a very public campaign of picketing and media pressure, the women were able to force five of the six agencies to agree to use the Bill of Rights.[35] The Workplace Project also started several worker-run cooperatives as a way for workers to exert more permanent control over highly variable work like construction day labor and domestic work.

Similar organizing was done among construction day laborers and domestic workers across the nation. In Los Angeles the National Day Laborer Organizing Network (NDLON), the country's largest day laborer association, founded in 2001, won the right to put a hiring hall right on the premises of corporate giant Home Depot, providing a dignified space for workers as well as tighter controls over wages and conditions.[36] The Domestic Workers Union, based in New York City, became a "collective voice" for that city's six hundred thousand housekeepers—who were scattered among nearly as many individual workplaces—by encouraging workers to use a standardized contract requiring employers to provide fair wages and conditions. The union has won over $500,000 in back pay for workers since it began.[37]

Over twenty thousand domestic workers are members of the National Domestic Workers Alliance (NDWA), which connects state, regional, and national campaigns. Founded in 2007, by 2011 it had expanded to thirty-three affiliate organizations in seventeen cities.[38] After years of persistent organizing, activists got a Domestic Worker Bill of Rights signed into law in New York State in 2010; Hawaii, California, Oregon, and Massachusetts soon followed. In a report it coauthored, *Home Economics: The Invisible and Unregulated World of Domestic Work*, the NDWA recommended enacting policies "that rectify the exclusion of domestic workers from employment and labor laws," including "the right to organize, earn the minimum wage, get paid for overtime, take regular rest and meal periods, claim workers' compensation and unemployment insurance, have healthy and safe work environments, and have effective remedies for discrimination, abuse, and harassment."[39] The Domestic Worker Bill of Rights addressed many of these issues and has served as an industry-wide "contract."

Organizing the "Unorganizable"

Until recently many trade unions have been reluctant to organize undocumented workers, claiming that their legal status made the task too difficult. But the successes chronicled above demonstrate that undocumented immigrants can exercise control over their labor—whether through worker cooperatives, street corner solidarity, or formal unions. As Hector Delgado points out in his study of undocumented workers in Los Angeles, the difficulties are not attributable "so much to their legal status as [to] the factors that make it difficult to organize *any* worker—native or immigrant, documented or undocumented."[40]

Management's attempts to divide workers along race, gender, ethnicity, or citizenship lines undermine broader labor solidarity and lead to lower wages for all workers. This is particularly true in areas where undocumented immigrants make up a large portion of the workforce, such as Los Angeles, where an estimated 55 to 90 percent of workers in the food, textile, apparel, lumber, and furniture industries are immigrants.[41] But employers who rely on undocumented workers may also be trapped by their location in the production process. Because undocumented workers fill the US economy's "hidden" jobs, they are virtually indispensable to their employers, who sometimes fear high turnover and interruptions of the production process more than unionization. One worker told Delgado he wasn't afraid of being fired for union activity, because he could get another job easily: "There are places in Los Angeles that hire only people like me. Everywhere I've worked, everyone . . . was illegal." In addition, companies who betray their workers to the DHS may become government-identified illegal employers, which would limit their ability to attract undocumented workers in the future.[42]

Employers in low-wage occupations often prefer undocumented workers. Bosses can intimidate workers into accepting lower wages and can ignore labor laws and mandated benefits like social security, workers' compensation, and disability payments. Undocumented workers are protected by the Fair Labor Standards Act (which governs minimum wage and overtime laws); they are eligible for workers' compensation if they are injured; and they have the right to unionize under the National Labor Relations Act. However, these rights can seem more theoretical than real for immigrant workers who have no collective structure to support them in fully exercising their rights.[43]

These labor law protections are also undercut by immigration laws such as "employer sanctions," which require employers to keep records of each worker's citizenship status. The employer theoretically faces a small fine for hiring undocumented workers, but in practice employers are rarely fined and the real burden falls on workers defined as "illegal." If workers complain about conditions, employers threaten to call the DHS, or simply fire them, to attempt to circumvent any incipient legal action or union organizing. New York State's enforcement arm, the Division of Labor Standards—like many other government agencies around the nation—has a reputation of treating immigrant workers' claims with indifference and postponing its investigations of wage and hour law violations for months or even years.[44] The workers' center model—teaching immigrant workers to protect themselves through collective action as well as legal action when necessary—gives these workers the foundation to organize themselves and effectively use their rights.

Defining undocumented workers as "illegal" has wide-reaching effects. Raising the specter of illegality—equated with criminality—not only effectively lowers wage levels in entire industries and increases the vulnerability of immigrant labor but also makes it easier to deny immigrants education or medical care. As journalist David Bacon puts it, "The original premise that undocumented immigrants have no right to work or earn a living has been broadened to include the denial of rights to most other basic elements of normal life, including the right to be a part of a community."[45]

Trade unions can join workers' centers and immigrant rights groups in the fight against this trend by opposing regressive laws and enforcing immigrants' workplace rights. But not every union does so, either out of ignorance of immigrants' needs or, in a few cases, because of outright racism. On Long Island, noted Jennifer Gordon in 1993, "unions with thousands of Latino members frequently write their contracts only in English, and do not employ field personnel or organizers who speak Spanish. Union efforts to communicate with their immigrant members are often so limited that workers do not know which union they belong to."

Gordon recalls a worst-case scenario presented by undocumented Guatemalan candy-factory workers who asked for assistance from the Workplace Project. "Their employer required them to change names every six months or be fired," recounts Gordon. "This rule arose from the union contract, which gave new workers the right to join the union after six months." The union ignored the practice since it did not want the Guatemalans as members, and management's name-change requirement effectively kept them out.[46]

A decade later, much of the trade union movement had adopted a more progressive stance, as evidenced by organizing campaigns by HERE, SEIU, and others, and by the AFL-CIO's own February 2000 resolution reversing its support of employer sanctions and favoring amnesty for undocumented immigrants. By the late '90s the Workplace Project occasionally partnered with trade unions, such as the United Food and Commercial Workers (UFCW), which asked for its assistance with several organizing campaigns among food service employees.[47] The Workplace Project's innovative organizing made it a model for other workers' centers around the country and a respected force on its home turf of Long Island, where it helped inspire a culture of organizing among immigrant workers and increase consciousness among trade unionists about the exploitation of immigrant workers. A testament to that consciousness: when two Latino day laborers were violently attacked on Long Island in September 2000, the president of New York City's AFL-CIO Central Labor Council pledged, in a letter to the *New York Times*, to work together with community groups to protect the rights—and lives—of immigrant workers.[48]

Creating this kind of worker solidarity is a goal of all workers' centers as they reach out to build alliances with traditional labor unions and religious and community groups. In Austin, Texas, the Workers Defense Project, founded in 2002, has become known as one of the most creative, often using construction liens to get contractors to cough up illegally held pay for workers, or using complaints to the Occupational Safety and Health Administration to get investigations of dangerous construction sites, leading to large fines. The group even took on corporate giant Apple, organizing at the local level to successfully force the multinational to provide a higher minimum wage and workers' compensation in exchange for Austin's $8.6 million in city tax incentives.[49]

The Workers Defense Project also handles a large volume of wage theft claims—up to $7 million every year—from Texas construction workers, many of them undocumented immigrants. Because of their immigration status, these workers bear the brunt of this problem. "The level of abuse has been unsettling, particularly during the economic crisis," staffer Emily Timm told *Dollars and Sense* in 2009.[50]

The Coalition of Immokalee Workers (CIW), based in the small town of Immokalee, Florida, took up the problem of low wages in a different way—by pressuring tomato growers to raise wages for thirty thousand workers and adhere to stricter workplace protections, from rest breaks to respect. Through CIW's Fair Food Program the coalition's activists got retailers to buy tomatoes only from growers who pledged to follow the standards—which are formally enforced by a retired New York judge—and pay an extra penny a pound, which goes directly to farmworkers' pay. A "fair food" label lets consumers know the produce complies with the program. It took four years of activism to get the corporation that owes Taco Bell on board; other national chains, such as Whole Foods, Trader Joe's, Chipotle, Subway, and Walmart, followed. Since its beginnings in 2011 the program has added $15 million to the paychecks of Florida farmworkers.[51]

CIW's worker-consumer model has been replicated by other farmworker activists, such as Migrant Justice / Justicia Migrante in Vermont, which is working for better protections and wages for the state's dairy workers, and the Farm Labor Organizing Committee, a group active in North Carolina's tobacco fields.[52] Indeed, workers' centers have spread among those involved in food-related industries— more than half of the nation's worst-paid jobs are related to food, from cultivating it in the fields to serving it in restaurants. Sara Jayaraman has documented the struggles of the nation's nearly ten million restaurant workers, most of whom make the "special" subminimum wage of $2.13 per hour and don't get any benefits. A national workers' center, the Restaurant Opportunities Center, has helped win back pay and paid sick leave for these workers.[53]

Consciousness Raising, North and South

The workers' center model has also been used by nonimmigrant workers fighting for economic and social justice, especially in the nonunion South. Black Workers for Justice (BWFJ) has organized primarily African American workers around a variety of issues—including workers' rights in the contingent economy, union organizing campaigns, environmental racism, and welfare reform. Along with other southern community and labor activists, BWFJ has sought to create a renewed culture of organizing in the region.

The move of many multinational corporations' operations overseas has been accompanied by a parallel move, often by the same corporations, to reestablish plants in the mostly nonunion US South. In the late '80s BWFJ pointed to the region's historical role as a "third world" within the US borders, home to a cheap, nonunion industrial workforce, with many of the "old racist structures still intact." Sharply critical of business unionism, BWFJ emphasized that unions should start paying attention to the structural causes of organized labor's decline. Unless the trade union movement "moved quickly to organize unions in the South," BWFJ editorialized in its newspaper *Justice Speaks* in 1989, "it runs the risk of losing more union members in the North to plant closings and concessions because of the threat of runaway shops."[54]

The South's labor activists had long been eager for unionization following the failures of both the AFL's organizing in the late 1920s and the CIO's Operation Dixie in the late 1940s. "We live here," activist Shafeah M'Balia told reporters in 1995 as she described BWFJ's work. "We're not going anywhere. . . . We have one foot in the black community and one foot in the labor community."[55] Many of BWFJ's members were, in fact, active in what limited trade-union presence there was in the South. Their agenda was not only to organize the unorganized but also to reconfigure the face of the labor movement nationally. Organizing the South, they hoped, would lead to more Black leadership in the labor movement and a realignment of labor away from dependence on the Democratic Party and toward a more independent and radical labor politics.[56]

In a few cases, trade unions responded to Black Workers for Justice's call—after its activists phoned the big unions in Washington, DC, such as AFSCME, the Communications Workers of America (CWA), SEIU, and UAW in the fall of 1991, asking for help in the form of full-time organizers and other resources for a variety of independent union campaigns in the South. CWA moved to affiliate the independent Raleigh Alliance of City Workers after its representatives spoke at a local Martin Luther King Jr. Day rally in 1990 about "union rights for all workers in 'the right to work as a slave' South." The AFSCME local representing city workers employed in Durham, North Carolina— some of whom were members of BWFJ—lobbied national AFSCME leadership in 1990 to commit more organizing resources to North Carolina, relaying their experience as a small local organizing without collective-bargaining rights. As a result of these efforts, by late 1991 both CWA and AFSCME had launched new organizing campaigns among the region's public workers.[57]

As this demonstrates, BWFJ operated as more than a typical workers' center—its members' political work sometimes resembled the caucus strategies that workers of color and women have practiced within unions since the 1960s. Like those caucuses, it emerged from groups of workers who were already formally represented by trade unions but who felt changes were needed in those unions. But their work differed from the caucuses of the '60s and '70s: it was carried out simultaneously through several unions, collectively bringing poor workers' voices to the larger issues of regional economic policy and overall trade-union organizing strategy. Members of BWFJ also reached out to neighbors and coworkers about their rights to organize and fully participate within any union that might represent them.

In the mid-'80s BWFJ began running "workers' schools" in North Carolina's African American neighborhoods. Students of these schools discussed questions such as "Why are the black freedom movement and the labor movement natural allies in spite of historical and current problems?"[58] This close attention to consciousness raising and intellectual development is shared by several other workers' centers. Involving the hearts and minds of workers in the struggle takes active groups of rank-and-file activists who can push the campaign forward—whether in a shop-floor organizing drive, a community-wide wage battle, or a legislative program. Workers' center activists draw on indigenous US traditions such as the Highlander Center's worker education model, as well as theories of popular education such as those of Brazilian teacher Paulo Freire, centering on the idea that learning is inherently political and that political consciousness develops through participatory learning. These approaches argue that critical reflection and analysis are developed through practical action.[59] Not only are these critical abilities useful in organizing, but they can also be turned inward to evaluate and transform the institutions that represent poor workers. Classes on labor history, legal rights, the environment, and gender relations are central facets of many workers' center programs.

This innovative consciousness raising has helped engender new tactics and a resurgence of organizing in parts of the South. Given the problems of organizing in the region, winning a union election can be difficult. Employers often throw huge amounts of money into fighting union drives and undermine rank-and-file leaders by firing them or through other types of intimidation. BWFJ employs a workplace-organizing strategy based in "worker labor organizations" (WLO, also sometimes also called "minority unions" or "pre-majority unions") as an end run around NLRB requirements that a union formally represent a majority of employees to be given bargaining status.

The WLO is a rank-and-file group consisting of at least 30 percent of the members in a given workplace, whose objective is to build coalitions with other labor and community organizations across multiple industries in its geographic area before taking on a fight with an employer.[60] This is a movement-style organization that seeks to build horizontal solidarities. The WLO makes no demands on the employer for recognition or contract bargaining. Instead it actively seeks help from its allies to construct broad-based campaigns of resistance to employer power. This results in collective struggles, where participants owe each other a debt of solidarity, rather than the more usual go-it-alone approach of organizing unit by unit.

Labor Rights Are Civil Rights

This horizontal coalition building was at the center of Black Workers for Justice's organizing in the 1980s and '90s. Shortly after its founding in 1981, BWFJ launched, and won, a community-based picketing campaign against multinational department-store chain Kmart in North Carolina, which had been paying lower wages to its African American employees. The group's campaign in 1988 against Shoney's, a restaurant chain with outlets across the state, included petitions, pickets, a boycott, and church "pray-ins" in a successful effort to end racial discrimination in its employment.[61]

Such campaigns in the South often had the flavor of civil rights organizing of the 1960s. In one of the most watched southern union battles in decades, the workers at the Delta Pride Catfish plant in Indianola, Mississippi, mostly African American women, voted for union representation in 1986. It was the largest union vote ever held in the Mississippi Delta, involving over one thousand workers, and the campaign faced the usual antiunion tactics employers have perfected. Just twenty-four hours before the vote, plant owners gave workers time off to attend a company barbecue at which they displayed a pile of cash—$182,000, to be exact—which the company said represented what workers would be "squandering in dues" over the next year if they voted the union in. The United Food and Commercial Workers Union (UFCW) won the election by building a strong coalition with BWFJ and civil rights and religious leaders in what was widely termed a new southern "civil rights struggle." Of the victory over the world's largest catfish company, Cleve McDowell, state field director of the Mississippi NAACP, told the *Washington Post*, "This is the beginning of a second era of civil rights for us here. We are going past public accommodations and the right to vote, and looking at economic power."[62]

In 1990, Delta Pride catfish workers went on strike against the company's "starvation" wages, speedup on the assembly line, and unhealthy working conditions. Again, with the backing of the UFCW and a strong community coalition, the workers won their strike.[63] In another key struggle, BWFJ helped take on Kmart a second time in 1996, when African American workers at one of its distribution plants launched a nationwide boycott to pressure the company to bargain with UNITE (the Union of Needletrades, Industrial and Textile Employees), which they had elected as their representative in 1993. Dozens of labor, community, and religious supporters—and even a few state representatives—were arrested in sit-ins targeting Kmart's racist and antiunion policies.[64] Framing the campaign as a community-based living-wage struggle, activists eventually negotiated their first union contract and simultaneously launched a citywide discussion about the politics of fair wages, race-based wage discrimination, and the role of a $35 billion corporation in their community.[65]

As with other workers' centers, community and political issues were central to Black Workers for Justice's agenda. It did not hesitate to get involved in opposing a planned radioactive waste site in North Carolina, writing that under Reagan-era budget cuts, communities of color in particular were "easy prey for exploitation by the big companies who are in search of cheap labor and places to dump their death causing hazardous wastes."[66] Side by side with union news in the organization's newsletter were editorials against the 1991 Gulf War and articles opposing the death penalty, among many other issues. By the mid-'90s, BWFJ had expanded from its original base in Rocky Mount, North Carolina, with chapters in Virginia, South Carolina, and Georgia. It joined a rich brew of independent multi-issue people's organizing projects across the South, such as the Gulf Coast Tenants Organizations fighting environmental racism in Louisiana, poultry workers' unions from Mississippi, and the multi-issue Southern Organizing Committee (a successor to the Southern Conference Educational Fund).

The situation for public-sector employees in the South was just as difficult as it was for private-sector workers. North Carolina law makes it illegal for any state institution to bargain with a union. So labor activists had to turn to other methods. The independent University of North Carolina (UNC) Housekeepers Association, heavily supported by BWFJ, won its demand for a living wage through a class-action racial discrimination lawsuit against the university over poverty wages, increasing workloads, and institutional racism. The housekeepers at the Chapel Hill campus—who were 88 percent Black and 70 percent female—argued that their low pay and status were a vestige of slavery (slaves had actually worked on the campus) and therefore discriminatory. The university challenged the suit, brought on behalf of the housekeepers by the Center for Constitutional Rights, all the way to the state supreme court, but the housekeepers were finally victorious in 1996 with a settlement giving them more than $1 million in back pay and other benefits. As part of the settlement, UNC's chancellor agreed to meet and confer with the Housekeepers Association on other workplace issues.[67]

In 1997 the UNC Housekeepers Association had joined the independent North Carolina Public Service Workers Union, which had evolved out of BWFJ's multiple organizing efforts across the state. The North Carolina Public Service Workers Union approached several unions seeking affiliation (including SEIU, AFSCME, and CWA) but received a proposal only from the United Electrical Workers, with which it affiliated as UE Local 150. UE, true to its long interest in worker-driven organizing campaigns, had backed the housekeepers' struggle because of "the incredible courage of the lowest-paid state workers in the least unionized state in the union," wrote Bob Kingsley, UE organizing director, whose creative campaigns enabled them "to fight and win workplace battles even in the absence of a signed collective bargaining agreement."[68]

UE Local 150 lead organizer Saladin Muhammad also served as national chairperson of BWFJ. UE's organizing spread to the nineteen thousand housekeeping staff scattered at the University of North Carolina's other fifteen campuses across the state. They faced an administration that had declared their union "illegal" and threatened to outsource their jobs. Knowing the university would cite state law in refusing to bargain with the union, UE Local 150 instead turned to the university's own grievance procedure and the US Constitution's free-speech protections to build the union, with its Grieving for Justice Campaign in 1999.

"Creating a culture of protest is part of what we do," said Muhammad, and to do that effectively the organization needed allies. "Grievance brigades" made up of workers, students, and community supporters fanned out to collect over eight hundred grievances to be presented en masse to UNC's chancellor. The local also launched a community-based solidarity campaign, in which workers and their supporters leafleted on Martin Luther King Jr. Day, wore armbands during Black History Month, picketed the chancellor's inaugural, and met with legislators, while local ministers conducted "walk throughs" of the campus to highlight dangerous and unjust working conditions. This widespread community support was also aimed at affirming workers' rights to free speech and protecting them from intimidation by management. It worked: the university officially recognized the workers' right to join the union without retaliation, changed its policies to allow union representatives to assist employees with grievances, and set up mechanisms to "meet and confer" with the union. Over the next few years, workers began winning formal grievances, and racist supervisors were forced to leave due to pressure from the union.[69]

The victories fueled organizing. "Many workers signed union cards within sight of their supervisors," reported the *UE News* in 1999, "in what could be regarded as either acts of defiance or statements of empowerment." The local had also branched out to organize the state Department of Health and Human Services, another large public-sector workplace. In its short existence, UE Local 150 had grown tenfold—from fewer than three hundred members at its birth in 1997 to some three thousand statewide in 2003. A decade later, the local's activists were a key part of North Carolina's "Moral Monday" coalition, which mobilized tens of thousands to pressure state legislators on workers' rights and other issues.[70]

In a region where trade union failures are common, Black Workers for Justice shows how labor organizing can take root and make a real difference, given the right approach. While the cultural and economic conditions under which it grew were specific to the South, the methods it uses are the same community-based solidarity and social movement–oriented tactics that other poor workers' unions have found successful. Like other workers' centers, Black Workers for Justice holds on to a staunch independence even when interacting with trade unions on organizing campaigns. Maintaining independent voices rooted in their communities gives Black Workers for Justice and other workers' centers flexible positions in terms of both politics and organizing, a freedom they value and seek to preserve.

Separateness and Unity: Building Coalitions

Many trade unionists express admiration for workers' centers' innovative tactics and ability to organize the nation's most exploited workers. But others see the use of ethnicity, race, and gender by workers' centers as an inherent limitation to their organizing capacities. "Sure, they organize the Chinese community, or low-wage Latino workers," one unionist told me, referring to CSWA and the Workplace Project, "but what about building unity with other workers, across ethnic or racial divisions?"

Organizing is always shaped by specific historical and social contexts and rooted in specificities such as race, ethnicity, and gender. Throughout US history, trade unions have organized within workplaces, industries, or labor markets that were segregated by race, ethnicity, or gender, with obvious consequences for their memberships. The Brotherhood of Sleeping Car Porters was almost entirely African American; the United Farm Workers' membership is mostly Latina and Latino; educational workers' unions like the AFT and NEA are overwhelmingly female; some AFL craft unions were exclusively white and male (and to an extent some remain so today, decades after membership restrictions were ruled illegal).

Workers' centers also similarly face divisions created by employers and by the labor market. They have consciously chosen to organize around race, ethnicity, and gender in addition to class because these are real forces at work in their members' lives, not just on the job but also in their communities, with segregated housing, inadequate public transportation, poor health care, and deficient schools. Trade unions frequently encourage class unity while minimizing racial, gender, or ethnic differences—as if class solidarity might simply cancel out race, for instance, or sweep it under the rug. The workers' center model is led by a new generation of activists that has intentionally chosen not to privilege class, race, or gender. Underlying workers' centers' practices are neither so-called identity politics nor simplistic ideas of class-based universalism. Rather, at work is a deeper understanding of how intersecting oppressions simultaneously construct workers' identities.

Acknowledging these complexities leads to broader organizing tactics and the gradual formation of new coalitions, often bringing about multicultural solidarity among poor workers. For instance, in New York City CSWA's early organizing was carried out within a fairly homogenous group of workers. Shared culture, language, and ethnicity provided some of the cohesiveness for the campaigns, along with a class awareness that workers' interests were different from those of restaurant owners. But CSWA's work later expanded to include a multinational, multiracial ethnic workforce. At Shinwa, a pricey Japanese restaurant in midtown Manhattan, the union campaign in 1992 started with "front-of-the-house" Japanese, Chinese, and Korean servers but soon included the Latino busboys and kitchen workers at the "back of the house." The campaign targeted management's divisive racism among the various groups of workers and was actively supported by a wide array of community groups, including Harlem Fightback, the Center for Immigrants' Rights, and the Committee Against Anti-Asian Violence (also known as CAAAV: Organizing Asian Communities).[71]

CAAAV launched labor-organizing projects of its own, such as the Lease Drivers' Coalition among the city's taxi drivers. Over 90 percent of the drivers are immigrants—primarily from Africa, Bangladesh, the Caribbean, China, India, and Pakistan—surviving on a take-home income as low as $45 a day as independent contractors of big cab companies. In 1998 the Lease Drivers' Coalition changed its name to the Taxi Workers' Alliance and organized two highly successful twenty-four-hour strikes in which thousands of drivers demonstrated against new repressive rules proposed by then-New York City mayor Rudolph Giuliani.[72]

Following its successful foray into multiethnic organizing, CSWA and other community-based groups established the Latino Workers' Center on the Lower East Side of Manhattan, with the goal of creating a base of operations among non-Chinese immigrants.[73] Hundreds of thousands of Latino and Latina workers were scattered across New York's small- and medium-sized workplaces, and strategies to organize them included training courses in labor rights for immigrants and legal aid to help workers with unpaid wages, unjust firings, and discrimination, as well as direct actions and demonstrations on the doorsteps of offending employers. The Latino Workers' Center had its own Spanish-speaking staff that used workers' shared experiences of culture, language, and anti-immigrant discrimination as a basis for organizing. CSWA and the new Latino Workers' Center worked together cooperatively on countless local organizing projects.[74]

The workers' center movement has grown in just this way, with one center giving inspiration to another, or a group of community activists deciding to start a center after witnessing their usefulness elsewhere in the community. In New York, for instance, CSWA's history inspired the Latino Workers' Center while CAAAV helped establish the Taxi Workers' Alliance and Workers Awaaz/Sakhi (which organizes primarily Indian and Pakistani domestic workers). By 2007, the Taxi Workers' Alliance had formed an international alliance that stretched across eighteen US cities, as well as Montreal, Toronto, Sydney, Nepal, and the Punjab region of India, mirroring a large slice of the global South Asian diaspora.[75] The founders of Asian Immigrant Women Advocates in Oakland looked toward their Spanish-speaking sisters' example in La Mujer Obrera and Fuerza Unida in Texas as they began organizing garment industry workers. Trade unions have also taken inspiration from independent workers' centers: UNITE (formerly ILGWU) drew on the models of CSWA, La Mujer Obrera, and Fuerza Unida in its establishment of garment workers' centers in New York, San Francisco, and Los Angeles. While progressive foundations and dues provide financial support for most workers' centers, trade unions have also contributed funding on occasion.[76] Empowering workers through education and consciousness raising are seen as essential tasks, and most workers' centers have democratic structures in which rank-and-file workers fill leadership and decision-making roles.[77]

The supposition that workers' centers represent homogenous racial, ethnic, or gender groupings breaks down with a closer look at their internal dynamics. For instance, Sebastian Quinac, a Guatemalan organizer at the Latino Workers' Center, observes: "Here in New York City you have Salvadorans, Dominicans, Ecuadoreans, Mexicans, Peruvians—many different ethnicities who do not have the same experiences, and their cultural backgrounds are very different. Some have experience organizing unions, some come from countries where being in a union was dangerous."[78] Workers' centers connect those who may speak the same language but who, because of their histories or political beliefs, may also have vastly different understandings of community and workplace organizing. The centers can also end up connecting those who come from very different cultural places: Los Angeles's Korean Immigrant Workers Advocates initially started as an advocacy center for a single immigrant group, but having encountered the realities of its South Central neighborhood, it quickly expanded to include Latina/Latino and African American workers as well.[79]

In North Carolina the Latina/Latino population grew from seventy-seven thousand in 1990 to three hundred thousand in 2000 to 828,000 in 2011. Multinational corporations often pitted newer, often undocumented workers against an existing low-wage labor force that was mostly African American. The Farm Labor Organizing Committee (FLOC), BWFJ, and UE Local 150 were among several organizations forging a "black-brown" alliance to foster better communication and mutual support between African American and Latina/Latino workers. Although FLOC represented agricultural workers and UE Local 150 public service workers, neither held any formal rights under state labor law. Joint projects included a petition drive supporting amnesty for undocumented workers and collective-bargaining rights for public sector workers, as well as joint community-based organizing in the Latina/Latino and African American communities.[80]

This sort of expansive alliance building was mirrored by a similar philosophy in these organizations' internal operations. Workers' centers embody a holistic approach to organizing, combining workers' everyday life struggles with the fight for workplace justice. The women activists whom Miriam Ching Yoon Louie interviewed in *Sweatshop Warriors* said workers' centers helped fill many of their

needs, among them, as one activist put it, "to learn English, to become enfranchised citizens, to break their isolation, to get out from
under the thumb of domineering partners, to give themselves space
outside the sweatshop grind, and to taste the freedom of remaking
themselves as fuller human beings."[81] These basic changes in culture
are, in many respects, as important to building a workers' movement
as winning a union contract. Women who don't often speak in public
have learned to make their voices heard. Poor people who rarely have
power in any capacity become practiced at running their own organizations and campaigns. Immigrant workers, targeted by nativist laws
and attitudes, speak up collectively to win justice for themselves and
their families. The politicization of these new activists supports, in
both small and large ways, a broader movement for social and economic justice.

The expansion of low-wage employment has, in part, fueled the
growth of workers' centers around the nation. Only five workers' centers existed in the United States in 1992, according to Janice Fine and
Ruth Milkman, but by 2012 there were two hundred and sixteen.[82]
Most organize urban workers but some are in rural communities, such
as the Coalition of Immokalee Workers (Florida-based organization
of Latino/Latina, Haitian, and Mayan agricultural workers), and
Piñeros y Campesinos Unidos del Noreste (Latina/Latino farm and
forestry workers in Oregon).

The South, in particular, has become a mecca of multiracial organizing and solidarity across industries and issues. This has been fos-
tered in part by the absence of trade unions and by the presence of a
wide variety of alternative labor organizations (workers' centers, contingent worker groups, welfare unions) in coalition with hundreds of
environmental, community, and religious groups. These local groups
were linked by regional or national networks such as Southeast Regional Economic Justice Network (calling itself a southern "indigenous, multiracial, gender-mixed, non-profit membership association,
comprised of 37 worker and community groups"), the Federation for
Industrial Retention and Renewal (formed in 1988 by fifteen community and labor organizations to share organizing strategies to save blue-
collar jobs), Southerners for Economic Justice (based in Durham,

North Carolina), and the SouthWest Organizing Project (representing over seventy organizations in the US-Mexico border region engaged in environmental and worker organizing).[83]

The vast demography of workers' centers and their allies reflects their decentralized organizing strategies. Intentionally local, workers' centers rarely have had the "national vision" of MEJ or ACORN or a large trade union like HERE or SEIU, although the workers' center phenomenon itself and the problems it addresses—wage exploitation, racism and sexism, and anti-immigrant discrimination—are clearly national. In the summer of 1994 some dozen groups across the nation formed the National Consortium of Independent Workers' Centers with the goal of building a national movement. While the formal coalition structure lasted only a short time because commitments to local organizing left little energy to develop a national strategy, many centers maintained close ties over the years.

In 2006 the AFL-CIO began working more closely with workers' centers, encouraging them to affiliate with local and state labor councils and signing a national "partnership agreement" with the National Day Labor Organizing Network. NDLON and the AFL-CIO pledged to work together to enforce existing state and federal rights, as well as develop new wage and hour laws, health and safety protections, and immigration reform. As well, the Domestic Workers Alliance entered a strategic partnership with the AFL-CIO, SEIU, AFSCME, and several community-based nonprofits to press for changes to immigration law that would support immigrant domestic workers.[84]

In June 2010, at the US Social Forum in Detroit, the National Domestic Workers Alliance, Jobs with Justice, and NDLON brought together an Excluded Workers Congress, composed of nine "sectors" of workers who faced explicit or implicit legal exclusions that affected their ability to organize. The initial sectors were domestic workers, farm workers, taxi drivers, restaurant workers, day laborers, guest workers, workers from southern right-to-work states, workfare workers, and formerly incarcerated workers.[85] The group later changed its name to the more positive United Workers Congress, aiming to "leverage power and resources that would otherwise be impossible with one sector or alliance on their own."[86]

The workers' center movement has been built on such cooperation. One early project was the Unpaid Wages Prohibition Act, which
we caught a glimpse of in this book's introduction. Immigrant workers
successfully lobbied for the bill in the New York legislature in 1997.
The activists won an increase in the penalty for employers who re-
peatedly and intentionally violated wage and hour laws, from a slap
on the wrist (25 percent of back pay owed) to a real fine (200 percent
of withheld wages). The act also upgraded such violations from mis-
demeanors to felonies and prohibited the Department of Labor from
settling cases for less than the full amount owed without the express
consent of the worker. The Workplace Project's members worked col-
laboratively with members of the Latino Workers Center and Chinese
Staff and Workers Association on the campaign.[87]

The organizing story behind the bill's passage is remarkable. Undocumented immigrant workers, most of whom did not speak English
and had no right to vote, convinced several of Long Island's most conservative Republican senators to sponsor the bill—despite their track
records of supporting anti-immigrant legislation. (Workers and senators wore simultaneous-interpretation equipment to communicate.)
Coming at a time of anti-immigrant hysteria, with measures like the
federal Anti-terrorism Act, the Illegal Immigration Reform and Responsibility Act, and California's Proposition 187, passing the Unpaid
Wages Prohibition Act was an enviable feat. Workplace Project
founder Jennifer Gordon credited the rank-and-file nature of the
process. "That the bill's provisions were developed by immigrant
workers rather than being designed by advocates," she wrote in *The
Nation*, "gave the workers a passion for the bill that would have been
impossible to achieve otherwise."[88]

It was also, she added, a real life lesson in political activism in
their adopted country, a lesson infinitely more valuable than the usual
required "citizenship" classes on the founding fathers. This is but one
example of how workers' centers have been able to transform fights
over workplace conditions into a broader consciousness of politics
and activism and, like most of the other poor workers' union activism
examined here, into political and community-based rather than contractual struggles. This kind of rank-and-file involvement—which re-

lies not on paid "professionals" but on workers themselves—accounts for much of the effectiveness of workers' centers and for the broad reach they have had across the nation. It can also be credited in part for a reemerging culture of solidarity, which may be poor workers' best weapon against the "new" flexible economy.

Front to back, Emma Harris, Roxanne Trade, and R. G. Goudy, all members of People Organized to Win Employment Rights, make their voices heard at a San Francisco Board of Supervisors meeting. *(Photo courtesy of POWER)*

6

Knocking at Labor's Door

Organizing Workfare Unions in the '90s

C hicago's crisp fall air crackled with excitement in October 1997 as hundreds of community and union activists gathered to strategize about the growing problem of workfare at the tenth annual convention of Jobs with Justice, a national labor and community network founded in 1987. A steady stream of workfare workers, union members, religious leaders, and politicians took the podium at the conference's Workers Rights' Board to testify about the devastating effects of workfare programs on them and their communities. In the series of workshops that followed, workfare activists and trade unionists talked about local organizing projects, exchanged ideas, and made promises to support each other's struggles across the nation.[1]

That same fall a different—and perhaps more characteristic— scene emerged at a national Labor/Welfare Summit between union and workfare activists on a balmy weekend in San Francisco. A deep gulf existed between some AFL-CIO trade unions—whose public-sector bargaining units were most affected by workfare programs—and energetic workfare union-organizing projects run by community organizations, such as the Association of Community Organizations for Reform

Now (ACORN) and the San Francisco–based People Organized to Win Employment Rights (POWER). The National Lawyers Guild, which had organized the summit, consciously sought to mend the divisions. But here, beneath the words of formal solidarity, notes of disagreement, anger, and resentment hung in the air.

Nowhere was this more evident than when Bill Pastreich, a former welfare rights activist turned union organizer who had been hired by the AFL-CIO as its workfare consultant, announced at the summit that the AFL-CIO was ready to "take the lead" in workfare organizing, making good on its resolution of February 1997 to support "aggressive organizing campaigns" for workfare workers "by integrating them into bargaining units [and] organizing new units."[2] A long line of workfare workers rose to respond critically, pointing out that they were already organizing themselves, and voicing a fundamental distrust of what they saw as AFL-CIO unions' belated interest in them.

This kind of scenario was replayed across the nation as community-based workfare organizations and trade unions—who were often in ideological agreement about the evils of workfare—tried to determine how organizing would be carried out on the ground. As tens of thousands of welfare recipients were forced into workfare programs in the '90s, a new generation of poor workers began to organize, forming independent community-based unions opposing what they called "workfare slavery." Their grassroots organizing techniques were quite similar to those of United WREP Workers, which organized thousands of workfare workers in New York City in the early '70s, as recounted in chapter 3. What differed dramatically was the national scope of their work as well as trade union responses to their efforts.

There were two main reasons that trade unions had begun to pay attention. First, the vast numbers of potential workfare workers being thrown into the labor market by new federal regulations meant they simply had no choice. Now more aware of their sharply declining strength, unions couldn't afford to ignore this new and growing sector. Workfare was vastly enlarging capital's traditional "reserve army of labor," which had always served to undercut union wages and working conditions. As Frances Fox Piven noted in 1997, "These workers, most of them poor mothers, are being hurled like hostages into the frontlines of the campaign against workers. The plan is simple, bold, and big, and could be devastating to the affected unions."[3]

Second, the '80s had brought a strengthening of community-based unionism both within independent poor workers' unions and within the AFL-CIO. With the success of community-based organizing on both fronts, the potential for a strategic alliance between trade unions and the independent poor workers' movement was greater than it had been in decades. While the historical separateness of poor workers' unions and trade unions made such an alliance problematic, several joint organizing projects showed how the labor movement could effectively respond to shifting economic conditions.

Shrinking Budgets, Indentured Workers

The explosive growth of mandatory workfare programs throughout the country in the late '90s, which created a huge pool of super-exploitable workers, presented a difficult challenge to both community and union organizers. The Personal Responsibility and Work Opportunity Reconciliation Act, passed by Congress in 1996, ended six decades of guaranteed support for poor people under Aid to Families with Dependent Children (AFDC), which the act renamed Temporary Assistance for Needy Families (TANF). While limited workfare programs had existed in some states since the 1940s, the new law transformed welfare from a federally administered entitlement program into a state-determined program of coerced labor with a five-year lifetime limit on benefits.[4] Nationally, hundreds of thousands of people participated in workfare programs after its inception.[5]

At the same time, the budgets of many state and local governments were shrinking during the recessionary '90s. The new welfare law handed politicians an opportunity to solve their budget woes by replacing high-wage union workers with unwaged workfare workers. As in the '70s with New York City's WREP program, by the late '90s thousands of workfare workers were performing the same work that cities, counties, and sometimes private employers had paid real money to unionized workers to do. In some communities, nonprofit and religious organizations were major beneficiaries of workfare labor. Corporations were also increasingly taking advantage of workfare as a plentiful source of cheap labor, along with generous tax subsidies provided by the federal government as an incentive for their participation.[6]

The earliest, largest, and by some accounts most draconian workfare system began in New York City in 1995 under Republican mayor Rudolph Giuliani. As attrition thinned the ranks of unionized city workers by some twenty thousand, Giuliani filled their positions with about twice that number of part-time workers from the city's Work Experience Program, or WEP. Rather than receiving actual wages, WEP workers were "paid" from the welfare benefits they already received—the equivalent of $5,000 to $12,000 a year (depending on size of family and rent costs). A unionized city worker made from two to eight times that amount—about $20,000 a year plus benefits for clerical or service workers, $40,000 for tradespeople like painters and carpenters. An average workfare worker cost the city only $1.80 an hour for a twenty-hour workweek (based on a $577 monthly welfare check, of which one-quarter was paid by city, the rest by state and federal funds).[7]

More than 120,000 workfare workers rotated through thirty-seven thousand positions in 1996. The sheer size of the WEP workforce meant a union of these workers could potentially be among the city's largest and most powerful. With the city's welfare caseload at over four hundred thousand, the number of workfare workers threatened to eventually far outstrip public employees in the city, who numbered about two hundred thousand.[8] WEP workers accounted for about three-fourths of New York City's Parks Department workers and a third of the Sanitation Department. Until they began organizing, these workers had no right to grievance procedures. Those who contested their assignments or conditions, or even showed up ten minutes late for work, could be "sanctioned" by the welfare authorities and lose all benefits. Basic needs like protective gear and proper safety training in handling hazardous wastes largely went unmet until WEP workers started organizing.

"There's no other way to look at it but modern-day slavery," said WEP worker Edriss Anderson. "They're not paying you wages, they don't care if you get hurt, and they threaten to cut off your benefits if you complain. . . . We need our own union."[9] To indicate her workfare status, Anderson and her fellow "WEPs" were required to wear special orange vests—"like a chain gang," as one WEP worker put it. (The similarities between workfare and prison labor are more than rhetorical; in one case a Georgia recycling plant fired thirty-five trash sorters on a workfare program to replace them with prison contract laborers who made even less.)[10] Major problems included access to fresh drinking water and time for rest breaks. WEP workers also faced discrimination at times from paid city workers who, laboring side by side with them, refused to share restrooms or safety equipment.

To some, workfare made sense: why not require welfare recipients to "give back" something to the community in exchange for benefits, especially if the goal was to prepare them for paid jobs? But workfare doesn't work: neither the welfare recipient nor the public gains. It's a rerun of what happened to CETA workers nationally and WREP workers in New York in the '70s, as described in chapter 3. Assignments rarely led to permanent living-wage employment—less than a third of New York City's workfare workers obtained full- or part-time jobs afterward. One study of over one hundred thousand welfare recipients revealed that those few who did find work ended up shuttling between a succession of low-wage jobs "at a dizzying pace, with only 17 percent employed by one company for more than three years."[11] Moreover, communities are economically damaged by workfare, which displaces paid workers, depresses wages, and leads to lower labor standards.[12] Workfare compensation is mostly in the form of food stamps or rent vouchers, the rest in cash welfare benefits—a combination that put workfare workers, on average, far below the federal poverty line. Workfare does benefit employers, who reap the benefits of a subminimum wage workforce coerced into labor.

In this massive process of job restructuring, welfare recipients replace waged workers, who often ended up on the welfare rolls themselves. While it was technically illegal to replace laid-off workers with workfare workers under WEP, in practice it was common. Tales abounded of workers who were once employed at union wages but, as in a Kafkaesque game of musical chairs, later ended up as WEP workers. Fifty-year-old Hattie Hargrove, for instance, was laid off from her custodial job at the Long Island County Department of Social

Services. After her unemployment benefits ran out, she went on welfare and was handed a workfare assignment back at her old job, doing exactly the same work for the same supervisor. The difference: a $53.50 welfare check and $263 in food stamps instead of her previous union wages for the same work. Her response was to demand a union. "I would feel better because I'd be getting a paycheck and people wouldn't look down at me like I was crazy anymore," she said.[13]

As for getting on-the-job training or a new career, WEP workers complained of several problems with the system. Workfare actually had the effect of reducing job openings, since employers had a ready supply of nearly free labor in the form of WEP workers to fill jobs. "Why should they actually hire anyone?" asked Pat Simmons, a forty-nine-year-old woman on a WEP assignment at Bellevue Hospital, where she changed beds and transported patients. Of her two-year-long work experience there, she said, "We all but work for free."[14]

Another example of the dishonesty behind the claim that workfare helped recipients transition into real jobs: WEP worker Brenda Stewart was a clerk in the social services department for two years, but because she was on a workfare assignment rather than hired as "regular staff," she was not allowed to apply for permanent positions. Workfare also established a two-tiered employment system, undermining possibilities for solidarity between paid workers and workfare workers. "They don't consider us workers," said Stewart. "As soon as they found out I was on welfare, they felt they didn't have to treat me in a certain way, because now, I'm just a WEP instead of a worker."[15]

Stewart also said a practice of "racial steering" was used by some WEP supervisors to discriminate against workers of color in job assignments. In February 2004 four New York City workfare workers won a federal lawsuit over sexual harassment at their worksites.[16] And in Los Angeles, discrimination complaints based on language and ethnicity were common among Spanish-, Russian-, and Vietnamese-speaking workfare participants, who sued the county in 1999 for preventing full access to job training.[17]

While New York City's workfare program provides the most dramatic example of exploitation and displacement, several other cities had similar programs. In Los Angeles some twenty-five thousand workfare participants labored in area schools and hospitals, and in Wisconsin tens of thousands of welfare recipients worked "for benefits" as Republican governor Tommy Thompson attempted to end welfare altogether. Active ACORN workfare organizing campaigns developed in both locations. In San Francisco, People Organized to Win Employment Rights represented some three thousand workfare workers. The city's mayor, Willie Brown, though a progressive Democrat and longtime civil rights leader, backed the program fully, saying workfare workers were merely "volunteers" whose attempt to organize a union was "silly."[18]

Jurisdiction Wars: Trust and Turf

In New York City the question uppermost in the minds of workfare workers was who would help with organizing, and when. Some trade unions—notably Communications Workers of America Local 1180, representing some seven thousand white-collar city workers, and several United Auto Workers (UAW) locals—had been vocal in their denunciations of workfare and later became active supporters of the community groups organizing WEP workers. CWA Local 1180 "took a leading role in turning labor's attention to WEP," write Benjamin Dulchin and Sharryn Kasmir, establishing "a monthly roundtable meeting attended by advocacy groups and unions to deal with the crisis that WEP presented" and outfitting WEP workers with red CWA T-shirts during the city's 1996 Labor Day parade to acknowledge their identity as workers.[19]

The painters' and carpenters' unions sued the city, arguing that workfare took jobs from their members. Some trade union leaders came out with public support for workfare organizing, among them CWA's Arthur Cheliotes, who said that WEP not only exploited workfare workers but "violate[d] every right the labor movement fought for, every basic right we've won." New York Jobs with Justice, a community-labor coalition including some local AFL-CIO unions, contributed to the public debate in 1997 by holding a Workers' Rights' Tribunal in New York City aimed at pressuring governments and corporations to reject workfare. "Embarrassment is our primary tool," said chair Dominic Chan. "We want to tell them this is unacceptable."[20]

But the leadership of the city's biggest public sector union and the one whose members had been most affected by workfare—AFSCME District Council 37, with 120,000 members—largely sat out the battle. District Council 37 executive director Stanley Hill, a close political ally of Mayor Giuliani, supported the city's workfare program for many years—that is, until April 1998, when nearly a thousand AFSCME-represented hospital workers were laid off, to be replaced by WEP workers. "All of a sudden, the giant—some would say, the pussycat—has stirred," wrote Steven Greenhouse in the *New York Times*, referring to Hill's long-awaited denunciation of the workfare program.[21] But the extended period of acquiescence by Hill—the labor leader most able to pressure the mayor—had allowed Giuliani room to continuously expand the workfare program.

In the face of District Council 37's inaction, two community-based organizations began organizing WEP workers—first WEP Workers Together (WWT, initiated by a coalition of three neighborhood nonprofits) in 1996, and then ACORN in 1997.[22] Using direct actions such as pickets, sit-ins, work slowdowns, and public demonstrations, WEP workers in both organizations demanded better conditions, grievance rights, and benefits like childcare and health insurance. For instance, WWT staged a takeover of the parks commissioner's office after he refused to meet with WEP workers over a denial of warm clothing, gloves, rest breaks, and sanitary facilities in the parks. Echoing the 1960s National Welfare Rights Organization's welfare office occupations, twenty-five workers marched into his office, followed by television news cameras, and shut it down.[23] Though threatened with arrest, the workers won most of their demands. In another action, workers held a "baby-in," crowding into the welfare office along with their children to demand day care.

ACORN organized over thirty demonstrations across the city during 1997 and filed collective grievances—including one on behalf of nearly a thousand workfare workers—as a way of bringing workers together to support each other and winning job protections. WEP workers blocked trucks leaving sanitation garages as a way to force meetings with welfare officials. Demands for real pay instead of welfare benefits were also on the agenda: hundreds of workfare workers descended on a welfare office in Manhattan's Union Square in April 1997 chanting, "A day's work for a day's pay."[24] These demonstrations resulted in numerous improvements in working conditions and a formal grievance procedure for workfare workers, but no actual wages.

ACORN's effort was by far the larger, with seventeen staff committed to the project at its height, compared to WWT's three. There was tension between the groups—WWT accused ACORN of moving in on its territory, and ACORN insinuated that WWT's efforts were insignificant. After much negotiation, both groups agreed to respect each other's organizing and collaborate on some projects.[25]

ACORN began collecting signed cards authorizing it as the collective-bargaining agent for the city's WEP workers, and by June 1997 had the support of over thirteen thousand—more than a third of all workfare workers in the city, and above the percentage required to call for an election under labor law. But because WEP participants didn't have legal status as workers, labor law didn't apply. When the city refused to voluntarily recognize the union, ACORN held a symbolic election. The New York chapter of Jobs with Justice facilitated the October election, setting up polling booths at over two hundred sites, including WEP workplaces, check-cashing centers, and other locations in low-income neighborhoods. Prominent politicians, clergy, and labor leaders, such as former mayor David Dinkins and Amalgamated Clothing and Textile Workers Union president Jack Schankman, served as election observers. WEP workers voted for ACORN by a margin of 16,989 to 207.[26] Although for workfare workers the vote for representation was only symbolic, the process publicly expressed their desire for union representation and put political pressure on the city to recognize the workers.

Shortly before the election, Hill announced that AFSCME District Council 37, too, would begin a union drive among WEP workers. Hill said pushing the legislature for the legal right of WEP workers to unionize was higher on his agenda than actually organizing them at the workplace, noting, "We have the power to do that more than ACORN does."[27] But that strategy, according to a top AFSCME workfare organizer who spoke anonymously, "went down in flames" before New York's Republican-controlled legislature.[28] Afterward Hill and Giuliani signed a "statement of principles" saying that workfare workers should receive safety training and assistance from transitional employment programs leading to real jobs. However, no such programs materialized.

Welfare rights groups and progressive lawyers had similar misfortune on the legal front. They won a prevailing wage lawsuit in May 1997 that argued workfare participants were workers entitled to the same wages paid unionized city employees, but lost in February 2000 after the city appealed the decision. ACORN sued the city over the lack of drinking water, bathrooms, and protections from oncoming traffic for street sweepers—winning two cases, both of which the city appealed. Still, the community-based groups tended to take the long view and didn't expect quick victory in the courts. As Jon Kest, organizing director for New York City's ACORN office, told a *New York Times* reporter, "I'd liken [the situation] to the farm workers' struggle in the early '60s and mid-'70s . . . it was fifteen years before they were classified as employees in the state of California."[29] Mobilizing in the streets rather than lobbying in the legislature was clearly a more productive strategy for workfare workers, and one that could potentially lay the groundwork for future legal changes.

District Council 37 also began collecting authorization cards in the summer of 1997 and subsequently gathered about ten thousand, although Hill acknowledged that many WEP workers, eager for any union, signed cards for both ACORN and District Council 37.[30] Since WEP workers had no collective bargaining rights, and the cards had a solely symbolic value, District Council 37's ten thousand signatures had meaning only if workfare workers mobilized to back them up. But unlike ACORN's strong rank-and-file committee structure, District Council 37's campaign was conducted primarily through the efforts of District Council 37–represented WEP supervisors, or "crew chiefs," who encouraged the workers they supervised to sign authorization cards. According to a highly placed District Council 37 workfare staffer, workfare workers themselves weren't active in the campaign, the union did not commit sufficient resources to the organizing, and there was widespread frustration among AFSCME staff with Hill's continued unwillingness to use his political power to strongly advocate for WEP workers with the mayor.[31] Other unions were reluctant to get involved directly in organizing, since WEP workers were filling public service jobs that had been overwhelmingly held by District Council 37 members.

Despite talks aimed at bringing the District Council 37 and ACORN organizing campaigns together, a wide gulf remained. "Their bottom line was they wanted us to stop doing organizing and let them do it," according to lead ACORN organizer Milagros Silva. "It was a question of trust and turf. If we were to win collective bargaining rights, they said they should represent WEP workers." She admitted that District Council 37 had more resources, but she said ACORN didn't want to bow out until the workers themselves had a chance to choose who would represent them under any future contract.[32]

Power in the Streets

Similar jurisdictional skirmishes happened in other cities. In San Francisco, People Organized to Win Employment Rights (POWER) was begun by antipoverty activists to organize that city's workfare workers. POWER started collecting authorization cards for union representation in early 1997, and within five weeks it had gained majority support from San Francisco's three thousand workfare workers. Because California's workfare workers, like those in New York, lacked formal collective-bargaining rights, POWER organizers turned to direct action to supplement more traditional union-organizing methods like signature collection.

Demonstrations and workplace actions were POWER's specialty, and with them workfare workers won proper work breaks and equal access to restrooms and eating facilities. Following in the traditions of both community organizing and unionism, POWER started with the small daily fights that could build a sense of confidence in workers so that larger battles could be won. By obtaining California Occupational Safety and Health Administration investigations at several worksites, POWER forced the city to comply fully with state safety requirements, such as providing proper protective gear. In late 1997, after a raucous demonstration at San Francisco's largest workfare placement site—the bus and streetcar terminal—management agreed to consult with POWER representatives before making any changes in working conditions, essentially recognizing the organization as a collective-bargaining agent for workfare workers.[33] POWER officially declared itself an independent union at a founding convention in July 1998.

The relationship between POWER and San Francisco's city workers' unions got off on the wrong foot when three Service Employees International Union (SEIU) locals, representing the majority of city workers, tried to negotiate an apprenticeship clause for workfare workers in their contracts and form a joint city-union task force on workfare in 1997, all without consulting POWER. "We said, 'Look, there have to be representatives of workfare workers on that committee,'" recalls POWER organizer Steve Williams, "'because the decisions will affect us.' The union's initial response was, 'Well, you're not members of the union, and this is a union contract, so you have no place in it.'" After POWER threatened to speak out against the contracts at a San Francisco Board of Supervisors hearing, the unions agreed to accept workfare worker participation on the committee.[34]

At POWER's request, SEIU also supported the creation of a separate job title for workfare workers, a mechanism though which workfare experience could be used to qualify for regular jobs. In February 1999, SEIU Local 790 executive director and San Francisco Central Labor Council president Josie Mooney told reporters that workfare workers should get job credits so they could obtain civil service jobs.[35] But area unions did not commit any resources to the organizing campaign. Three-fourths of POWER's $120,000 annual budget came from foundation grants, the rest from member dues and "solidarity memberships" from the community. POWER, like ACORN in New York City, was eager for joint organizing plans with trade unions for several reasons—because it needed the resources, believed such a plan was more likely to succeed, and hoped that some workfare workers would end up in AFL-CIO-represented jobs in the future.

But SEIU's perspective was very different. Even though San Francisco hadn't experienced widespread displacement of union workers, as in New York City, some union members were hostile to their new workfare coworkers. "We don't really know what it's costing in real jobs," SEIU Local 790 spokesperson Bale Butler admitted, but whatever the numbers, serving existing members rather than organizing new ones was the union's top priority. While voicing general support for workfare workers, Butler also expressed a very common perception among unionists: "POWER's not a union but an organization of welfare recipients. They do their work well, but that's not the work that a trade union can do. We organize people who are salaried as employees."[36]

Comrades or Rabble? Redefining Who's a Worker

This perception of a fundamental difference between "regular" workers and workfare workers has long created a stumbling block for joint organizing attempts. It is not a new one. "To white working-class people, and even to many Black workers," wrote Frances Fox Piven and Richard Cloward in 1968, "it appears that the welfare recipient is enjoying a free ride on their hard-earned tax dollars, meanwhile, scorning the value of work and the self-esteem of workers."[37] Unions more often than not have kept their distance from welfare recipients, viewing them less as unemployed or unpaid workers and more as a problematic and sometimes even dangerous underclass that threatens their own members' pocketbooks (as taxpayers) or their jobs (if hired as strikebreakers).

Against such attitudes, workfare activists continue to reassert their standing as legitimate workers. The expansion of mandatory workfare has handed some welfare recipients a new way of seeing their situation: not as surplus people cast out of mainstream society and the economy but as workers performing valuable labor and deserving of rights and protections. "We are not deadbeats, we are not 'volunteers,' as the mayor calls us," said POWER member Garth Ferguson. "We are workers, and we want equal work for equal pay, dignity and respect like any union person gets."[38]

Workfare workers find that their counterparts in unions sometimes need to hear this argument as much as the general public. "Workfare workers are scabbing on themselves," one SEIU representative told me. "I guess that's the wrong term, but they work and the employer won't hire them since they're already working for nothing."[39] Another union activist, chair of his local's committee on welfare reform, guessed

that at least 70 percent of the workfare participants he supervised cleaning buses were just people down on their luck. However, he rejected
the notion that they deserved compensation. "Workers performing
work? I have to disagree with that. If they were not supervised, nothing
would be done," he claimed. "People have very bad attitudes," he
added, claiming that workfare workers were often themselves to blame
for their unemployment.[40] These opinions are not far from those of the
Wall Street Journal, which editorialized in response to New York City's
workfare-organizing campaigns that poor people are unemployed not
because of structural economic problems but because "they can't get
to work on time, they don't wear the appropriate clothes, they won't
treat customers courteously."[41]

Union officials acknowledge that members express abundant
fears not only about job displacement but also about workfare workers
themselves, who sometimes differ from union members racially, eth-
nically, or in terms of class. Those prejudices are often rationalized by
claiming that union members' jobs need "protection"—which is true
enough, when corporations or governments are trying to lower labor
costs by using workfare workers. But with those valid fears comes a
massive amount of historical baggage and moralistic judgment about
the poor—such as their supposed lack of responsibility for their families and their unworthiness for work. Scratch the surface and a subterranean rush of allusions to poverty, race, or ethnicity flows out.
Some union activists have tried to bring this out in the open where it
can be challenged. Asked by the Massachusetts AFL-CIO to be its
representative on a state welfare advisory board, Elly Leary, vice president of UAW Local 2324, agreed only on the condition that the AFL-
CIO help fund an independent coalition where welfare rights activists
would be on equal footing with unions. Locals of SEIU, AFSCME,
and the UAW became active in the coalition, Working Massachusetts,
along with many community-based organizations.

Initially, Leary said, unions joined the coalition because "they
were afraid that 'those people were going to take our jobs unless we
did something.'" To break down the "us vs. them" attitude, coalition
members visited nearly every AFL-CIO Central Labor Council in the
state to facilitate conversations between welfare recipients and union-

ists. One particularly useful exercise asked unionists to think of three stereotypes about welfare recipients, then three about unionists. Leary said the exercise almost always revealed both groups to be stereotyped as "lazy, corrupt, [and] a drag on the economy," with one crucial difference: "welfare recipients are perceived to be Black women, while labor is perceived to be white men." The exercise was liberating, Leary said. It opened the way to understanding and healing divisions between union members and poor people.[42] Working Massachusetts activists hoped discussions like these would help change how unions saw welfare recipients—now as working-class comrades, no longer as enemies—and lay the groundwork for cooperative organizing.

Changing the Terms of Debate

Just as negative beliefs about the unemployed—that they are somehow different from other workers—are not new, neither are government programs to put unemployed people to work. Throughout recent US history, such policies have alternated between "fair work" (i.e., voluntary training or job creation programs like the Depression-era Works Progress Administration, usually intended for men and those seen as "deserving" real wages) and "workfare" (mandatory, usually punitive, unwaged work programs targeted at the "undeserving poor").[43] Activists in the 1990s confronted the latter: sustained right-wing attacks on welfare, downsizing of state and federal governments, and a vast expansion of workfare programs.

While financially strapped municipalities employed the majority of workfare workers in the mid-'90s, corporations were also eager to benefit from what they accurately perceived to be a plentiful source of cheap labor. In 1997 the Clinton administration promised generous tax subsidies to private employers who hired welfare recipients. As *Forbes* magazine noted, the private sector was "the only potential source for as many as 2 million [workfare] jobs that will need to be found in the next 5 years."[44]

For conservatives, welfare has always been about the regulation of labor, its object not to eliminate poverty but to use and discipline low-wage workers. Their justification for doing away with entitlements

and instituting punitive workfare programs is that welfare recipients
are unemployed not because of a lack of jobs, adequate childcare, or
sufficient benefits but because they lack motivation, skills, or a work
ethic. In the late '80s and throughout the '90s, racial and gender stereotypes were again rife within the lexicon of welfare revisionists. Conservative discourse continued to present poor people as "naturally"
deficient in the characteristics that made a responsible citizen and
good worker and to represent poverty as a moral condition rather than
joblessness or insufficient income due to structural problems of the
US economy. As Michael Katz noted in *The Undeserving Poor*, the
language surrounding welfare policy slipped "easily, unreflectively,
into a language of family, race, and culture rather than inequality,
power and exploitation."[45] Poverty was individualized as pathology,
obscuring its origins in social and economic inequalities.

Some conservatives were less interested in imagined pathology
and more concerned with their own pocketbooks: they said workers
were simply no longer willing to perform entry-level work. The fear
that welfare gave workers greater leverage in the job market—because
they had a "safety net" to fall back into should working conditions or
wages become unacceptable—accounted for much of the right-wing
distaste for welfare, matched only by the desire to use social and economic policy to resurrect the "traditional" heterosexual nuclear family
of wage-earning husband and dependent wife.

This kind of racist and sexist rhetoric blamed poor people for
larger economic problems. It bore no resemblance to the real lives of
most welfare recipients, the majority of whom were independent single
mothers working a "double shift" on workfare and at home. Such workers often had extensive work experience in the unstable, low-wage
labor market and suffered not from a missing work ethic but from an
economy that provided neither the jobs nor the support systems, like
childcare, they needed to work. For instance, in New York City there
were just 91,000 job openings each year through the late '90s, while
some 320,000 city residents were officially unemployed and another
419,000 received public assistance. At the same time, 9,000 welfare recipients studying at city universities were forced out of classrooms and
into WEP assignments, while tens of thousands more were forced to

leave adult literacy, English-as-an-additional-language, or job-training programs—programs that, statistically, gave welfare recipients a much better chance of getting a job than did workfare.[46]

With the safety net itself full of holes and giving way to universal workfare requirements, activists created their own counterdiscourse by consciously recasting welfare struggles in terms of social equality and civil and economic rights. In response to New York mayor Rudolph Giuliani's campaign to bring nonprofits on board as workfare employers in 1997, sixty-eight New York churches, synagogues, and nonprofits came together to denounce workfare using the language of abolitionism. With signs directed at the mayor—"Rudy, we will not be your slave drivers"—clergy and nonprofit leaders called workfare "unjust" and "evil."[47]

Like their predecessors in the National Welfare Rights Organization and the Movement for Economic Justice in the '60s and '70s, activists emphasized the commonalities that joined low-wage workers and welfare recipients, connections that reached across differences of gender, race, and ethnicity. Just as the civil rights and feminist movements influenced the dynamics of welfare organizing in the '60s and '70s, workfare organizing in the '90s took place within the context of multiracial solidarity and coalition building. Nationally, 42.5 percent of welfare recipients were white, 34 percent were African American, 19.2 percent were Latina or Latino, and 4.3 percent were classified as "other."[48] In New York City welfare recipients were overwhelmingly Latina or Latino and African American. Workfare organizers consciously built on this diversity by formulating ideologies and movement-building practices in terms of multiculturalism and unity between working people. Workfare organizing in most cities across the nation is similarly multiracial and shared by women and men. It is explicitly about obtaining jobs, and just as explicitly about building a broad economic-justice movement that values diversity and democracy.

In addition to campaigns aimed at transforming public consciousness and changing policy, activists used state and federal labor laws to protect their rights. Community activists bolstered their arguments with the guarantees of freedom from poverty and forced labor contained in the Universal Declaration of Human Rights and the

United Nations Child Rights Convention, as well as the US Constitution's Thirteenth Amendment, which states, "Neither slavery nor
involuntary servitude . . . shall exist within the United States."[49] In
Maryland a community-labor coalition convinced the governor to
issue an executive order prohibiting the use of tax credits to hire welfare recipients to cut payroll costs. In May 1997 a broad coalition of
civil rights, women's, community, religious, and labor groups successfully pressured then-president Clinton to protect workfare workers
under federal employment laws such as the Fair Labor Standards Act
and the Occupational Safety and Health Act. The federal government
filed suit against New York City, charging it with not doing enough to
protect female workfare workers from sexual and racial harassment
by supervisors.[50]

Conservatives opposed these actions, which enhanced the power
of workers and undermined employers' ability to divide workers by
race, ethnicity, gender, or welfare status. One businessperson told the
Los Angeles Times (apparently without intended irony) that extending
employment rights to workfare workers "sucks people onto welfare"
by providing better benefits than those accorded to other low-income
workers who aren't on welfare.[51] Of course, what he and other busi-
nesspeople were opposing was the logical outcome of workfare organizing: the creation of living-wage jobs that would enable people to
leave welfare; jobs that would also have the effect of bringing up the
wages and benefits of other poor workers.

Changing Union Cultures

By the late '90s several experiments in joint organizing between trade
unions and community organizations made connections between
workfare, the expansion of low-wage jobs in the private sector, privatization, and the subsequent lowering of wages in the public sector.
Efforts like these opened up new and fruitful directions for the labor
movement as a whole.

For instance, the Campaign on Contingent Work in Massachusetts set out to organize low-wage and unwaged workers, including
day laborers, workfare workers, and immigrant workers. "This is

clearly a high-risk, no-guarantees project," observed Elly Leary, "but it's exciting as well." Organizing began in 1998 with the distribution of a brochure, printed in English, Spanish, Creole, Portuguese, Chinese, and several other languages, informing workers of their existing rights (minimum wage, health and safety, rest breaks) as well as the rights they didn't have but should have (protections against job loss, healthcare benefits).[52]

Workers, including a large group of African American women who heard about the project from ACORN, began contacting the campaign for assistance. The women had been temping for Polaroid until they were thrown out of work and onto welfare when management replaced their temp agency with another, one that paid lower wages to a largely immigrant workforce. Workfare workers also sought the campaign's help. Leary said workfare workers "tend to be the most fearful of all," worried about losing welfare benefits if they "talk back to the boss, refuse an assignment, or complain about their placements." Workers wanting to start union drives were referred to AFL-CIO unions for help.

In New Jersey the Communications Workers of America and ACORN launched innovative joint workfare-organizing campaigns in New Jersey and Milwaukee. Impressed with ACORN's success in organizing workfare workers in New York City, David Weiner, president of CWA Local 1081, had approached his national union in 1998 with the idea of cooperating with ACORN to organize New Jersey's ten thousand workfare workers. Weiner's local, which represented social workers at the Essex and Passaic County welfare offices, was joined by five other CWA locals in the project. Their organization was called People Organizing Workfare Workers (POWW). Half of its board of directors was chosen by ACORN and half by CWA, and CWA provided significant financial backing. The first two organizers hired were from ACORN; they in turn hired and trained rank-and-file workfare workers as organizers. By August 1998, POWW had thousands of authorization cards in hand to pressure nonprofit and religious organizations, the largest workfare employers in New Jersey, to voluntarily recognize the union.[53]

CWA represented most of New Jersey's state employees, and the combined threat of privatization and workfare increasingly loomed over its members' jobs. For instance, childcare in Jersey City used to be run by the state, and it provided living-wage jobs with benefits, according to Ed Sabol, organizing director of CWA District 1. But after the system was privatized, workfare workers were placed in those jobs, and, said Sabol, "basically they're run with indentured servitude." While unions needed strong antiprivatization contract language, Sabol said, ambitious and sustained organizing was also necessary.[54] Workfare not only displaced employees lucky enough to have union jobs, taking away jobs with decent wages that could provide a way out of poverty for low-wage workers and welfare recipients; it also depressed the job market in both the private and public sectors.

Meanwhile in New York City, the resignation of AFSCME District Council 37 executive director Stanley Hill in February 1999, on the eve of a corruption scandal, led to new, more militant leadership and greater cooperation with community groups organizing around workfare. District Council 37 sued the city over its replacement of nearly two thousand unionized clerical workers with unpaid workfare workers. An AFSCME local in Kansas City pushed for a program to move four hundred welfare recipients into city jobs and give right of first refusal of entry-level jobs to workfare workers. Another AFSCME local in Indianapolis cosponsored twenty-five workfare workers in full-time jobs in various public agencies and offered them transportation and childcare support.[55] An SEIU local in Los Angeles became a key part of a community coalition organizing workfare workers there.[56] These are only a few examples from around the nation that indicated a progressive shift in trade union attitudes and actions toward workfare workers.

Building a New House of Labor

What did workfare organizing actually accomplish? In San Francisco, POWER activists forced the city to create 850 living-wage jobs for the city's workfare participants. They also won legal recognition of workfare workers from the state's Occupational Safety and Health Administration and got workfare workers included in the city's living-wage ordinance. Direct worker actions resulted in a formal grievance procedure, free public transportation for all workfare workers, and a 40 percent reduction in their work hours. San Francisco's POWER also participated in the movement to raise the city's minimum wage and began organizing domestic workers.

In Los Angeles and New York, workfare workers represented by ACORN achieved access to a grievance process when they were faced with unsafe working conditions, racial discrimination, or gender harassment. "People use it . . . it is a pain in the ass to the city," according to ACORN's Jon Kest. New York unions and community groups worked together to win legislation that allowed for training and education, including college attendance, to satisfy welfare-reform work requirements, instead of workfare.[57] Perhaps most important, all of the workfare unions act as de facto collective-bargaining agents for their members, defending their rights primarily by direct action and worker solidarity.

Organizing for labor rights has changed the way welfare recipients see themselves—as workers, joining together for equal pay for equal work and a safe working environment, rather than as people begging for a handout. "We're workers just like anyone else," said New York City WEP worker Brenda Stewart. "We want real job creation and all the benefits afforded to any other worker."[58] Workfare activists themselves are agents of change, working to transform the ideology surrounding welfare away from racist and sexist notions about poor workers and toward the goals of fair wages and job creation—as well as continuing the political fight for state support of caregiving activities in the home.[59] They eloquently redefine welfare in terms of economic justice—the right to a decent job at livable wages. On a broader level, workfare activists advocate an economy based on social and economic justice, rather than exploitation.

By 2004 the number of people on workfare had declined in San Francisco, New York City, New Jersey, and elsewhere. Where did all the recipients go? As writer Vijay Prashad notes, "Poverty remains, but the poor have been banished from state care."[60] Forcing poor people into unsustainable and exploitive workfare jobs, without support for childcare, transportation, or education, forced many off the welfare rolls and into the arms of private charities. Others were cut off after they exhausted their limited period of assistance. Between 1996 and 1999, AFDC/TANF enrollment declined by over 50 percent, and some six million recipients lost benefits.[61] For those who remained, the fight against workfare mounted by community organizations and unions mitigated its effects and played a role in limiting its spread. Organizing campaigns, grievances, massive publicity, and lawsuits made it more politically difficult for city governments to expand workfare programs.

In terms of movement building, workfare organizing profoundly affected the relationship between independent poor workers' unions and AFL-CIO unions. In New York, workfare organizing led to strong relationships between ACORN and some progressive unions such as CWA Local 1180, which worked with ACORN to gain permanent ballot status for the state's Working Families Party.[62] In San Francisco, POWER developed a close relationship with Hotel Employees and Restaurant Employees (HERE) Local 2. The relationship developed in part because the hospitality industry took an economic nosedive, so that some of HERE's members ended up on welfare and became active in POWER. The organizations began strategizing together, exchanging staffs, and showing up at each other's demonstrations. But POWER continued to have a problematic relationship with the union representing most municipal workers, SEIU, which did not consistently support workfare workers in their campaigns confronting city leaders. POWER decided to focus on workfare, said Steve Williams, "because it allowed us to explicitly talk about recipients as unemployed and underemployed workers. We thought, 'This is going to form an incredible synergy between us and unions, and we'll have an incredible fighting force to make some real, concrete change.' But then we started knocking on people's doors within [San Francisco] organized labor, and [most] weren't answering."[63]

It is just this "synergy" that could help renew the labor movement's spirit and rebuild its strength. Helping to organize against workfare offers trade unions the opportunity to look beyond the usual limits of their own institutions and join forces with community-based labor activists. Such collaboration has important implications for how the labor movement as a whole sees itself and how it operates. As trade unions join forces in workfare organizing, they move toward a broader notion of who "workers" are. As they respond creatively and work in mutual respect with the community organizations that have historically represented poor workers, the likelihood that such organizing will succeed increases. This success, in turn, will strengthen the labor movement in its fight against exploitation.

The reappearance of workfare programs also opens up new possibilities for organizing welfare recipients by tying welfare rights to workers' rights. How movements build upon each other is at the heart of this story. Welfare rights activists of the '60s and '70s attempted to bargain collectively for welfare recipients within the context of the civil rights, feminist, and Black Power movements. Contemporary welfare rights activists sense the possibilities of deep and lasting change that lie in organizing to demand economic justice within the context of the labor movement. By reconnecting workplace-based unions with community-based movements for economic, racial, and gender justice, workfare organizing is part of the reemergence of social justice unionism.

On April 15, 2015, some sixty thousand people took part in Fight for 15 demonstrations across the nation, in what the *Guardian* called the "largest protest by low-wage workers in US history." (*Photo courtesy of Fight for 15*)

7

Reviving an Activist Culture

The AFL-CIO's Turn toward Organizing

For tens of thousands of poor workers, the 1980s and '90s were decades of growth for their independent unions. Whether these unions were part of a nationwide campaign by ACORN-affiliated unions (chapter 4) or took the form of locally based workers' centers (chapter 5) or workfare unions (chapter 6), all adhered to a community-based vision of workers' organization that was democratic, antibureaucratic, and movement oriented, and that recognized the salience of race, ethnicity, and gender in reconstructing a unified labor movement from below. Building on the experiments of their forerunners in the '60s and '70s, these unions of the poor sought to effect lasting change not only in their members' lives but also in the larger movements for economic and social justice of which they were a part.

After years of quiescence, signs of change also appeared clearly on AFL-CIO trade union horizons by the late '80s. In part because of the successful examples set by poor workers' unions scattered across the nation, interest in community-based tactics within some sectors of the trade union movement had heightened considerably. While independent

unionists continued to develop their organizations, social justice unionists within the AFL-CIO were pushing for similar transformations. An
infusion of activists from poor workers' unions and community organizing also helped to revive these tactics within the mainstream labor
movement. An increasing number of social movement–type campaigns
were undertaken by progressive trade unions, some of them in coalition
with independent community-based organizations.

By 1990 there were enough examples to fill a thick volume edited
by veteran labor journalists Jeremy Brecher and Tim Costello, *Building
Bridges: The Emerging Grassroots Coalition of Labor and Community.*
The key question for the trade union movement, as Kim Moody
noted in his contribution to the volume, was a choice between "cooperation and concessions" and "confrontation and coalition."[1] The latter meant opening the doors of the trade unions to new members and
new tactics and learning not only from the independent poor workers'
movement but also from trade unions' own militant past.

Out of Your Meetings and into the Streets

One of the earliest and most confrontational trade-union organizing
efforts of this period was SEIU's Justice for Janitors campaign. Begun
in 1986, it sought to organize custodial staff through creative direct action and civil disobedience while bypassing National Labor Relations
Board (NLRB) election procedures. Like the independent poor workers' unions that came before it, Justice for Janitors knew that with a
hostile management environment and a high-turnover workforce, traditional organizing methods were unlikely to succeed. Justice for Janitors organizers, wrote journalist Zach Nauth, compared the NLRB
to "a black hole that sucks in the union's time, stalls momentum and
eventually bores workers to death."[2] Worse still, the lengthy legal
process tended to underscore unions' weaknesses, as it gave antiunion
employers time to conduct illegal activities, such as firing rank-and-
file activists, which then took the union's time and money to fight.

Instead Justice for Janitors turned to time-tested social-movement
strategies—including sit-ins, militant demonstrations, and civil disobedience—that physically interfered with employers' ability to con-

duct business. These were supplemented with corporate campaigns, boycotts, and community coalition building. In Los Angeles's Century City neighborhood, hundreds of janitors, mostly Latina and Latino, and their supporters poured into the streets in the spring and summer of 1990 for near-daily marches in support of demands to unionize janitorial services in eleven of the area's massive office buildings. Police attacked one such peaceful demonstration on June 15, 1990, injuring ninety and jailing forty; their excessive force elicited comparisons to the state's sometimes violent relationship to labor.[3] But far from scaring off potential union members, the actions inspired new activism. As Justice for Janitors director Stephen Lerner wrote in 1996, "People started calling up and saying, 'How do I do that strike thing? That's not a thing you usually get, non-union workers saying, 'I want to go on strike too.'" Television images of nonviolent strikers being beaten by police increased public sympathy for the janitors in their fight against wealthy building owners.[4]

The campaign involved a commitment to community and civil rights issues at more than a rhetorical level. For instance, in a spring 1987 Atlanta campaign that involved mostly African American women, Justice for Janitors worked closely with both ACORN and the Southern Christian Leadership Conference.[5] In Washington, DC, janitors blocked a major bridge and held class in the streets to protest educational cuts.[6] In November 1990 they chained themselves to the headquarters of the city's wealthiest developer, and in March 1995 they occupied city council offices to protest a real estate tax break. The tax reduction would have devastated social programs for the poor while benefiting big developers, including one that had resisted the union's attempts to organize its buildings. "This isn't just about 5,000 janitors; it's about issues that concern all D.C. residents—what's happening to their schools, their streets, their neighborhoods," a union leader told the *Washington Post*.[7]

This kind of activism won Justice for Janitors important allies among nonlabor progressives, who often showed up to put their bodies on the line during contract fights. By 1995 Justice for Janitors had won contract battles in Los Angeles, Washington, DC, and Denver and had become the most successful organizing campaign among private-sector service workers in decades, bringing thirty-five thousand new members into SEIU.[8]

There were other bright spots, too, where community-based organizing had percolated into the ranks of some AFL-CIO unions. The national working women's organization 9to5 had come from movement beginnings to represent some twelve thousand office workers after having established a cooperative "sisterly" relationship in 1981 with SEIU Local 925.[9] Former United Labor Unions locals in New Orleans and Chicago—which, as we saw in chapter 4, had affiliated with SEIU in 1984—grew at a rapid pace as they coordinated organizing rank-and-file intensive campaigns among home healthcare and hotel workers with their sister organization ACORN.

Around the nation, usually on a local level, progressive trade unionists and community-based labor activists were increasingly working together. For instance, San Francisco's multiethnic Hotel Employees and Restaurant Employees (HERE) Local 2 began a fruitful relationship with the independent Asian Immigrant Women Advocates in the late '80s, working toward the common goal of defending the rights of immigrant women hotel workers.[10] In another case, at Hilton Head, an island resort off the coast of South Carolina employing mostly poor whites and African Americans in hotel, food service, and bus-driving jobs, workers decided in 1992 to organize themselves but could find nothing under "unions" in the local yellow pages. They turned to a fourteen-year-old community-based workers' rights organization, the Carolina Alliance for Fair Employment (CAFE). Later, workers asked the Union of Operating Engineers, an AFL-CIO affiliate, to join the campaign. In October 1994, after two years of organizing with duties equally shared by the union and CAFE, workers voted overwhelmingly for union representation.[11]

Several other AFL-CIO unions, notably UNITE, HERE, and CWA, began to adopt community-based techniques and expand their organizing beyond its usual boundaries.[12] In 1990 the United Mine Workers of America announced it would raise the percentage of its budget devoted to organizing from 18 to 50 percent and expand its use of rank-and-file organizers, extending its reach past the coalfields to any workplace "where workers are being exploited by their employer."[13] The United Farm Workers union, after a period of difficulty in the '80s, broadened its organizing from its base in California to Arizona, Washington, Texas, and Florida in the early '90s and won several representation victories from 1994 through 1996.[14]

One ambitious multiunion collaboration was the Los Angeles Manufacturing Action Project (LAMAP), founded in February 1994 by a group of labor and community activists to launch a regional organizing drive in Los Angeles's massive manufacturing corridor. During its first year, nine unions contributed tens of thousands of dollars each to the project, in hopes of organizing a mostly Latino workforce of 650,000 in the sprawling area of some 120 square miles. LAMAP supported a tortilla delivery drivers' strike and an organizing campaign among truckers. But it folded in 1997 when the unions that had pledged money withdrew support upon realizing that much larger sums were needed to make the project viable.[15] Still, as an attempt at innovative large-scale, cross-industrial, community-based organizing, LAMAP captured the imaginations of progressive activists in the labor movement, who saw it as the wave of the future.

Immigrant-driven campaigns also made headlines elsewhere. For instance, Salvadoran factory workers in Everett, Massachusetts, organized with UNITE in the fall of 1996, in an extremely short but energetic campaign built on worker and community solidarity. The 170 workers, mostly women, began organizing at Richmark, a highly profitable firm producing curtains for big retailers like J.C. Penney, against degrading sweatshop conditions, low wages, and lack of benefits. Richmark's $20 million in annual sales translated into only $5 per hour for its workers. A group of ten women workers at the factory initially contacted a community-based religious organization for help, which then contacted UNITE, which represented textile workers in the area. When activists began leafletting their coworkers, the company fired six of them; most of the rest of the plant walked out in support of the fired activists, then brought family and friends from surrounding neighborhoods to the picket lines each day. Civil disobedience by prominent community members, resulting in arrests, added further pressure on Richmark. Through it all, union officials followed "the lead of the workers," and within three weeks the company gave in and recognized the union.[16]

What these campaigns had in common was an aggressive organizing outlook that relied on community-based, social movement–style tactics. Like the work of most of the independent unions, this organizing tended to be based in communities of color and among the growing immigrant workforce. Networks of activists, both inside and outside of mainstream labor, spread the philosophy of this new militant unionism. By the late '80s, organizers with social movement or community-organizing experience had made headway inside local, regional, and national trade unions. Experience with the UFW and ACORN was quite common; others came with backgrounds in international solidarity movements and antiapartheid struggles.[17] Some were in high positions, such as Rhode Island Workers Association organizer George Nee, who had become head of that state's AFL-CIO; Eliseo Medina, who had worked with the UFW before becoming head of SEIU's West Coast organizing division in the late '80s; Miguel Contreras, another former farmworker organizer, who in 1996 became head of the second-largest local federation in the country, the Los Angeles County Federation of Labor; and Mark Splain and Stewart Acuff, both former community organizers with ties to ACORN, who later directed the AFL-CIO Organizing Department.

Still, these kinds of initiatives were rare within the AFL-CIO universe. In 1995 an astonishing 97 percent of AFL-CIO union locals had no organizing programs, and most had no community outreach.[18] And though the new initiatives provided the movement with working examples of a different organizing culture, the public picture of the labor movement remained one of an increasingly irrelevant bureaucracy protecting a small enclave of privileged workers. A report commissioned by the AFL-CIO in 1994 from a prolabor consulting firm concluded that "mostly, unions are discussed as something no longer relevant, as symbolized in the frequently used short-hand, 'they're dinosaurs.'" Only 25 percent of those surveyed felt that unions were concerned about all working people, while 65 percent said unions were concerned only about their members. "Labor unions are seen by many people," wrote the consultants, "as bastions of older, white men who are looking first after their power and institutions, then after their members' interests and only then—if at all—the rest of the nation."[19]

The steady decline in union membership did nothing to refute this widely held view. In 1995 only 14.9 percent of US workers were union members, a level not seen since the Great Depression.[20] However, this number masks the fact that the drop actually occurred only in the private sector. Public-sector membership rates had actually increased slightly through the '80s and '90s, from 35.9 percent in 1980 to 37.7 percent in 1995, while private-sector union membership plummeted from 20.1 percent in 1980 to 10.3 percent in 1995.[21]

No longer could trade union leadership put the blame on the Reagan and Bush administrations and their antilabor policies. By 1992, Democrats were in control in both the White House and Congress, heavily supported with trade union PAC money, but this made no significant difference in labor's ability to reform the NLRB in a more pro-worker direction or get favorable laws passed. Though globalization and other economic changes were intensifying union decline in some parts of the private sector, such as manufacturing, not all of the decline could be attributed to these economic forces. Overall manufacturing employment totaled less than 8 percent between 1980 and 1994, yet union membership in the sector declined by over half, in large part because manufacturers relocated their plants to nonunion states in the South and the sunbelt.[22] During the same time, the number of private-sector nonmanufacturing jobs—a good portion of which constitute the high-turnover "service sector" in which poor workers are concentrated—had grown by over 39 percent.[23] Few trade unions even attempted to follow those employers or take up service-sector organizing in a major way. The time had come to acknowledge collectively that many trade unions had been asleep at the wheel during the US economy's decades-long journey toward a new configuration in which low-wage "marginal" workers played a leading role. It was time to wake up before it was too late.

An Organizing Renaissance?

All of this set the stage for the first contested election in the AFL-CIO's history. With experiments in social justice–style organizing blossoming successfully while trade unionism's overall fortunes continued to sink, some in the federation realized they desperately needed a new national organizing strategy that would begin to take the movement back to labor's more successful days. Opportunity for leadership change came when Lane Kirkland, lackluster president of the AFL-CIO since George Meany's retirement in 1979, stepped down. Kirkland's aide Tom Donahue promptly declared his candidacy; so did SEIU president John Sweeney.

Critiques of the AFL-CIO were now advanced from its innermost leadership circles. A group of reformers led by Sweeney and AFSCME president Gerald McEntee formed a "New Voice" slate, which fully acknowledged the weakened state of the labor movement. "American workers look about and see no one who speaks on their behalf," their platform of June 1995 noted. "We cannot wait for a change in the political climate. . . . We must first organize despite the law if we are ever to organize with the law." If elected, the New Voice leadership pledged to "organize at a pace and scale that is unprecedented" and to "lead a movement that speaks for all American workers."[24] This would be no small task: just to stay even with the losses, trade unions would have to organize three to four hundred thousand new members each year, and far more would be required if they wanted to expand the movement.[25] As the New Voice platform stated, for the AFL-CIO to regain the strength of its postwar years, when it represented one in three US workers, a million new members would be needed each year for the next two decades.[26]

How did the reformers propose to accomplish this? First, they promised to increase the AFL-CIO's organizing budget to at least $10 million and use it both for direct federation organizing and to provide matching grants to national unions engaged in organizing. Second, they would use the already-existing AFL-CIO Organizing Institute to create a "brigade of top organizers from various unions who can be deployed into important, highly visible, strategic campaigns." Third, they would establish an organizing department within the AFL-CIO, which—amazingly—had never had one before. The New Voice platform included other goals, chief among them reforming the public's perception of trade unions, reinvigorating the regional Central Labor Councils, and opening up "new opportunities for women, minorities and young people at all levels of the movement."[27]

In October 1995 Sweeney, along with running mates Richard
Trumka of the United Mine Workers and AFSCME's Linda Chavez-
Thompson, won the election with 56 percent of the vote. It was, in the
words of historian Paul Buhle, a stunning and remarkable defeat for
the old guard: "Middle-of-the-road business unionists facing the near-
collapse of their dues-paying constituency suddenly escorted a new
type of leadership . . . through the front door."[28] Progressive unionists
hoped the change would lead to deeper involvement of people of color,
youth, women, and LGBTQ people in the labor movement.

The new leadership announced its organizing plan in March 1996,
five months after taking office, unveiling a "Union Summer" training
program for a thousand college students modeled on the civil rights
movement's Freedom Summer.[29] In an important and long-overdue
move, it also embraced the LGBTQ trade union group Pride at Work.[30]
AFL-CIO rhetoric became more openly critical of the past. "Instead
of organizing," the new leadership wrote in 1996, "unions [had] hun-
kered down" and "collectively chose the shortsighted strategy of trying
to protect current contracts of members instead of organizing new
members."[31] The federation's $10 million would provide matching
grants to unions with innovative organizing plans—up from about $2
million in previous years—but unions would have to match AFL-CIO
dollars four to one.[32] Because most of the funding needed for organizing resided not within the AFL-CIO but in the hands of individual
unions, those unions held the key to large-scale organizing. The AFL-
CIO, as an umbrella group, could set the ideological pace and coordinate multiunion campaigns, but much of the actual organizing would
need to be done—and paid for—by constituent unions themselves.

Organizing Institute head Richard Bensinger was appointed AFL-
CIO organizing director. Among his chief duties was convincing the
federation's affiliated unions to spend at least 30 percent of their budgets on new organizing.[33] Most spent much less, with the vast majority
of organizing done by a few larger unions. The resources needed to
recoup the strength that labor had lost in the previous forty years were
massive. Unions estimated they would need to spend $300 million on
organizing just to maintain membership nationwide.[34] Clearly, re-

building the movement would take much more than the New Voice slate's election-year commitment plus the efforts of those few unions that had stepped up to the plate with more money for organizing.

Nine months later, the AFL-CIO increased its 1997 organizing budget to $30 million.[35] It was a dramatic increase, but compared with other expenditures by the AFL-CIO, the sum was not so impressive. For instance, the AFL-CIO had already spent $5 million on pro-union television ads during 1996 and—to the chagrin of many organizers— was preparing to spend another $40 million. Some $20 million alone was spent in the mid-'80s for renovating the AFL-CIO's headquarters in Washington.[36] Moreover, the AFL-CIO spent over $30 million in campaign contributions during 1996.[37]

But the promised numbers kept climbing. By the AFL-CIO's 1997 convention—at which the New Voice slate was reelected unopposed— the federation was making it clear that unions themselves would have to foot the bill for new organizing: it argued for having $1 billion dedicated for organizing, most of it collected from affiliate unions, in the year 2000 alone. That would amount to just under 20 percent of the approximately $6 billion collected in dues by AFL-CIO unions.[38]

Every Worker Is an Organizer

The move to spend more on organizing was opposed in some quarters. In some unions, internal political pressure was applied by both members and paid staffers to retain the vast majority of funds for "servicing" existing worksites instead of organizing new ones. "Don't they realize," one delegate said with barely concealed racism and classism at the 1997 AFL-CIO convention, "if they really push this organizing, the labor movement is going to wind up being a movement of strawberry pickers and chicken pluckers?"[39] Though few unionists openly expressed similar feelings, a defense of what had become de facto divisions within the labor movement was strong in some union meeting halls.

Trade union progressives argued that spending money to reach out to enlarge the movement was essential to labor's health. But among the pro-organizing forces themselves there was another, perhaps more elemental, debate. If funds were liberated from union coffers for organizing, how should such massive resources be used? Should they foster rank-and-file involvement in order to build a stronger movement, or pay for campaigns that were institutionally driven and controlled from above?

The question was thus not just organizing per se but also how to organize and under whose control. As Fernando Gapasin and Michael Yates wrote in 1997, "For all of its good features [the AFL-CIO's program] is still a sort of 'revolution from above.'"[40] Sweeney pointed to his success at SEIU, a union that had nearly doubled its membership since 1980, from 635,000 to 1.1 million members. But much of this growth, critics alleged, was not the result of organizing efforts but of mergers and "accretion"[41]—that is, affiliating independent associations and unions that had organized themselves (among them some of those I have been discussing here, such as the Rhode Island Workers Union and United Labor Unions). Merging independent unions into AFL-CIO-affiliated ones built numbers, brought in new activists, and strengthened the federation overall. But it could only go so far: oceans of workers remained outside the gates of labor, "as likely to be struck by lightning as to be approached to join a union," as activist Janice Fine put it.[42]

Who would do all this new organizing? Unions would need virtually an army of organizers to sign up the numbers they were hoping for. The AFL-CIO's answer was to "staff up" with paid professionals, often upper-middle-class young adults right out of college, who would hop from campaign to campaign, organizing across the nation—a model quite different from the alternatives presented by the grassroots labor organizing flourishing elsewhere. The federation's Organizing Institute and its highly publicized Union Summer internship program brought hundreds of young people into labor's ranks as new organizers, while promises about involving existing rank-and-file members in organizing went largely unfulfilled. In a widely circulated critique of the AFL-CIO's Organizing Institute published in April 1996, veteran organizer Steve Early wrote, "Unions should avoid over-reliance on young staffers recruited from college campuses, given a crash-course in organizing, and parachuted into workplace campaigns. . . . Peace Corps-type cadre who lack local ties, union experience, or any organizational context for their work are no substitutes for rank-and-file organizers recruited from and working off a base of existing members."[43]

These newly trained organizers, Early added, could seem to be delivering "a sales pitch like any other peddler of a product . . . even if the organizers involved are young, multi-cultural women who don't fit the traditional stereotype of middle-aged, white, male union reps." Sociologist Dan Clawson suggests this design was part of a larger mass-marketing strategy on the part of unions, imitating liberal "public interest" groups' reliance on direct mail and phone solicitations to recruit members rather than on labor's traditional—and more powerful—tactic: mobilizing its members to "disrupt the economic functioning of the system."[44]

Early, Clawson, and other critics of the marketing model advocate instead the development of "organizing locals" committed to fostering rank-and-file involvement and a lively organizing culture rooted in local unions and in communities. In this vision, members themselves would reach out to their coworkers to join and participate, encouraging worker empowerment and rank-and-file "ownership" of the union drive. Such an approach would promote activism regardless of whether an NRLB election "is won or lost or is even an immediate possibility," Early writes.[45]

Workplaces organized in this fashion have stronger bonds of solidarity that are more likely to be sustained through struggles for union representation, employer attacks, and contract battles. Labor researchers Kate Bronfenbrenner and Tom Juravich demonstrate quantitatively that aggressive organizing campaigns relying on rank-and-file workers have the best chances of winning elections, bargaining strong contracts, and resisting decertification.[46] Moreover, large-scale organizing has never been successfully done by paid organizers alone, argues labor activist Kim Moody, but requires "workers organizing other workers." Paid staff are essential to facilitating this process but should not control it. In the AFL-CIO's new approach, some unions have been willing to use militant tactics such as mass demonstrations and civil disobedience only until they win recognition. Afterward, Moody writes, "power passes to the hands of the existing union staff or officialdom and the 'service model' recommences as ever." Like the glass ceiling that bars women and people of color from leadership, the "bureaucratic polyester ceiling" of this paid managerial class presents a "barrier to rank-and-file participation and power."[47]

This trend is, ironically, most visible within SEIU, one of the AFL-CIO's leading "organizing" unions, and one that has historically reached out to innovative independent unions as part of its revival. SEIU deserves credit for its energetic organizing work but has come in for justified criticism for its centralization and top-down practices. While SEIU rank-and-filers are routinely mobilized to support union drives and contract battles, they are less often in control of the substance and tactics of such campaigns. SEIU, though politically progressive, is known throughout the labor movement as one of the most heavily staffed and highly centralized unions, often exercising harsh control through trusteeships when local leadership doesn't fall into line, such as in the highly publicized 2009 split of the member-led National Union of Healthcare Workers (NUHW).[48]

The Justice for Janitors campaign, among SEIU's most successful, employed some 110 professional organizers in 1995, at a cost of about $2 million per year.[49] Its 1990 Los Angeles victory was marked by a centralized, top-down structure, and the Justice for Janitors model itself was "exported through trusteeships" and imposed by the national union on locals across the nation.[50] Organizing decisions were often made among paid leadership, with little consultation at the local level. Black Workers for Justice activists, for instance, questioned why SEIU staffers in Washington, DC, pulled the plug on a drive to organize some two thousand service workers at the Atlanta airport in May 1996 without consulting the workers themselves. Organizing for a movement, they wrote in October 1996, "must be *different* and not just new."[51]

No More Business Unionism as Usual

New union members were not the only ones who felt this polyester ceiling's weight bearing down on them. Rank-and-file activists had long pondered the problem of top-down control and the bureaucratic inflexibility that came with it—the extent of which differed widely between unions, and even within the same union. In the 1970s, democratic reform groups such as Teamsters United Rank and File and Steelworkers Fight Back fought for change within trade unions. In the late '80s within several AFL-CIO unions, antibureaucratic movements such as Teamsters for a Democratic Union and the UAW's New Directions were gaining speed. Sweeney's own SEIU had an active reform group, Service Employees for Democratic Reform, which worked for increased democracy and an end to corruption within the union, such as double-dipping on union salaries and monitoring op-position activists.[52]

Union reformers and their allies argued not only for democratic control by members but also for increased gender and racial diversity among union leadership at all levels. During the 1995 AFL-CIO election, union activists questioned both the Donahue and Sweeney election slates' commitment to diversity, pointing to the federation's ruling executive council, where twenty-nine of thirty-three positions were held by white men, "all middle-aged to elderly," and challenged the lack of a substantive proposal from either side to remedy the situation.[53] Labor activists had put forward proposals to greatly expand the size of the elected council so it could be more representative of diverse communities, as well as proposals for direct elections of AFL-CIO representatives.[54] The Coalition of Black Trade Unionists endorsed neither slate, giving both low scores on their efforts to include women and people of color, and criticized Sweeney for creating a new position for AFSCME's Linda Chavez-Thompson—a Latina— instead of nominating her for one of the two existing top posts.[55]

Since the 1990s, challenges to bureaucratic control within AFL-CIO unions have been regular occurances, and often include critiques of racial and gender hierarchy, especially in unions where women and people of color predominate. Three examples serve to illustrate this, some white collar and some blue collar, but all occurring within national unions that officially backed the "new" AFL-CIO.

In one of the more numerically significant actions of the '90s, local union leadership at the huge nine-campus University of California system rebelled against a hierarchical AFSCME council and national union structure that took more than 90 percent of their dues but refused to provide resources for organizing campaigns in the difficult "open shop" of the university workplace. Activists had originally affiliated with AFSCME back in 1967, when they perceived it as the leading edge of social justice unionism, but by the '80s, rank-and-file female leadership saw the male "suits" in Washington, DC, as the primary obstacle to successful organizing. In 1990, one group of activists broke with AFSCME to form the University Professional and Technical Employees (UPTE, which affiliated with CWA in 1993). By 1997 they had racked up a string of representational elections for some fifteen thousand workers in several major bargaining units. UPTE had adopted CWA's one-on-one organizing model and built a strong union run by its members, putting it in a healthy place to win a difficult but historic fight to preserve the single-tier pension at the university in 2013.[56]

In 1997, activists frustrated with the lack of organizing assistance in another University of California bargaining unit of some eighteen thousand clerical and administrative workers—overwhelmingly female—left AFSCME to found the Coalition of University Employees (CUE). In a state-run recertification election, workers voted by a more than two-to-one margin to decertify AFSCME as their collective bargaining agent and simultaneously to certify the new independent union. It was one of the largest such actions in decades. All the more remarkable, the campaign was conducted almost entirely without paid staff and under the direction of a loose network of organizing collectives at each campus.[57]

Over the next few years, CUE organized thousands of new members, worked in campus coalitions, and held a series of successful strikes over bargaining issues.[58] But after thirteen years of independence, CUE's internal structure began to weaken. Little attention was being given to training new activists or keeping locals viable, and membership fell to historic lows. By 2010 an internal struggle on CUE's executive board became externalized in the form of an new affiliation battle. Three unions—AFSCME, CWA, and the Teamsters—competed to affililate CUE, an independent union. An army of paid Teamsters organizers fanned out across the multicampus system, undercutting the slower one-on-one organizing by CUE members. The Teamsters' victory gained them a gigantic new unit, complete with a treasure trove of agency shop dues. The national union then quickly imposed a trusteeship over the protests of members, "with officers operating in a shroud of secrecy," according to Teamsters for a Democratic Union, a union reform group.[59] Campus locals were merged into less accessible regional councils, while university management continued on a path of pension and benefits cuts.

Even with SEIU's better track record of organizing, a similar dynamic around democracy played out in SEIU's Justice for Janitors campaign. That drive had brought tens of thousands of rank-and-file janitors—many of them Mexican, Central American, and African American—into the union in the late '80s and early '90s. Many of those new members were in SEIU's Local 399 in Los Angeles, one of the largest union locals in the state with some twenty-five thousand members. The local's tactics had drawn on the militance of the largely immigrant workforce, filled with workers who, as journalist David Bacon wrote, had "faced down government terror in El Salvador or Guatemala . . . workers who learned, as children in Mexico, that while they have a right to a fair share of the wealth of society, they have to fight to get it."[60] In 1995, critical of what they saw as the local's "old boys' network," Latino/Latina, African American, and white SEIU janitors and health-care workers formed the Multiracial Alliance to run against existing officers in the first contested elections in Local 399's history.[61]

A 120-member mobilization committee spent months talking with voters about the need for democratic reforms and leadership diversity within Local 399, and on June 8, 1995, Multicultural Alliance candidates won all twenty-one contested seats on the executive board in one of the largest election turnouts in the local's history. A showdown shortly ensued with the local's president, whose election had not been challenged by the Multicultural Alliance, when the new officers wanted to fire some of the local's staff, whom they accused of undermining democratic practices in the union. The president refused to fire the staff or allow the new officers to meet in any official capacity. In August 1995, Alliance members launched a twenty-one-day hunger strike outside the union's headquarters in protest. "We built this union," strike leader César Oliva Sanchez told the *Los Angeles Times*. "We want to be able to make the decisions."[62]

In September negotiations broke down; SEIU stepped in and

placed Local 399 in trusteeship for eighteen months, voiding the entire election. "It was chaos, and impossible to function," said Michael Baratz, an SEIU staffer involved in the trusteeship. "We didn't have time for all the internal fighting."[63] But for many rank-and-file members, it was about moving beyond the idea that members were just the frontline troops at demonstrations to building empowerment and democracy in *their* union.

The situation at Local 399 was not unique. Members of SEIU Justice for Janitors locals around the nation—including locals in Washington, DC, San Francisco, San Jose, San Diego, Atlanta, and Providence—encountered similar roadblocks in their attempts to run their own locals. From 1996 through 2004, some forty SEIU locals, or about 14 percent of SEIU affiliates, were forced into trusteeship with newly appointed officers from the national union, usually from outside the units they headed. Even at the peak of the court-ordered cleanup of the Teamsters in the early 1990s, only 10 percent of its locals were put into trusteeship, and this was under a Justice Department indictment for "racketeering."[64]

In San Francisco, SEIU merged its three-thousand-member Local 87 into a larger Bay Area–wide local, saying that the only way to defend janitors against the economic power of the huge contractors employing them was to obtain larger "master" contracts covering more workers. Richard Leung, president of Local 87 for two decades, said the local was already "the crown jewel of the West Coast janitors' unions, with the best contract outside of New York City."[65] When members refused to go along with the merger, the local was put into trusteeship in January 2002.

But for the local's members, the issue was democratic control of the institution they had built. "Instead of making it more responsible to the rank and file," said Leung, "they decided to take the corporate route through merger and acquisition to streamline their operations." SEIU avowed that such consolidations "build industry power" by creating larger, more uniform negotiating entities, but from local activists' perspective, merging locals hands important control over to the national union, since rank-and-file activists lack the resources to run expensive regional or statewide election campaigns, or even travel to more distant meetings where decisions are made. In these geographically dispersed statewide or multistate mega-locals, members end up having less power over bargaining decisions and organizing drives.

Although janitors in other cities made gains, the first round of bargaining with janitorial companies by the new larger local resulted in significant takebacks in benefits for San Francisco janitors.[66] "They're trying to mirror the corporations we bargain with, but we shouldn't be a mirror," according to Olga Miranda, former organizing director of Local 87. "We don't want to look like the corporations we're fighting against." Former Local 87 activists launched a recertification drive to simultaneously decertify SEIU and elect their own independent union, United Service Workers for Democracy, as the bargaining agent for San Francisco janitors. They won the election, held in August 2004, by nearly a two-to-one vote, despite SEIU's attempt to thwart the decert by bringing in large numbers of out-of-town organizers.[67]

During labor's revival, these kinds of situations posed fundamental questions: How were labor's new recruits changing the demographic and political topography of the labor movement? Would those changes translate into more activist unions, and ultimately into more power for the labor movement? If trade unions could simply withdraw financial resources or suspend democracy when new members took control or bureaucratic prerogatives were questioned, how could they convincingly claim to be the grassroots voice of America's workers? For many unionists, democracy was no longer merely an abstract ideal; it was fundamental to the discussion of institutional transformation.

Such talk of union democracy is "too narrow" for others, like Justice for Janitors organizer Stephen Lerner, who argues that the number of workers organized is more important. "If only 10 percent of workers in an industry are unionized it is impossible to have real union democracy because 90 percent of the workers are excluded," Lerner writes.[68] But for many activists, democracy cannot be secondary to organizing. After decades of failed top-down organizing campaigns and increased union bureaucratization, internal union democracy was the key not only to signing up new members but also to getting them active. For them, speaking of democracy as separate from movement strength created an entirely false dichotomy. Their vision was not one of neatly partitioned trade union institutions but one that incorporated the messiness of a movement, with all of its unpredictable energy.

Community Work Is Union Work

Such energy was harnessed in the practical work of creating community-labor coalitions to build a broad-based social justice movement. The AFL-CIO's New Voice election platform had acknowledged in 1995 that union politics "must start in the neighborhoods where our members live and vote."[69] But well before that, forward-thinking union activists had founded Jobs with Justice, an independent nationwide community-labor organization. Its first meeting, on July 29, 1987, in Miami, drew eleven thousand participants, who vowed to stand in solidarity with other labor and social justice struggles as well as their own. Their "I'll Be There" pledge was based on the "old Wobbly principle of 'an injury to one is an injury to all.'"[70] In addition to labor, its affiliates included women's, environmental, consumer, and student groups, as well as civil rights organizations. Jobs with Justice sought to connect workplace and community activism to create a better climate in which to organize.

Much of its work was directed at creating bridges between unions and community people, putting pressure on local antiunion employers, and coordinating national protests, such as one in May 1993 in which over seven thousand demonstrators descended on NLRB offices in twenty-five cities to denounce the board's failure to process unfair labor practice complaints; more than four hundred protesters were arrested. By its tenth anniversary in 1996, Jobs with Justice had thirty local chapters scattered across the nation and the backing of eleven national unions as well as major community groups like ACORN and Citizen Action. It sponsored a "National Day of Action for Welfare/Workfare Justice" on December 10, 1997, with more than eighty organizations in sixty cities participating.[71]

All this was done on a shoestring budget and driven by rank-and-file volunteers in unions and community groups. Jobs with Justice's main sponsoring unions (CWA, the Teamsters, SEIU, AFSCME, and

UNITE) each contributed about $10,000 a year to the organization, and CWA, which has been a prime advocate of the organization, has provided many additional special grants. After Sweeney's New Voice slate took power, the overt hostility that had prevailed between Jobs with Justice and the AFL-CIO during the Kirkland administration diminished markedly. Still, appeals to the new leadership of the AFL-CIO to help fund the organization were only moderately successful—the AFL-CIO donated only $100,000 in 1997 out of a total operating budget of some $95 million. Critics of the AFL-CIO's lack of enthusiasm for Jobs with Justice, such as Suzanne Gordon of *Labor Notes*, said the federation provided little real backing because "it's not a program they initiated, can control, or call their own."[72] Others worried that if the AFL-CIO did adequately fund Jobs with Justice, the organization would lose its independence and its militant edge.[73] Some AFL-CIO leaders were less than supportive of Jobs with Justice because they felt it competed with the federation's Central Labor Council structure, which they had been trying to resurrect from a largely moribund bureaucracy into a geographically based structure for mobilizing demonstrations and strike support.

Throughout the '90s, Jobs with Justice continued to help lay the groundwork for community-based, cooperative organizing in a number of US cities. Workfare unionization efforts, such as those described in chapter 6, accounted for some of these relationships, as did living-wage and affordable-housing campaigns in a dozen or so cities across the nation.[74] But a commonly perceived problem with some of these ad hoc collaborations persisted: trade unions often expected community support without fully reciprocating when community groups called for aid in their struggles.[75] In an attempt to overcome the problem, trade union and community groups launched a few efforts to formalize their partnerships. For instance, in late 1998 in Stamford, Connecticut, community groups and four local unions (UAW, SEIU, Hospital Workers 1199, and HERE) began a wide-ranging campaign for social and economic justice among the city's poor. The AFL-CIO paid the salaries of five full-time staffers to help coordinate the effort. The Stamford project was one of a handful of experiments initiated by the AFL-CIO's own national organizing department, and was successful in many ways, albeit "extremely controversial" among national unions, in part because they believed such projects would divert attention from industrial strategies.[76] But cooperative work such as this, said Kirk Adams, AFL-CIO organizing director at the time, was a necessity for trade unions: "The labor movement understands a little better now that we'll never be strong enough to carry a social agenda by ourselves."[77]

This "new" community-based attitude on the part of the AFL-CIO didn't emerge from thin air; it had deep roots in the work of previous decades. Poor workers and their social-movement union allies within the AFL-CIO advocated by word and deed the idea that the labor movement's relevance in the lives of all workers depended on its ability to facilitate grassroots organizing and democratic institution building that would equally include the large number of poor workers who had been left out in decades past. The collaboration also grew from the simple reality that many activists who got their start in social movements later became rank-and-file members of local unions, bringing new tactics and perspectives to the labor movement. Their "fusion" between labor and social justice movements might well lay the groundwork for the "next upsurge," in Dan Clawson's terms, redefining the face of the labor movement with a burst of expansive growth, much as happened in the 1930s.[78] The revival of militancy stems from the very real and evolving connections between community activists and trade unionists, who despite myriad problems and differences are now closer than they have ever been.

Reviving the Activist Tradition

Organizing methods continued to be a subject of debate at many levels within the federation, even as the AFL-CIO went through four organizing directors in as many years. In June 1998, AFL-CIO organizing department director Richard Bensinger was replaced with the federation's southern regional director Kirk Adams, a former United Labor Unions organizer. By April 2000, Adams himself was out, replaced with the AFL-CIO's West Coast organizing director Mark Splain, who got his start doing community and welfare organizing with Massachusetts Fair Share and the Movement for Economic Justice back in the '70s, before working with United Labor Unions in the early '80s. Former ACORN organizer and Atlanta Central Labor Council president Steward Acuff replaced Splain as organizing director in 2001, serving until 2008.

In October 2000, Bensinger told *Businessweek* that AFL-CIO unions' plans to organize weren't making much headway. "Only a handful of unions have even started down this road," he said. "The truth is, we're still in big trouble and everyone in the labor movement knows it." Bensinger noted that trade unions overall still spent 90 percent of their resources servicing existing members. What little growth there was came largely from a few innovative campaigns, such as SEIU's February 1999 win among home healthcare workers in Los Angeles County, which brought seventy-five thousand workers into the AFL-CIO in the largest union election since the historic autoworker struggles of the early '40s. In 1998 all the AFL-CIO member unions combined had added only one hundred thousand members.[79]

Home health care and "residential care" (nursing homes) are two of the three fastest-growing industries in the United States.[80] The SEIU campaign stemmed directly from the home healthcare organizing of ACORN's United Labor Unions in the mid-'80s. SEIU's California staff had visited SEIU 880 in Chicago, the former United Labor Union's home health care local, to learn its techniques, developing a relationship that continued over the course of the campaign. The California home health care campaign recruited some members through outreach from community-based workers' centers, and it also drew from the Justice for Janitors model of targeting workplaces industrywide with strikes, civil disobedience, and street demonstrations. Several more campaigns followed. By 2015, SEIU represented about 600,000 of the nation's 2.1 million home healthcare workers, the vast majority of them African American and Latina women.[81]

There were a few large private-sector victories, such as the ten thousand US Airways workers who won CWA representation in August 1999. The campaign was member-run, with rank-and-file activists participating in every aspect of the organizing drive against an intensely antiunion employer. An organizing committee of several hundred workers conducted one-on-one meetings with their fellow workers, laying a solid base for the union's successful contract negotiations after the election was won. CWA used the same strategy in a southern regional organizing campaign at telecommunications giant Cingular Wireless. The union trained member organizers to reach out to their coworkers, and after the drive's start in late 2001, some fifteen thousand wireless workers joined, almost all in right-to-work states.[82]

The Hotel Employees and Restaurant Employees (HERE) also launched major organizing campaigns, mostly notably in Las Vegas, where thousands of food service and hotel workers labored at low-wage jobs. Direct-action tactics were common. For instance, when the antiunion Ark Restaurants Corporation fired eight activists for organizing their coworkers, HERE held a "sip-in" at the restaurant, in which hundreds of union members clogged business by ordering only water and staying to drink it for hours. The "sip-in" harked back to the successful "shop-in" tactic CORE employed in the '60s. Some ten thousand unionists and their supporters then marched on the hotel to demand union recognition for the restaurant's workers.[83]

Labor historians now refer to the leadership of the trade union movement post-1995 as "New Labor," so sharp was its break with the old. But even with these new campaigns, there was little growth overall for the trade union movement. The gains did not keep pace with employee turnover and the growth of new, nonunionized jobs. For instance, only nine unions added more than five thousand new members in 2002, among them the American Federation of Teachers, AFSCME, SEIU, and CWA. Overall union membership continued its steady erosion, falling from 14.1 percent in 1997 to 12.9 percent in 2003. In raw numbers, AFL-CIO membership actually dropped by nearly half a million members during Sweeney's first eight years in office.[84]

At the AFL-CIO's 2003 organizing summit, participants gathered to take stock of the Sweeney administration's years of urging unions to "organize, organize, organize." While more resources were being devoted to campaigns, "some unions—SEIU, UNITE, HERE and AFSCME—still fervently believe in 'staffing up,'" observed attendee Steve Early. "By hiring, training, and rapidly deploying large crews of full-time organizers and researchers—often recruited from outside their own ranks—they approach the 'challenge of growth' like a corporation retooling its sales force."[85]

Upping Labor's Market Share

In September 2003 the Sweeney administration came under fire from a new group of reformers who thought such restructuring was key. Five national union presidents—Andy Stern of SEIU, John Wilhelm of HERE, Bruce Raynor of UNITE, Terrance O'Sullivan of the Laborers' Union, and Doug McCarron of the Carpenters' Union—unveiled their challenge to the Sweeney administration before the 2005 AFL-CIO elections: the New Unity Partnership (NUP). Reminiscent of SEIU's large-scale merging of locals, the NUP plan called for drastically consolidating the federation's sixty-plus unions into twelve to fifteen larger ones, carving out new jurisdictional lines and instituting a "strategic growth plan." Instead of what the NUP called "general unions," where any group of workers could approach any union for organizing help, it advocated "industry-focused unions," which would represent only workers in the same industries, giving them a bigger market share.[86] This reorganization, the theory went, would build union density (the percentage of organized workers in each industry), handing unions more bargaining clout. Unions would swap locals, if need be, to achieve the correct industry alignments.

Activists welcomed the debate but raised critical questions about the NUP strategy as well as issues of democracy. Who would decide where to draw the new jurisdictions, and would such changes enhance unions' ability to organize? Would strict adherence to industrial lines even be desirable in building a movement, the nature of which crosses boundaries and creates horizontal linkages at both the workplace and community levels? Poor workers' history tends to support a more expansive formation than a narrow, industrially based one. Commitment to broader goals like the right to organize promised to get short shrift if industrially focused organizing was prioritized. Those who worked for smaller employers—like many of the poor workers covered in this book—might find it even harder to attract unions' attention if they were concentrating on larger workplaces.

As JoAnn Wypijewski observed in her critique of the NUP plan, "Unions have to be more than columns of numbers, grouped by industry sector."[87] Workers organize with a particular union for many reasons, including organizing philosophy, political perspective, local connections, or because the union to which they logically should belong isn't interested in organizing them. And while industry-based campaigns can make good sense, union density hasn't historically always equaled power, as is obvious from the case of union workers in other countries like Mexico, who have great density but low wages, or the opposite case of France, where workers have high union density and a lot of economic power but are split into many unions.

Several unions and other labor groups responded to the NUP plan with alternative proposals to revive the movement. CWA activists were among the most vocal critics of the NUP's proposed restructuring, advocating instead that unions focus their energies on expanding the right to organize and on developing their social vision and activist base. Collective bargaining is a "public good," and fighting for it "positions us to appeal for public support based on gains that are good for everyone," declared Larry Cohen, who was CWA's executive vice president at the time. According to Cohen, unions needed to fortify their strike funds to guarantee workers support during walkouts and build stronger networks of shop stewards, the frontline troops of the labor movement who play crucial roles in organizing and political action. Above all, they should not, in the name of "density-driven restructuring," dictate which unions workers can join. To do so, Cohen wrote, would mean "losing any public debate about collective bargaining being an essential element of a democratic workplace."[88]

An open letter from the presidents of twelve AFL-CIO Central Labor Councils cautioned that change at the national level wouldn't succeed without stronger regional movements rooted in community-labor coalitions. The nation's Central Labor Councils, they wrote, should become "truly representative structures," throwing open their doors to "community groups, minority unions, and non-AFL-CIO unions. Exclusivity is a luxury union members can no longer afford."[89]

There was concern about how much control, under the NUP plan, workers themselves would have had in choosing who would represent them. The NUP's architects went forward with a high degree of secrecy. Two of the NUP's unions, UNITE and HERE, had already merged without giving their membership a vote in the matter,[90] and indeed rank-and-file members "played no major role in the development of positions or directions for the unions. Communication travelled one way, from the top to the bottom," wrote Bill Fletcher Jr. and Fernando Gapasin in their excellent study *Solidarity Divided*, which covered the transformation.[91] The NUP's "left-right alliance" was also troubling: the Carpenters' McCarron was a Republican close to George W. Bush and leaked NUP documents indicated a willingness to work with antiunion politicians in the Bush administration, including key strategist Karl Rove. In 2003 SEIU's Stern, HERE's Wilhelm, and the Laborers' O'Sullivan urged unionists to "follow their example by giving $1,000 or more" to the reelection campaign of Republican House Speaker Dennis Hastert, and their unions also bought tables at a Republican congressional campaign dinner.[92]

Low-wage workers and immigrants made up a good part of most of the NUP member unions, but the NUP's planners seemed to have a limited vision of their role in running a reorganized AFL-CIO. The NUP's initial plans called for power to reside in "chief operating officers," who would not be elected by members but appointed by the national leadership. State- and city-based AFL-CIO formations, like Central Labor Councils, would have lost all autonomy: delegates would have been appointed by national unions and funding controlled by the AFL-CIO.

But just as the debate was heating up, in January 2005 the NUP suddenly disbanded itself, even while its leaders promised to continue advocating for its vision of large-scale restructuring. Publicly, NUP leaders said the partnership had "served its purpose" in jump-starting discussion, but political differences among the NUP unions—particularly over whether or not to leave the AFL-CIO—also played a role in the dissolution.[93]

The NUP echoed the structure of trade unions' past, a "combination of old AFL conservatism with its strictly assigned jurisdiction," writes activist Herman Benson, "and the old radical industrial unionism with its imaginary unions concocted out of wheels and charts."[94] The NUP ended up more like the short-lived Alliance for Labor Action of the 1970s—top-down, obsessed with numbers, and lacking a broad base.

In 2005 the NUP formally dissolved and its five member unions, along with the Teamsters and the UFCW, created a new alliance, Change to Win. The new organization's leaders put it forward as an alternative to the AFL-CIO and pledged to spend 75 percent of its resources organizing the unorganized. But just three years later, as an internal feud erupted in SEIU, resulting in the trusteeship of its third largest local, and SEIU went to war with its ally UNITE HERE, the coalition swiftly began to disintegrate. Over the next four years, four of the seven member unions left the coalition to rejoin the AFL-CIO.[95]

The new alliances' backers liked to compare them to the CIO's industrial organizing in the 1930s, '40s, and '50s, but that was largely driven by a revolution from below, whereas the NUP and Change to Win came from the minds of five highly placed union staffers. "Real change in this country has never happened because of a few smart guys," notes Wypijewski. "It took at least fifty years for workers to figure out industrial organizing," she writes, "[and] when it finally had lift-off it was part of a mass movement. In the meantime locals developed, as the name implies, locally, through a combination of job actions, mutual aid, cultural activities, political education, party activity, target practice, newspapers, picnics, the warp and woof of life."[96]

Managerial efficiency was high on the NUP and Change to Win agendas, driven by a desire to straighten the lines of labor's historically overlapping institutions or, as the NUP's founders called it, creating "a united movement with discipline and accountability" instead of the existing federation of autonomous affiliates, each with its own political and strategic tactics. But bigger is not always better. Centralization and bureaucratization have historically gone hand in hand, and contributed not to labor's revival but to its slow death. Swallowing up small unions into larger ones promised to reduce variation and with it innovation, leaving labor's institutions more bureaucratically rationalized but likely less able to creatively cope with capital's challenges.

AFL-CIO Opens Its Doors

Neither the Sweeney-led AFL-CIO or its critics succeeded in enlarging the universe of workers under union protection. Union membership numbers continued to drop, sinking to 11.1 percent of the workforce by 2014.[97] Still, traditional trade unions' views of the larger working class slowly underwent an evolution over the next decade, and increasing numbers of victories were won by community-labor coalition building. A deeper understanding of the interrelationship of class, race, ethnicity, gender, and sexuality pushed the union movement toward advocating for broader economic and social justice issues rather than limiting itself to only contractual or workplace issues. "Not only does class go beyond employer versus employee," wrote Fletcher and Gapasin, "it is also about more than bargaining units, collections of bargaining units, or even sectors of the economy. Class speaks to the relationship of individuals and groups of individuals to the production process and power. As such, twenty-first century unionism must recognize that struggles beyond the workplace are as legitimate as struggles within the workplace."[98]

By August 2006 the AFL-CIO had signed a "partnership" agreement with the National Day Laborer Organizing Network (NDLON), following a decision by the fifty-three-union federation that it would institute formal ties with workers' centers.[99] In 2009 former United Mine Workers president Richard Trumka, who had served as AFL-CIO secretary-treasurer from 1995 to 2009, was elected to head the federation. Trumka told the National Press Club in 2010 that trade unions could not "win economic justice only for ourselves, for union members alone. It would not be right and it's not possible. All working people will rise together, or we will keep falling together."[100]

By the AFL-CIO's 2013 convention, the press was abuzz with news that the organization was finally making widespread connections with poor workers' unionism—fashionably titled "alt-labor"—from immigrant workers to Walmart activists to fast-food employees. And not a moment too soon, wrote Josh Eidelson, as "labor's perceived and often real estrangement from causes (and communities) beyond current union members' compensation has fueled its isolation and vulnerability."[101] The AFL-CIO's move opened up real possibilities for enlarging the labor movement, by helping to organize the unorganized into unions, as well as expand community support for union struggles.

"This convention marked a long overdue strategic shift," wrote activists Jeff Crosby and Bill Fletcher Jr. "The shift is to speak for the whole working class. . . . [Labor] recognized that there is no way forward for current members without a re-direction of the movement, to construct an alliance of working class forces and allies to change the country."[102] The president of the New York Taxi Drivers' Alliance joined the AFL-CIO executive council. Critical voices pointed out the danger of merely adding members on paper rather than actually creating a sound infrastructure for organizing, or championing alliances without making them real and useful.[103] But most labor activists and observers welcomed the development. "Having banged its head against a wall for years with nothing to show for it but a headache," labor commentator Harold Meyerson wrote, "the American labor movement is devising a plan to bypass the wall altogether."[104]

Labor and Community Fighting Back

The AFL-CIO was responding not only to the numbers of independent poor workers organizing but also the work of its own rank-and-file members, many of whom had waged labor fights with deep community support or connections to poor workers' unions. While some of these coalitional struggles took place in the embattled public sector, others occurred among the vast, mostly unorganized private service sector.

In February 2011, the war on public services and education came to a head when Wisconsin governor Scott Walker set out to destroy union bargaining rights and dues collection systems for state, county, and municipal employees and teachers, provoking a historic uprising with up to 150,000 marching on the state's capitol. Seemingly every progressive group in the state showed up in support—from the Wisconsin Farmers Union, which fired up fifty tractors for a march, to graduate students at the University of Wisconsin, Madison, to African American and Latino high school students.[105] Following tactics embraced by the right wing after Barack Obama was elected US president in 2008, Wisconsin legislators' attacks were part of a broad narrative aimed at both public workers and social service recipients, alleging that they were "stealing" benefits from taxpayers. While Walker and his right-wing colleagues were legislatively victorious, the Wisconsin labor movement was strengthened and enlarged by the coalitions that were created during the fightback.

The attacks on public-sector workers in Wisconsin and elsewhere hit at trade unionism's heart. Union membership in the public sector had remained remarkably stable since 1979 at about 35 to 37 percent. In 2014, public sector union membership stood at 35.7 percent, more than five times higher than the rate for private-sector workers of only 6.6 percent in that year.[106]

Likewise, the landmark 2012 Chicago Teachers Union strike was built on community solidarity and democratic rank-and-file activism. The twenty-six-thousand-member organization was transformed from a staid, bureaucratic union to an activist one after the Caucus of Rank-and-File Educators was elected to leadership positions in 2010. The union's new leadership decided to take on more than workplace issues. "The union made publicly funded corporate subsidies, most notably through the city's Tax Incremental Financing [TIF] system, a major issue," wrote labor journalist Micah Uetricht, "and worked alongside community groups and other unions to expand the CTU's organizing to include the issue of austerity for poor neighborhoods of color throughout the city." Teachers themselves were "carrying out the union's broad agenda for educational justice," convincing students and parents to support the cause.[107]

Nationally, adjunct faculty members at colleges and universities are one of the biggest new groups organizing via community-labor coalitions. "Tens of thousands of them have won organizing drives in the past couple of years, and hundreds of thousands more are ripe for replicating those successes," wrote Lance Compa in the *American Prospect* in 2015.[108] In the previous two decades, colleges and universities had begun shifting the work of teaching to temporary academic workers, so that contingent faculty now make up the majority of faculty in US higher education. Doing essentially the same work as full professors, these "freeway flyers" may have elite job titles, but their wages and working conditions resemble those of poor workers, with multiple part-time workplaces and wages so low they qualify for food stamps.

Unions have conducted large nontraditional campaigns in the private sector as well, such as SEIU's Fight for 15, which began in November 2012, when about two hundred New York City fast-food workers walked off their jobs.[109] The campaign was a coordinated effort in ten states by SEIU, which funded it as part of its backing for Barack Obama's presidential run in 2012.[110] By spring 2013, fast-food and retail workers had taken job actions in New York, Chicago, St. Louis, Milwaukee, Detroit and Seattle. A second week of one-day strikes followed that July, writes activist Trish Kahle, then a worker at Whole Foods and a member of the SEIU-backed Workers Organizing Committee of Chicago, and "on August 29, sixty-two cities and more than one thousand workers struck around two principal demands: $15 an hour minimum wage and the right to form a union without retaliation."[111] In September 2014, workers walked off the job in 150 cities nationwide; nearly five hundred fast-food workers and supporters were arrested, some as they sat in at their places of employment and sang civil rights songs.[112]

The movement spread to over two hundred cities on April 15, 2015, and with a reported sixty thousand workers taking part, the *Guardian* called it the "largest protest by low-wage workers in US history," as it expanded to include "home care assistants, Walmart workers, child-care aides, airport workers, adjunct professors and other low wage workers."[113] The demonstrations fueled a national debate on the minimum wage and income inequality as US president Barack Obama and many progressive politicians came out in favor of a $15 minimum; even a few Republican 2016 presidential candidates backed the idea. The $15 wage proposal faced stiff opposition from business groups, who claimed that raising wages would cause consumer price increases and worker layoffs, although economic studies on the effects of wage increases did not back up their dire predictions.[114]

Seattle, San Francisco, and Los Angeles adopted a phased-in $15 minimum to begin in 2015, and a state panel appointed by New York's governor recommended a $15 minimum wage to cover 180,000 fast-food workers, to be phased in over six years.[115] The huge University of California system, the second-largest employer in that state, adopted a $15-per-hour minimum wage.[116] Other cities and states were considering similar policy changes.

Using a tactic of "minority unionism" whereby activists organize a core group and its supporters to advocate for demands, the SEIU-backed campaign had produced tangible results after three years of organizing and publicity. Some say the Fight for 15 is *mostly* a publicity campaign, bankrolled by SEIU without much rank-and-file involvement (except in its Chicago local, which by most accounts was quite activist-driven). It's clear that SEIU pours millions into the campaign, hiring several high-power communications consultants who have created a "media frenzy" around the strike events, writes *In These Times*' Arun Gupta.[117] Fight for 15 activist Kahle acknowledges the criticism of SEIU's role but gives the union credit for opening up "space" that may have "possibilities far beyond what organizers and even workers ourselves have imagined." Fight for 15, she writes, is "social movement unionism in embryo. . . . The Left needs to move beyond conceptualizing workers' institutions like SEIU as monoliths incapable of change. It's difficult to change them, but not impossible."[118]

The AFL-CIO's transformation over recent decades has been uneven. It is important to remember that the federation is a tenuous collection of its affiliate unions, only some of which have taken the organizing path. Others are declining and dysfunctional, more focused on retaining or "servicing" current members and less interested in movement building. Changes have come from the bottom up—originating from locals—but also from the top down, as the federation itself has tried to institute broad ideological and structural changes among its members.

Still, many AFL-CIO trade unions have come around to a deeper understanding of the importance of a more broadly conceived labor movement, even if their organizing projects have not yet produced the numbers required for movement revival. At its 2013 convention, the change in thinking was epitomized by the slogan of American Federation of Teachers president Randi Weingarten, "Community is the new density!"[119] In a movement in which "density" was always defined numerically, by the number of union members in an industry, this represents a real paradigm shift.

Such ideological changes are crucial to expanding labor's reach and relevance. But institutional bureaucracy remains a structural fact in most unions and in the AFL-CIO, creating a huge stumbling block for building a movement that can successfully confront continuing attacks on working people's rights. Whatever direction trade union institutions decide to take in reinventing themselves, resources spent building labor's activist base to transform those structural impediments are essential to its health. Democratic, rank-and-file activism is as crucial as ever to reversing the dynamic of movement decline.

Jose Villareal, a worker from Los Angeles, at the rally that capped the historic Immigrant Workers' Freedom Ride, October 2003. *(Photo by Peter Holderness)*

Conclusion

Imagining a New Movement

A crowd of one hundred thousand spread out across New York's Flushing Meadows on October 4, 2004, to welcome busloads of "freedom riders" converging from ten cities across the nation. "We are all immigrants," read large handmade signs in the crowd. Others, lettered in bright red, orange, and green, insisted, "No human being is illegal!" Some participants wore "I am a man" T-shirts, commemorating the 1968 Memphis sanitation workers' strike, or held crosses in the Central American tradition, bearing names of friends and relatives who had died on the job or crossing the border. They had come as part of a new civil rights movement.

The day marked the end of a three-week cross-country collective act of resistance called the Immigrant Workers' Freedom Ride, in which over a thousand participants of some fifty nationalities had traveled thousands of miles to demand equality for immigrants—both as workers on the job and as community members targeted in the wave of post-9/11 immigration hysteria. Stopping in over one hundred cities along the way, the freedom riders had held rallies, walked picket lines, and met with legislators to build support for immigrants' civil and workplace rights. Under the Patriot Act, some risked arrest or deportation merely by going on the ride. Riders on the southern leg of the cross-country journey were detained at a DHS checkpoint near

El Paso, only to be released when supporters flooded the agency with protest calls.

Most of the freedom riders were union members. Rider Julie Quiroz-Martínez, writing in *The Nation*, recalled "an Afghan homecare worker on my right, a Chinese hotel housekeeper on my left, an African American custodian in the seat ahead." Some were new to the labor movement; others were longtime activists in their locals, like Doretha, a Black woman and union steward in a predominantly immigrant workplace. "It took me a long time to get it," Doretha confessed. "The way they treat immigrants is how they treated us in the sixties."[1]

Modeled on the freedom rides of the '60s, which challenged segregation in the South, the event was intended to honor that history and connect the struggles of civil rights movements past and present. Its goal was to make the struggles of immigrant workers more visible, encouraging them to see unions as their allies, and to advocate for legal changes such as amnesty for undocumented immigrants. The ride had been conceived by AFL-CIO affiliate HERE but soon gained the support of many trade unions, religious and community groups, and immigrants' rights organizations. Initially skeptical, community-based groups joined the planning process only after trade unions agreed to share power in an equal partnership.[2] The Immigrant Workers' Freedom Ride gives a glimpse of what a renewed labor movement looks like with poor workers included as equal partners, and with a deep commitment to social justice guiding its practice.

Incubating the Revolution

As independent poor workers' unions have evolved over the decades, they have provided distinctive examples of social movement unionism, as well as real-life examples of how workers organize themselves. What can their histories teach activists in today's movements? These unions serve as incubators of the idea that labor movement organizing should address all the issues in workers' lives, not only those in the workplace, and should include all workers, not just those in industries where trade unions already exist. They have helped promote a different logic for the labor movement, built on a broader conception of

work and workers and on a deeper understanding of how racial, ethnic, and gender equality manifests itself within working-class institutions and movements.

The poor workers' unions we've examined here are rooted in
community-based movements for change. Their vision entails a real
commitment to democracy and diversity and includes such needs as
fair welfare, affordable public housing, tenants' rights, health care,
childcare, safe neighborhoods, and public transportation. Struggles
are not won without community support and involvement, nor without engagement with key social problems in workers' communities.

Poor workers' unions exhibit a melding of social movement and
workplace union characteristics. Class is only one element in the construction of these unions; race, gender, and ethnicity equally shape
their struggles for social change. They take for granted the insepara-
bility of economic and political demands and often consciously link
cultural and material politics. Growing primarily out of communities
of color and of immigrants, their struggles against racism, sexism, and
anti-immigrant discrimination and their visions for large-scale social
change are central to their campaigns.

The post–World War II trade union movement, with a few exceptions, had separated itself from popular movements during the
'60s and '70s, at least on an official level. Trade unions were mostly
perceived as self-interested, with little concern for building bridges to
movements representing nonunionized workers. Several independent
poor workers' unions (such as the civil rights and working women's
groups, the Distributive Workers, internal union caucuses, and workers' centers) came into being in reaction to that exclusion. The ten-
dency to reject rather than embody solidarity is still alive in some trade
unions, even—as we saw with the dilemmas over workfare unionization in the '90s, described in chapter 6—within what are widely considered progressive unions.

Poor workers, on the other hand, have advocated the idea, both in
words and in action, that there is a different way to build the labor movement, one that is based on inclusive social justice principles and that
aims to increase not only membership numbers but also democratic activist involvement. Trade unions' neglect of new organizing has gone

hand in hand with an overreliance on legal maneuvers and large staffs paid to manage grievances, keep the labor peace, and, in the lexicon of business agents, "service the unit." Rank-and-file activists, by contrast, are the center of poor workers' unions and nurture a culture of inclusion and solidarity—with fellow workers, community allies, and other unions—that is fundamental to their organizing philosophy. Community-based worker organizations value above all else the cultivation of movement energy—demonstrations, sit-ins, one-on-one organizing, and collective actions of all sorts—which they believe generates a more powerful force for social change than legal or procedural appeals.

Poor workers' unions have targeted low-wage occupations that employ a transient workforce, workers who could at times be found in the welfare office or standing in line to pick up unemployment checks. Organizing strategies have to be different to reach workers who move from job to job in this largely contingent and often informal economy. Campaigns have often had regional or cross-industry aspects, such as the organizing of private-household workers and hotel workers together in New Orleans by United Labor Unions, or targeted the community's poorest workers across the board rather than just those at a particular worksite, in the Chinese Staff and Workers Association model. Poor workers' unions successfully use a wide range of organizing tactics among populations that most trade unions have regarded as unorganizable.

Success, however, cannot always be gauged by traditional measures. While some poor workers' unions (such as the Distributive Workers of America, 9to5, the Rhode Island Workers Union, and ACORN's United Labor Unions) signed up thousands of workers in representational campaigns and eventually obtained contracts to cover them, others (such as the independent workers' centers) often have smaller memberships yet still play powerful roles in their communities.

Born in the social upheavals of the '60s, poor workers' unionism has survived through many decades in part because efforts to create lasting and flexible institutions worked. The existence of poor workers' unions no longer relies on spontaneous movement-based protest; those that survived have flexible, small-scale organizational forms that allow for organizing to continue even with a transient membership base. Poor workers' unions have evolved into a diverse group, existing on a continuum from community-based organizing centers with loose structures to organizations that have adopted the basic institutional outlines of trade unions. Some, such as the Distributive Workers, Rhode Island Workers Union, and United Labor Unions, entered the mainstream through affiliation with the AFL-CIO, helping broaden the federation and the kinds of workers it represented. The organizations that have affiliated tend to be those that most resemble progressive trade unions. While broadly community-based, their central methods—maintaining worker solidarity, holding workplace elections, taking direct action on the job—primarily target the workplace. In general, the closer they have moved to traditional union forms, the further they have traveled from contingent, welfare, and unemployed organizing. Their institutional structures mirror the AFL-CIO unions they have merged into, complete with constitutions, executive boards, dues schedules, and meetings governed by Robert's Rules of Order.

Other poor workers' unions, such as the workers' centers and workfare unions, have pursued different strategies. Some see even progressive trade-union structures as incompatible with their mission of creating primarily community-oriented organizations for economic justice among the poor, the unemployed, low-wage workers, welfare recipients, and immigrants. These poor workers' unions have also tended to favor a greater diversity of methods, including activities not directly tied to employment, such as language and educational programs or assistance with housing and health needs. Like other poor workers' unions, the workers' centers and workfare unions are highly democratic but are not necessarily modeled after trade union structures. Instead they are run as membership-based organizations, worker collectives, or nonprofit organizations with boards of directors drawn from the community. Trade unions generally have not expressed interest in affiliating such groups, seeing their work as too different from trade union organizing. However, tentative collaborations on joint campaigns between these poor workers' groups and trade unions are occurring more frequently and with some success.

Whether they venture into or remain outside the AFL-CIO, however, poor workers' unions have collectively affected the course of the labor movement, pushing it toward a broader conception of itself both politically and organizationally. For this reason, the history of poor workers' organizing is integral to a complete understanding of the US labor movement, in terms of both where it has been and where it is headed. With their various organizational forms, poor workers' unions collectively represent a vital democratic force pushing to organize and strengthen the labor movement from below.

Toward a Local and Global Economic Justice Movement

Poor workers' unions closely resemble other grassroots organizations around the world that operate at both local and global levels. Trade unions, too, have long attempted to put together transnational networks that can uproot corporate capital. This kind of decentralized organizing can often challenge power effectively from below, throwing big bureaucratic institutions off balance or weakening the footing of corporate capital with creative actions.[3] Antipoverty, welfare, civil rights, and feminist activists since the late 1960s visualized and put into practice a broad movement for economic justice, and this movement has remained at the center of an evolving poor workers' unionism ever since.

During roughly the same period a growing global movement for democracy and against economic exploitation became visible in myriad organizations around the world that resemble poor workers' unions in the United States. A few examples of these include India's Self-Employed Women's Association (representing some one million street laborers and contingent workers who are not organized by mainstream Indian trade unions), organizations of tens of thousands of farmers protesting corporate and state destruction of their livelihoods in South American rainforests and South Asian forests and river valleys, and Brazil's Workers' Party, whose work unites traditional class-based economic issues with demands for environmental rights and racial equity.[4] Principles of economic and environmental justice were explicitly taken up in 1999 by top AFL-CIO leadership in opposition to World Trade Organization policies—a global cause for which US trade unionists turned out by the tens of thousands in Seattle. Since 2001 a wide variety of social justice organizations has met annually at the global World Social Forum to continue the collaboration.

Many of these struggles exhibit a strong sense of transnational solidarity against global capital and an understanding of how larger economic transformations affect local communities. Others are remarkably local, organizing against smaller-scale day-to-day economic oppression coming from the more "traditional" quarters of local and national capital. Poor workers' unions in the United States—many of which organize among service-sector workers whose jobs are unlikely to be shipped overseas—usually fall into the latter category. Still, while "acting locally" they also "think globally," as when the Chinese Staff and Workers' Association assisted garment workers in the late '80s, or young United Labor Unions activists took on multinationals like Burger King, McDonald's, and Hyatt in the late '70s. But no matter what the focus—multinational, national, or local capital—poor workers' tactics of bottom-up organizing and solidarity have been strikingly similar.

Their organizing is also qualitatively different from narrow class-based organizing: it consciously confronts environmental, cultural, racial, and gender oppression along with economic concerns. This kind of multilayered organizing forces us to pay closer attention to the ways class conflicts actually take place in everyday life and how such conflicts are bound up with, and often inseparable from, other types of oppression.[5] Aiming to enlarge the sphere of the political to encompass daily life, this organizing also attempts to consolidate a diffuse and democratic power capable of effectively challenging injustice and oppression.

Within the labor movement, progressive trade unions are increasingly reaching out across borders, either with joint organizing campaigns or in solidarity with workers' struggles abroad.[6] Poor workers have also begun building bridges to each other, both locally and globally, through regular dialogue and exchanges of activists. There are multiple networks of workers' centers and like-minded organizations that meet to discuss strategy and plan joint actions. For instance, activists in Los Angeles formed the Multi-Ethnic Workers Organizing Network in 1999 to collaborate on joint organizing, and in 2010 poor workers' organizations from coast to coast launched a federation called the United Workers Congress. San Francisco's POWER developed ongoing relationships with the Congress of South African Trade Unions, and considered collaborating in campaigns against transnational corporations, such as Citibank, that profit from electricity deregulation in Soweto and from welfare privatization in San Francisco.[7]

Many AFL-CIO unions have robust international connections. As sociologist Peter Evans notes, "Much more than other transnational social movements, the global labor movement is a set of historically layered organizational and institutional forms going back at least 150 years."[8] CWA has done extensive transnational movement building, winning accolades from the International Labor Rights Forum for its work with Brazil's largest union federation and its strong relationship with Germany's largest union, ver.di, with which it has worked to pressure Deutsche Telekom to respect workers' rights in the key international sector of telecommunications.[9] The UAW, the United Steelworkers of America, and SEIU have carried out other notable transnational campaigns.[10] Expanding transnational cooperation with other grassroots organizations, the US labor movement stands to grow stronger in its confrontations with corporate economic exploitation at home and abroad.

Organizing a Divided Movement

The social movement–based economic initiatives of the 1960s and early '70s came into being within a relatively strong US economy, which fueled rising expectations. In the early '70s, however, the numbers of working poor began to grow as the economy slid into recession. Many poor workers simply did not have full access to the institutional vehicles—trade unions—that they might have used to organize protections against the downturn. However, doors were opening within mass-based social movements. Social justice organizing encouraged a heightened consciousness of racial and gender discrimination in all sectors of society, including the many institutions of the working class. Like others in those movements, poor workers saw the need to create new institutions and alternative cultures that would support their communities. The economic organizing initiatives for jobs, wages, and equality within the civil rights and women's movements were practical attempts to fill the organizing gap left by a cloistered trade-union movement.

The development of poor workers' organizations merely acknowledges what has long been the case: a discernible division exists within the contemporary labor movement between the organized and unorganized. It is a division rooted in race, ethnicity, gender, and citizenship status as well as in the structure of trade unions, which have historically separated workers by industry and skill. As oppositional movements, poor workers' unions are a counterhegemonic ideological, cultural, and political force that begins to transform that history of division. By offering a reconceptualization of what constitutes a "worker" in both ideology and practice, they encourage a redrawing of the boundaries of the labor movement.

These attempts to erase the conceptual line between the poor and other workers have had far-reaching implications for both workers' consciousness and movement practices. This organizing often leads to profound personal change for those involved in it, bringing new understandings of class oppression and workers' rights to many poor people who had previously seen themselves as outside the working class. On the larger front, this activism makes a unique contribution to the labor movement's sense of itself, demonstrating in a very real way how the movement might further expand to encompass all working people—including workers on unemployment and welfare, and workers whose labor is transient, unwaged, or carried out within the informal economy—by relying on democratic structures and methods of organizing.

Like broad-based labor organizing in the past, these evolving poor workers' unions welcome those outside the traditional boundaries of the factory floor. Their stance is reminiscent of the commitment made by the Knights of Labor to organize all workers, no matter what their place in society, or efforts undertaken by the Industrial Workers of the World to organize workers across industries into one big union. They also resemble the CIO at its best, to the extent that it sought to organize workers across lines of race, ethnicity, and gender. As such, poor workers' unions can be seen as a continuation of these strands in US labor history.

Poor workers' unions also help us reconceptualize the relationship between labor and "other" social movements in the post–World War II period. Just as demands for social equality can inhabit union institutions, so too can labor consciousness reside comfortably within the structures of social justice movements or community organizing. Manning Marable describes how in the 1950s and '60s "the massive efforts waged for desegregation and to a lesser extent, for Black Power, were basically Black workers' movements."[11] The trade union movement of the 1940s and '50s missed its chance to develop into a labor-based civil rights movement,[12] and most of those same institutions in the '60s and '70s missed an opportunity to embrace a social and economic justice agenda that could have convinced poor workers that it spoke for them. Instead that agenda, for much of the last half-century, has been advanced primarily by a disparate array of poor workers' unions.

As with social movements around the world, US movements—for civil, welfare, and women's rights, labor, diversity, and democracy—are closely related to each other by common histories, ideological debates, and questions of strategy, and often by common participants. For many activists the late 1960s and early '70s marked the beginnings of a deep transformation in the labor movement. By building alliances with poor people's movements, community-based activists, and neighborhood organizers, poor workers sowed the seeds for an expansion of independent labor organizing, as well as a revival of community-based tactics within the AFL-CIO.

Movements develop and change in complex yet grounded ways as participants share their experiences and strategies and transition from one movement to another.[13] It is this organic process that leads, along with larger political and economic changes, to evolution in movement institutions. Poor workers' unionism illustrates the integral relationship between labor and other social movements over the past half-century. Like the intricate web of personal and organizational ties in the '50s that laid the groundwork for the civil rights movement's explosion,[14] the renewed interest in social justice unionism within trade unions in the '90s owes much to the long history of independent community-based workers' organizations. The history of poor workers' unions shows how participatory democracy, feminism, and multiculturalism collided with mainstream bureaucratic unionism, pushing the labor movement as a whole toward new organizational forms and a new kind of politics. Their practices offer evidence that erodes the often false boundaries between labor and "other" social movements, boundaries rooted not only in misconceptions about movements but also in definitions of workers.

Inventing the Future

How can the AFL-CIO unions and independent community-based groups move forward with collaborative work and institutional transformation? The 2006 and 2013 AFL-CIO convention moves to welcome and more closely work with community-based labor groups were steps in the right direction, and the hard work is increasingly happening where it needs to, at the local and regional organizational levels.[15] While sharp differences persist between the cultures, politics, and structures of independent poor workers' unions and AFL-CIO unions, the potential for working toward common goals exists in abundance. Trade unions need to acknowledge the organizing work that community-based groups have undertaken for decades. A labor movement that appreciates the uniqueness and creativity of this kind of organizing will tend to encourage beneficial coalitions to flourish. The democratic transformation of labor organizations can succeed only if trade unions and independent poor workers' unions communicate and work side by side, learning from each other and developing the ties of mutual respect that are so important to movement building.

This work must go beyond typical coalition building, in which one side expects only that the other will show up for its rallies or endorse its campaigns. The Immigrant Workers' Freedom Ride exemplifies what is possible with mutual dialogue and sustained cooperation. Community-based organizations and AFL-CIO unions have different institutional structures, constituencies, and organizing cultures.[16] But they also have potential affinities in their talents for one-on-one organizing and principles of solidarity. AFL-CIO unions often excel on the political and legislative front and can bring a measure of institutional and financial stability to organizing campaigns. Community organizations bring extensive experience in bottom-up organizing among disenfranchised and poor people, but they sometimes have a difficult time maintaining stable funding and long-term organizing campaigns. Joint organizing projects hold the potential to radically transform the labor movement by nurturing a different kind of organizing logic—one that builds ties of solidarity between all workers and emphasizes mobilization and direct action. If successful, it may also help trade unions transform their own internal cultures so that activist community-based organizing becomes a greater priority.

Labor activists also need to think creatively about the structure of the labor movement. Harking back to CIO industrialism, some believe the labor movement should pick its battles carefully and focus only on "strategically important" areas or areas of "core strength" like manufacturing, but in the absence of more expansive organizing, this approach might reinforce unionism's already narrow, workplace-based character. While partisans of industrial unionism had hoped since the 1930s to counter the exclusivity of craft unionism, they achieved only limited success with the alternative model of "wall-to-wall" industrial-style organizing. With industrial organizing tactics, union membership has remained concentrated in particular economic sectors and as a result is still effectively split along existing lines of race, gender, skill, and citizenship status.

A more inclusive strategy would focus on the large, growing sectors of the economy dominated by low-wage work. These sectors already account for nearly one-third of all jobs and are projected to expand dramatically during the next decades. Cross-industrial, coalitional campaigns aimed not just at winning representation elections but also at building workers' power in the long run could dramatically improve the labor movement's prospects. If such organizing were successful, it would radically change trade unions into institutions with a more progressive social ideology, a much broader base, and even a different organizational structure. This new membership composition is already becoming visible among trade unions that have undertaken some of the more innovative AFL-CIO campaigns. This membership is not solely worksite or industrially based but "organized geographically along loose occupational lines," notes Howard Wial, and acts "both as an economic pressure group and a social movement."[17]

In the poor workers' movement, where an ideology of social justice has driven its practical social movement–style organizing, this structure has already been in evidence for a time. To transform itself, the labor movement cannot limit changes to style and strategy; it will have to extend them to structure, constituency, and union cultures. As Bill Fletcher Jr. and Richard Hurd note, "As the workforce becomes browner and more female, issues of transformation are not limited to matters of technique and alterations in the bureaucracy, but must address the fundamentals of what constitutes trade unionism." They predict that attempts to organize women and people of color "will not succeed on a grand scale unless there is a coinciding affirmative program to change the face and culture of the labor movement."[18] Organizers and rank-and-file leaders need to do more than reflect the diversity of their membership: they need to come from that more diverse membership and maintain ties to the world of the workers they represent. Poor workers' unions have long thrived on such a model, which builds rank-and-file involvement from the ground up.

Real change within trade unions also requires informed and active members. Winning the numbers game alone won't necessarily save the movement from decline—trade unions must take a hard look at their cultures of participation as well. Union strength and internal democracy are linked, as is clear from study after study showing that rank-and-file organizers build stronger unions. Union members need to be more than troops to mobilize for a street demonstration; they must be activists integral to the movement in all its aspects. They need to own their movement.[19]

Finally, unions must put forward a vision of a just society, where workers strive not only for bread but for roses too. This is what motivates all movements for change, but more than that—it is simply good strategy. Any special interest group can vie for more resources for its members, but a movement with a compelling vision of a more egalitarian society can become a force for major social, economic, and political transformation. If labor hopes to become a new movement in the cause of economic and social justice, its actions must equal its rhetoric. Unions must prioritize issues such as combating discrimination, sponsoring fair tax reform, and securing universal health care, fair welfare policies, a shorter workweek, state-paid childcare, and affordable housing for all workers. Social justice unionism means moving beyond the bargaining table and into the community and the political life of the nation. It also means working for justice within our movement institutions.

Democratic social justice unionism, as practiced both in poor workers' unions and in trade unions, has done much since the 1960s to move labor as a whole toward a renewed vision. It is the brightest possibility for the future of the labor movement. Poor workers' unionists and their allies inside trade unions have kept this bright flame of possibility alive within the labor movement for more than five decades. They have engaged in an extended historical conversation with the rest of the movement about the nature of work, the agency of workers, and the possibilities for movement building. Whether the vision they have put forward will prevail is still an open question. In the meantime, poor worker unionists and their progressive allies will continue to build solidarity wherever they can in preparation for a future in which all workers might be represented. And they will continue to fight for their vision of a more inclusive, democratic, and powerful labor movement.

Cristina Tzintzún, founder of the Workers Defense Project / Proyecto Defensa Laboral, with participants at a "thirst strike" in Dallas, pressuring the city's leaders to guarantee rest breaks to construction workers. Austin has passed a city ordinance requiring such breaks, which are not mandatory in the state of Texas. (*Photo by Jason Cato*)

Afterword

I remember finding *Poor Workers' Unions* back in 2007 at a local bookstore. I had just become the executive director of Workers Defense Project (WDP) at the ripe age of twenty-four. It was a position for which I was highly unqualified at the time and left me desperate to find books, organizations, and mentors from which and whom I could learn. Vanessa Tait's *Poor Workers' Unions* became my new organizing bible.

At the time, WDP was a small workers' center in Austin, Texas, that was focused on combating wage theft for Latino/a immigrant workers, most of whom were construction workers. Our few members and staff of two knew that we wanted our modest organization to do more than secure back pay for workers who had been stiffed of their hard-earned wages. While we reasoned that organizing and mobilizing workers—many of whom were undocumented—to get their back pay was powerful and important, in a conservative and antiworker state like Texas it simply wasn't enough to shift the power balance away from business in favor of workers. Furthermore, if we were truly honest, it was clear that by merely enforcing weak existing labor laws we were doing the work of the state, not actually advancing the rights of workers by winning new gains. If we wanted to build *power* for workers as we presumed to do, then we had to wrest concessions from business and government. To achieve this would require that we develop real relationships with traditional labor unions, which at the time saw us more as adversaries than as allies.

As a young organizer I was inspired by the collection of stories from *Poor Workers' Unions*. The book chronicled some of the most creative and innovative worker organizing strategies in the country. When I found *Poor Workers' Unions*, I was just beginning to grapple with the challenges and questions posed in the book: how to build power for workers outside of a traditional labor union; how to address issues of race, immigration status, and gender in our organizing work; and how to build ties with the traditional labor movement while challenging it to be more inclusive and intentional about building the capacity and leadership of women, people of color, and young people within its ranks.

At WDP, reading *Poor Workers' Unions* helped us situate our work in a broad and long tradition of organizing within and around the established labor movement. Tait's account helped me understand why some unions at the time saw us as adversaries instead of allies. The book was critical in helping WDP craft our own organizing strategy, tailored to our local context. Tait's work influenced our decision to focus on organizing in the construction industry and not to fear creating our own road map about how to build power for workers.

While in other parts of the country construction jobs are good blue-collar jobs, they are not in Texas. With building trades unions estimated to represent just 1 percent of the close to one million workers in the state, it's no surprise that Texas is the most deadly place in the country to work for construction workers. One in five workers in the industry experiences wage theft, more than half live below the poverty line, an overwhelming majority have no benefits, and close to 40 percent are misclassified as independent subcontractors.[1] Additionally, in the Lone Star state at least 50 percent of the workforce is undocumented,[2] and in this solidly conservative state the largest contributors to the Republican Party are developers and builders. To challenge one of the most powerful special-interest groups in the state with a workforce that has little political influence (more than half cannot vote) required us to craft new strategies and learn from the successes and mistakes of other innovators in the labor movement.

We took the lessons in *Poor Workers' Unions* about coalition building from civil rights groups that aligned themselves with progressive labor unions. When we decided to take on the construction industry, most unions observed our work with caution or outward hostility, and many met our attempts to collaborate with suspicion. But we stayed steadfast; we believed we had more in common than not. We worked to lift the voices of workers in the industry and bring union and nonunion workers together to find common ground. Today WDP has strong relationships, built on mutual trust and respect, with building trades unions across Texas. Moreover, at WDP actions, union and nonunion workers, citizens and undocumented workers, stand shoulder to shoulder to demand better working conditions and fight for immigration reform.

From *Poor Workers' Unions* we learned to imagine what it might mean to work on a large scale like ACORN (the Association of Community Organizations for Reform Now) when it organized home care workers. Today WDP has taken on some of the largest corporations in the world and won better working conditions for thousands of workers, including higher wages, better safety standards, training, and enforcement of those standards to make sure workers benefit.

But the most important lesson I learned from *Poor Workers' Unions* was how much more I had yet to learn. I learned that the best organizing requires learning from others' successes, challenges, and mistakes. In fact, our job as organizers is to regularly examine our efforts, craft new creative strategies, push boundaries about what is possible, and be open to new ideas about how to best achieve our goals.

With just 11.1 percent of US workers belonging to a union, and that number shrinking every year,[3] it should not come as a shock that today one in four American workers is a low-wage worker,[4] and growing numbers of the workforce are contingent (part-time, seasonal, or contracted) workers. Against these grim statistics, the labor movement should be trying new strategies to raise standards for thousands of workers and rebuild and create new institutions to give workers real power in shaping our country's economy. It is not a time to be tepid about trying alternative organizing strategies; it is the time for the labor movement to go full throttle and invest heavily in bold new organizing experiments. Millions of workers are dependent on the labor movement to push the boundaries of conventional organizing. Labor unions must seek to build real coalitions with community and alt-labor organizations—where the latter are seen as equals, not junior partners.

Organizing in one of the country's largest and most conservative economies has given me a unique understanding of the consequences of judging our economy solely by how well corporations (and not working people) are doing. Texas is the deadliest place to work in the country and the nation's largest minimum-wage job creator, and it has some of the skimpiest legal protections for workers of any state.[5] Republican leaders at the state and federal levels wish to export these economic models nationally. Texas's economic model—cut taxes for business, hand out millions to lure corporations to the state, and deregulate workers' rights and environmental standards—will take center stage in 2016 as Senator Ted Cruz runs for president. Cruz will undoubtedly tout Texas's economic "miracle" as one of his most important achievements and principal credentials to be named the Republican presidential nominee.

While the exportation of the Texas economic model alarms me for the millions of workers whose rights and quality of life could be further undermined, I am hopeful. In a short time WDP has proved that a small and determined group can win improvements and reforms for workers in a right-to-work state. If such an unlikely organization, with the odds so stacked against its members, can make such inroads in just seven years, imagine the possibilities for workers in this country when we think strategically about how to best leverage our resources for workers and work to implement new bold ideas.

Poor Workers' Unions shows what we are able to achieve when we refuse to believe that the odds against us are insurmountable. The questions, strategies, and challenges that Tait proposed to me as a young organizer continue to shape my work today. Her book is a must-read for all labor organizers and leaders.

Cristina Tzintzún

Acknowledgments

This book was possible only with the assistance of many activists committed to social change. My deep thanks to the long list of people who have lent their voices to this project through interviews and who are listed by name on pages 245–48. They are, of course, not responsible for my interpretations—indeed, the issues raised here are topics of healthy debate within the labor movement.

For help in finding sources and interviewees, or providing essential background information, I am grateful to Madeleine Adamson, Anu Advani, Ann Bastian, Deepak Bhargava, Edna Bonacich, the late Anne Braden, Fred Brooks, Cathy Cade, Larry Cohen, Terry DeAmicis, Gary Delgado, Hector Delgado, Steve Early, Bill Fletcher Jr., Jo Freeman, Jennifer Frost, Mike Gallagher, Florence Gardner, David Gerwin, Keith Hoeller, Ramsey Kanaan, Kitty Krupat, Kimi Lee, Gretchen Lemke-Santangelo, David Levin, Peter Levy, Nelson Lichtenstein, Miriam Ching Yoon Louie, Angela MacWhinnie, Mike Miller, Katie Quan, Michael B. Reagan, Virginia Rodriguez, Christina Roessler, Tony Santangelo, Ikuko Sato, Amy Schur, Rinku Sen, Holly Sklar, Jim Stockinger, Peg Strobel, Micah Uetricht, Robin Urevich, Cal Winslow, Barbara Winslow, Michael Yates, and Carol Zabin. Thanks also to Maurice Emsellem, Liz Krueger, and Steve Williams, who each came to my aid with hard-to-find statistics or other evidence, and to Rebecca Rosen Lum, who helped with rights issues.

My great thanks to those who read and commented on part or all of the text, in its various incarnations: Craig Alderson, John Brown Childs, Bill Fletcher Jr., Dana Frank, Michael Honey, Keith Kelleher, Peter Olney, Wade Rathke, Craig Reinarman, Kimberly Springer, Dana Takagi, and Michael Yates. Special thanks to Steve Early, who not only read the manuscript and provided sage advice but has been very supportive on a number of fronts. David Brundage and Barbara Epstein gave generously of their time during the early stages of this project, and the UC Santa Cruz Sociology Department provided several research grants.

My deepest thanks to two outstanding activists, Bill Fletcher Jr. and Cristina Tzintzún, for writing the foreword and afterword to this edition. I am delighted to have their views here on what poor workers' activism means on the ground and in the historical context.

It is a great honor to have Haymarket Books, one of our best movement presses, reissue this book. My editor, Dao X. Tran, has been wonderfully enthusiastic and a pleasure to work with, as are others from the press: Anthony Arnove, Julie Fain, Rory Fanning, Jason Farbman, Eric Kerl, John McDonald, and Jim Plank. Thanks to Rachel Cohen for designing a fabulous new cover around a photograph by Laura Emiko Soltis, to Ruth Goring for her careful and intelligent copyediting, to Nate Dorward for his excellent proofreading, and to Carrie Giunta for indexing.

For help locating photographs, I am indebted to Cathy Dang, Kate Donovan, Erika Gottfried, Shahana Hanif, Mary Hitchcock, Kathy Leichter, Joann Lo, Lisa Marine, Felicia Martinez, Marley Moynahan, Marissa Nuncio, Ai-jen Poo, Catherine Powell, Susan Sherwood, Casey Stoll, Cristina Tzinztún, Jim West, and Steve Williams. Thanks to David Bacon, Jason Cato, and Peter Holderness for allowing me to reprint their work.

A big thank-you to the staffs of the many archives and libraries I consulted, which preserve and make available our movement pasts. I particularly want to thank the late Debra Bernhardt, Sarah Cooper, Lincoln Cushing, Robert Dinwiddie, Lisa Hinzman, Louis Jones, Janice Kimball, Peter J. Roberts, Lisa Rubens, Mike Smith, Leon Sompolinsky, and Annie Tilden.

The work of digging up these histories was made easier by the support of family, friends, and colleagues. I am grateful to Jim Alderson, the late Pat Alderson, Ariel Ambruster, Elena Balashova, Martha Baskin, Scott Braley, the late Doug Brown, Maureen Chisholm, Celia Cody, Jean and Jonathan Eggenschwiler, Anitra Grisales, Katie and Bill Hart, Susannah, David, Ethan and Daniel Harte, Jelger Kalmijn, Ramsey Kanaan, Lisa Kermish, Paul Krantz, Joan Lichterman, Sasha Lilley, Floria Lupu, Steve Lussier, Karen MacLeod, Marion and Matt McCann, Lisa Petterson, Sherri Reeves, Alan Sanborn, Sara Sanderson, Libby Sayre, Kathy Seeburger, Eva Stigsdotter, Eileen Sutton, Janet Tait, Melinda Tuhus, Ken Wachsberger, Eric Weaver, Robert Weil, Margy Wilkinson, and Randi Zimmerman. My parents, Tess and Mark Tait, were always pleased that someone in our working-class immigrant family was writing about organizing. My wonderful KPFA friends Sarah Altshuler, Lynn Haug, Joe Ragazzo, Judith Scherr, Carla West, and especially Glenn Reeder cheerfully filled in for me when writing took me away from my radio duties.

My special thanks to two people whose advice and companionship have enriched this book, and my life, immensely. Dana Frank has generously shared her knowledge of movement history, union politics, and the joys and frustrations of writing, and wholeheartedly cheered on my research year after year. My partner, Craig Alderson, took time out from his own activist work to read many revisions, talk late into the night about issues raised here, and keep me nourished with love and divine Indian food.

I also thank my union sisters and brothers in University Professional and Technical Employees / CWA Local 9119, and my comrades in the successful 2000–2001 Pacifica Radio freelance reporters' strike who were scattered around the globe, for showing me what solidarity and committed organizing can accomplish.

Bengali leader Nayrin Muhith preparing statements for a press conference about public housing in New York City. She's an activist with CAAAV Organizing Asian Communities, a membership-based group working to unite low-income Asian communities for racial and economic justice. (*Photo courtesy of CAAAV*)

Archival Sources

ACORN Arkansas. Project and Campaign Records, 1970–1992. Wisconsin Historical Society, Madison (WHS).

Alliance for Labor Action. Collection, 1968–1973. Southern Labor Archives (SLA), Georgia State University, Atlanta.

Babson-Bernays Competition. Records, 1978. Schlesinger Library, Radcliffe College, Cambridge, Massachusetts.

Braden, Carl and Anne. Papers, 1960–1972, and Additions, ca. 1961–1990, Madison (WHS).

Center for Community Change. Records, 1960–1979. Archives of Labor and Urban Affairs, Wayne State University, Detroit, Michigan (WSU).

Center for Community Change. Records, 1969–1982. Record Group 4 of the Rockefeller Brothers Fund. Rockefeller Archive Center, Sleepy Hollow, New York (RAC).

Center for Popular Economics. Collection, 1978–1986. Special Collections and Archives, University of Massachusetts, Amherst.

Center for the Study, Education, and Advancement of Women. Organizational Files. University of California, Berkeley.

Chinese Staff and Workers' Association (CSWA). Records, 1979–1991. Wagner Labor Archives, New York University (WLA).

Davis, Michael. Papers, 1965–1970. Wisconsin Historical Society, Madison (WHS).

DeMuth, Jerry. Papers, 1962–1987. Wisconsin Historical Society, Madison (WHS).

Haymarket People's Fund. Records, 1974–1989. Special Collections, University of Massachusetts, Boston.

Haymarket People's Fund, Western Massachusetts. Records, 1975–1983. Special Collections and Archives, University of Massachusetts, Amherst.

Highlander Research and Education Center. Papers, 1960–1987. Wisconsin Historical Society, Madison (WHS).

Jobs or Income Now (JOIN). Papers. Wisconsin Historical Society, Madison (WHS).

Liberty Hill Foundation. Collection. Southern California Library for Social Studies and Research, Los Angeles.

Lynd, Staughton. Papers, 1960–1990. Wisconsin Historical Society, Madison (WHS).

Maupin, Joyce. Collection, 1952–1972. Wisconsin Historical Society, Madison (WHS).

McClendon, Mary Upshaw. Papers, 1969–1981. Archives of Labor and Urban Affairs, Wayne State University, Detroit, Michigan (WSU).

Mississippi Freedom Democratic Party (MFDP), Quitman County Chapter. Papers, 1965–1966. Wisconsin Historical Society, Madison (WHS).

Movement for Economic Justice (MEJ). Records, 1972–1980. Wisconsin Historical Society, Madison (WHS).

Newark Community Union Project. Oral history transcripts. Tamiment Institute Library, New York University.

Robinson, Cleveland. Papers. UAW District 65 Collection, Wagner Labor Archives, New York University (WLA).

Robinson, Jo Ann. Papers, 1960–1966. Wisconsin Historical Society, Madison (WHS).

Rockefeller brothers. Files, Record Group 1.2, Series 200. Rockefeller Archive Center, Sleepy Hollow, New York (RAC).

SEIU International Vice Presidents' Collection. Archives of Labor and Urban Affairs. Wayne State University, Detroit, Michigan (WSU).

SEIU Local 880. Records, 1983–1989. Wisconsin Historical Society, Madison (WHS).

Social Protest Collection. 1960–1982. Bancroft Library, University of California, Berkeley.

Southern Conference Educational Fund (SCEF). Papers, 1960–1972. Wisconsin Historical Society, Madison (WHS).

Special Collection on American Radicalism. Michigan State University, East Lansing.

SSEU Members for a Militant Caucus. Printed materials, 1968–1971. Wisconsin Historical Society, Madison (WHS).

Stromquest, Shelton. Papers, 1963–1980. Wisconsin Historical Society, Madison (WHS).

Student Nonviolent Coordinating Committee. Papers, 1959–1972 [microfilm]. Stanford University, Palo Alto, California.

Tamiment Institute Library, New York University, vertical files.

Tepperman, Jean. Papers, 1974–1975. Schlesinger Library, Radcliffe College, Cambridge, Massachusetts.

UAW District 65. Records, 1933–1992. Counsel Files. Wayne State University, Detroit, Michigan (WLA).

Union WAGE. Records, 1971–1982. Labor Archives and Research Center, San Francisco State University.

Vogel, Lise. Papers, 1964–1965. Wisconsin Historical Society, Madison (WHS).

Watts Labor Community Action Committee (WLCAC). Files. Southern California Library for Social Studies and Research, Los Angeles.

Wiley, George. Papers, 1960–1973. Wisconsin Historical Society, Madison (WHS).

Wisconsin Historical Society, Madison (WHS), vertical files.

Personal Interviews

All interviews conducted by the author.

Adamson, Madeleine (MEJ). Phone interview, April 14, 1998.

Anderson, Edriss (workfare worker). Interview, New York City, June 3, 1997.

Aska, Gale (Community Voices Heard). Phone interview, August 18, 1998.

Azcarate, Fred (Jobs with Justice). Interview, Chicago, October 25, 1997; phone interview, December 9, 1997.

Bacon, David (labor journalist). Phone interview, May 19, 2004.

Baratz, Michael (SEIU Local 1877). Phone interview, May 21, 2004.

Berger, Ilana (POWER). Interviews, San Francisco, December 10, 1997, and July 11, 1998.

Bonacich, Edna (Common Threads). Interview, Los Angeles, December 29, 1996.

Butler, Bale (SEIU Local 790). Phone interview, August 20, 1998.

Cantor, Daniel (United Labor Unions). Phone interview, March 6, 1998.

Chan, Dominic (NYC Jobs with Justice). Interview, New York City, June 2, 1997.

Cohen, Larry (CWA and Jobs with Justice). Interview, Chicago, October 24, 1997.

Delgado, Gary (Center for Third World Organizing, and welfare and workfare organizer). Interviews, Oakland, California, August 6 and 26, 1998.

Dodds, John (Philadelphia Unemployment Committee). Phone interview, July 29, 2003.

Dorow, Heidi (WEP Workers Together). Interview, New York City, June 9, 1997; phone interview, August 14, 1998.

Dulchin, Benjamin (Fifth Avenue Committee/WEP Workers Together). Phone interview, July 24, 2003.

Dymzarov, Megan (ACORN). Phone interview, September 16, 1998.

Emsellem, Maurice (labor and welfare lawyer). Phone interview, October 3, 1997.

Esakoff, Daniel (AFSCME District Council 37 workfare organizer). Phone interview, August 8, 1998.

Ferguson, Garth (POWER). Interview, San Francisco, July 11, 1998.

Gallagher, Mike (United Labor Unions and SEIU). Interview, Boston, June 7, 1997.

Galperin, Pam (Latino Workers' Center). Interview, New York City, June 13, 1997.

Gonzalez, Martin (ACORN). Interview, New York City, May 28, 1997.

Gordon, Jennifer (Workplace Project). Interview, Hempstead, New York, June 12, 1997.

Harris, Emma (POWER). Interviews, San Francisco, December 10, 1997, and July 11, 1998.

Haughton, James (Harlem Fightback). Phone interview, October 25, 1996.

Henriquez, Omar (Workplace Project). Interview, Hempstead, New York, June 12, 1997.

Hernandez, Gabriel (HERE Local 28). Interview, Lafayette, California, January 18, 1997.

Hill, Stanley (AFSCME District Council 37). Interview, New York City, June 2, 1997.

Honkala, Cheri (Kensington Welfare Rights Union). Interview, San Francisco, September 26, 1998.

Hui, Kwong (Chinese Staff and Workers' Association). Interview, New York City, May 30, 1997.

Janis-Apricio, Madelyn (labor and community organizer). Interview, Los Angeles, December 27, 1996.

Jimenez, Marta (Mexican American Legal Defense and Educational Fund attorney). Interview, San Francisco, March 23, 1997.

Kazis, Rich (Jobs and Justice). Phone interview, January 4, 2000.

Kelleher, Keith (United Labor Unions and SEIU). Interviews, Chicago, October 22, 1997, and July 24, 2003.

Kest, Jon (ACORN). Phone interview, September 15, 2003.

Kingsley, Bob (UE). Phone interview, September 8, 2003.

Koon, Stacy (Asian Immigrant Women Advocates). Interview, Oakland, California, October 29, 1996.

Leary, Elly (UAW Local 2324). E-mail interviews, August 31 and September 8, 1998.

Leung, Richard (SEIU Local 87 and United Service Workers for Democracy). Phone interview, September 19, 2003.

Levin, David (Latino Workers' Center). E-mail interviews, January 29 and 30, 1997.

Mayer, Eric (workfare worker). Interview, New York City, June 8, 1997.

Michaels, Sheila (CORE). E-mail interview, May 3–5, 1999.

Minnis, Jack (GROW). Interview, New Orleans, March 30, 1998.

Miranda, Olga (SEIU Local 87). Interviews, Berkeley, California, September 19, 2003, and August 30, 2004.

Mott, Andy (Center for Community Change). Phone interview, June 26, 1999.

Muhammad, Saladin (Black Workers for Justice and UE Local 150). Phone interview, September 16, 2003.

Nee, George (RIWA, RIWU, and Rhode Island AFL-CIO). Interview, Providence, June 5, 1997; phone interview, November 28, 1999.

Olney, Peter (LAMAP). Interviews, Berkeley, California, January 13, 1996, and May 29, 2004.

Pastreich, Bill (AFL-CIO workfare program). Phone interview, July 11, 1997.

Poland, Arthur (WEP Workers Together). Interview, New York City, June 9, 1997.

Portes, Alicia (workfare worker). Interview, New York City, June 30, 1997.

Quinac, Sebastian (Latino Workers' Center). Interview, New York City, June 13, 1997.

Rathke, Wade (ACORN and SEIU). Interview, New Orleans, March 31, 1998; phone interview, August 24, 1998.

Reyna, Irene (Fuerza Unida). Phone interview, October 25, 1996.

Ryder, Peter (AFL-CIO workfare program). Phone interview, August 19, 1998.

Sabol, Ed (CWA District 1). Phone interview, August 15, 1998.

Santana, Mónica (Latino Workers' Center). Interview, New York City, June 13, 1997.

Schur, Amy (ACORN). Phone interviews, July 30, 1997, and August 20, 1998.

Sen, Rinku (Center for Third World Organizing). Interview, Oakland, California, October 15, 1996.

Silva, Milagros (ACORN). Interview, New York City, June 11, 1997; phone interview, August 6, 1998.

Tejada, Freddy (Northern California Coalition for Immigrant Rights). Phone interview, March 23, 1997.

Turner, David (SEIU Local 790). Phone interview, August 20, 1998.

Weiner, David (CWA Local 1081). Phone interview, August 15, 1998.

Williams, Steve (POWER). Interviews, San Francisco, July 17 and December 10, 1997; phone interviews, August 14, 1998, April 27, 1999, and September 5, 2003.

Wise, Leah (Southeast Regional Economic Justice Network, former SNCC activist). Phone interview, October 30, 1996.

Zellner, Bob (GROW). Phone interviews, March 24 and May 7, 1999.

Frequently Used Abbreviations

ACORN	Association of Community Organizations for Reform Now (originally Arkansas Community Organizations for Reform Now)
AFDC	Aid to Families with Dependent Children
AFL-CIO	American Federation of Labor and Congress of Industrial Organizations
AFSCME	American Federation of State, County, and Municipal Employees
AFT	American Federation of Teachers
AIWA	Asian Immigrant Women Advocates
ALA	Alliance for Labor Action
BWFJ	Black Workers for Justice
CAAAV	Committee Against Anti-Asian Violence (also known as CAAAV: Organizing Asian Communities)
CCC	Center for Community Change
CETA	Comprehensive Employment and Training Act
CLUW	Coalition of Labor Union Women
CORE	Congress of Racial Equality
CSWA	Chinese Staff and Workers' Association
CWA	Communications Workers of America
DES	Department of Employment Security
DHS	Department of Homeland Security
DRUM	Dodge Revolutionary Union Movement
ERAP	Economic Research and Action Project
FLOC	Farm Labor Organizing Committee
GROW	Grass Roots Organizing Work

HERE	Hotel Employees and Restaurant Employees
HPF	Haymarket People's Fund
HWO	Household Workers Organization
IAF	Industrial Areas Foundation
ILGWU	International Ladies' Garment Workers' Union (later merged with Amalgamated Clothing and Textile Workers, renamed UNITE)
ILWU	International Longshore and Warehouse Union
JOIN	Jobs or Income Now
LAMAP	Los Angeles Manufacturing Action Project
MEJ	Movement for Economic Justice
MFLU	Mississippi Freedom Labor Union
MFU	Maryland Freedom Union
NAACP	National Association for the Advancement of Colored People
NCHE	National Committee on Household Employment
NDWU	National Domestic Workers Union
NEA	National Education Association
NLRB	National Labor Relations Board
NUHW	National Union of Healthcare Workers
NUP	New Unity Partnership
NWRO	National Welfare Rights Organization
OSHA	Occupational Safety and Health Administration
POWER	People Organized to Win Employment Rights
POWW	People Organizing Workfare Workers
RAC	Rockefeller Archive Center
RIWA	Rhode Island Workers Association (formerly UWU)
RIWU	Rhode Island Workers Union (formerly RIWA)
RWDSU	Retail, Wholesale, and Department Store Union
SCEF	Southern Conference Educational Fund
SCLC	Southern Christian Leadership Council
SDS	Students for a Democratic Society
SEIU	Service Employees International Union
SLA	Southern Labor Archives
SNCC	Student Nonviolent Coordinating Committee
TELACU	The East Los Angeles Community Union
UAW	United Auto Workers
UE	United Electrical Workers
UFCW	United Food and Commercial Workers Union

UFW	United Farm Workers
ULU	United Labor Unions
UNITE	(formerly the Union of Needletrades,Industrial, and Textile Employees, later merged with Amalgamated Clothing and Textile Workers, now merged with HERE and called UNITE HERE)
UWA	United Woodcutters Association
UWW	United WREP Workers
UWU	Unemployed Workers' Union (later RIWA)
WEP	Workers Experience Program
WHS	Wisconsin Historical Society
WLA	Wagner Labor Archives
WLCAC	Watts Labor Community Action Committee
WLO	Worker Labor Organization
WOE	Women Organized for Employment
WREP	Work Relief Employment Project
WSU	Wayne State University
WWT	WEP Workers Together

Notes

Introduction

1. *The State of Working America*, 12th ed. (Ithaca, NY: ILR Press, 2012); see pages 173–293 on measures of wage inequality, including fig. 4AD, "Real Value of the Minimum Wage."

2. Teresa L. Amott and Julie A. Matthaei, *Race, Gender and Work: A Multicultural Economic History of Women in the United States*, rev. ed. (Boston: South End, 1996), 92; National Immigration Law Center, "Facts about Immigrant Workers" (Los Angeles: National Immigration Law Center, 2004).

3. Robert Korstad and Nelson Lichtenstein, "Opportunities Found and Lost: Labor, Radicals, and the Early Civil Rights Movement," *Journal of American History*, December 1988, 786–811. On the expulsion of left unions from the CIO, see Steve Rosswurm, ed., *The CIO's Left-Led Unions* (New Brunswick, NJ: Rutgers University Press, 1992).

4. David Brody, *Workers in Industrial America: Essays on the 20th Century Struggle* (New York: Oxford University Press, 1980), 201.

5. The roots of business unionism lie earlier in the twentieth century. See Kim Moody, *An Injury to All: The Decline of American Unionism* (London: Verso, 1988), 55–69.

6. Barry Hirsch and David Macpherson, *Union Membership and Earnings Databook* (Washington, DC: Bureau of National Affairs, 2004).

7. Paul Buhle, *Taking Care of Business: Samuel Gompers, George Meany, Lane Kirkland and the Tragedy of American Labor* (New York: Monthly Review, 1999).

8. Kate Bronfenbrenner et al., introduction to *Organizing to Win: New Research on Union Strategies* (Ithaca, NY: ILR Press, 1998), 5.

9. Fernando Gapasin and Michael Yates, "Organizing the Unorganized: Will Promises Become Practices?" *Monthly Review* 49, no. 3 (July–August 1997): 47–63.

10. Barry Bluestone and Bennett Harrison, *The Deindustrialization of America: Plant Closings, Community Abandonment, and the Dismantling of Basic Industry* (New York: Basic Books, 1982).

11. Richard Belous, *The Contingent Economy: The Growth of the Temporary, Part-Time and Subcontracted Workforce* (Washington, DC: National Planning Association, 1989).

12. On the history of Taft-Hartley, see Nelson Lichtenstein, *Labor's War at Home: The CIO in World War II* (Cambridge, MA: Cambridge University Press, 1982). On how Taft-Hartley and NLRB rulings have affected unions, see Michael Yates, *Labor Law Handbook* (Boston: South End, 1987), 26–36.

13. See Staughton Lynd, ed., *"We Are All Leaders": The Alternative Unionism of the Early 1930s* (Urbana: University of Illinois Press, 1996), and Roy Rosenzweig, "Organizing the Unemployed: The Early Years of the Great Depression, 1929–1933," *Radical America* 10, no. 4 (1976): 37–60.

14. Leon Fink and Brian Greenberg, *Upheaval in the Quiet Zone: A History of Hospital Workers' Union, Local 1199* (Urbana: University of Illinois Press, 1989).

15. The United Electrical Workers union, which has always remained independent of the AFL-CIO, held different positions on social issues and organizing questions from those of other trade unions throughout the period covered in this book. See Ronald L. Filippelli and Mark McColloch, *The Cold War in the Working Class: The Rise and Decline of the United Electrical Workers* (Albany: State University of New York Press, 1995).

16. Jane Slaughter, *Concessions and How to Beat Them* (Detroit: Labor Education and Research Project, 1983), 27.

17. See, for instance, Frank Bardacke, *Trampling Out the Vintage: Cesar Chavez and the Two Souls of the United Farm Workers* (London: Verso, 2011); Randy Shaw, *Cesar Chavez, the UFW, and the Struggle for Justice in the 21st Century* (Berkeley: University of California Press, 2010); Richard W. Hurd, "Organizing the Working Poor: The California Grape Strike Experience," *Review of Radical Political Economics* 6, no. 1 (1974): 50–75; Margaret Rose, "From the Fields to the Picket Line: Huelga Women and the Boycott, 1965–1975," *Labor History* 31, no. 3 (1990): 271–93.

18. Julianne Malveaux, "The GOP's War against Poor Women," *Black Enterprise*, February 1995, 32.

19. Robin D. G. Kelley, "The New Urban Working Class and Organized Labor," *New Labor Forum* 1 (Fall 1997): 6–17.

20. Examples of labor histories that reach beyond the factory floor include Herbert Gutman, *Work, Culture, and Society in Industrializing America: Essays in American Working-Class and Social History* (New York: Alfred A. Knopf, 1976); Michael Honey, *Southern Labor and Black Civil Rights: Organizing Memphis Workers* (Chicago: University of Illinois Press, 1993); and Elizabeth Faue, *Community of Suffering and Struggle: Women, Men, and the Labor Movement in Minneapolis, 1915–1945* (Chapel Hill: University of North Carolina Press, 1991).

21. Nancy A. Naples, "Women's Community Activism and Feminist Action Research," in *Community Activism and Feminist Politics: Organizing Across Race, Class, and Gender*, ed. Nancy A. Naples (New York: Routledge, 1998), 1–27; Nancy A. Naples, *Grassroots Warriors: Activist Mothering, Community Work, and the War on Poverty* (New York: Routledge, 1998); Joseph M. Kling and Prudence

S. Posner, "Class and Community in an Era of Urban Transformation," in *Dilemmas of Activism: Class, Community, and the Politics of Local Mobilization*, ed. Joseph M. Kling and Prudence Sarah Posner (Philadelphia: Temple University Press, 1990), 23–45.

22. Gregory D. Squires, *Capital and Communities in Black and White: The Intersections of Race, Class, and Uneven Development* (Albany: State University of New York Press, 1994).

23. See, for instance, Mike Davis, *Fire in the Hearth: The Radical Politics of Place in America* (London: Verso, 1990); Susan S. Fainstein, "Local Mobilization and Economic Discontent," in *The Capitalist City: Global Restructuring and Community Politics*, ed. Michael P. Smith and Joe R. Feagin (Oxford: Blackwell, 1987), 323–42.

24. US Bureau of Labor Statistics, "The Employed Poor: Their Characteristics and Occupations," *Monthly Labor Review* 88, no. 7 (July 1965): 828–35.

25. John Kasarda, "America's Working Poor: 1980–1990," in *America's Working Poor*, ed. Thomas Swartz and Kathleen Maas Weigert (Notre Dame, IN: University of Notre Dame Press, 1995), 50.

26. US Bureau of the Census, Statistical Abstract of the US, "Table 613: Cash and Non-Cash Benefits for Persons with Limited Income" (Washington, DC: Bureau of Census, 1999), 389.

27. Mishel et al., "Share of Workers Earning Poverty-Level Wages by Gender," in *The State of Working America*, fig. 4E, 192.

28. Mishel et al., "Share of Workers Earning Poverty-Level Wages by Race and Ethnicity," in *The State of Working America*, fig. 4F, 193.

29. Kasarda, "America's Working Poor," 60.

30. Amott and Matthaei, *Race, Gender and Work*, 343–47.

31. William Humbert Form, *Divided We Stand: Working-Class Stratification in America* (Urbana: University of Illinois Press, 1985), 120, 123.

32. US Department of Labor, "Union and Non-union Earnings by Occupation, Full-Time Wage and Salary Workers' Median Weekly Earnings, 1999," *Employment and Earnings*, January 2000.

33. David Gordon, Richard Edwards, and Michael Reich, *Segmented Work, Divided Workers* (Cambridge: Cambridge University Press, 1982), 40.

34. David Roediger, ed., "The End of Whiteness? Reflections on a Demographic Landmark," forum, *New Labor Forum*, Spring/Summer 2001, 49–62.

35. David Roediger, *The Wages of Whiteness: Race and the Making of the American Working Class* (New York: Verso, 1991), 8–10.

36. Susan Porter Benson, response, "End of Whiteness?" ed. Roediger, 52.

37. Manning Marable, "Black Leadership and the Labor Movement," *WorkingUSA*, September/October 1997; on density, "Union Membership," in *Black Americans: A Statistical Sourcebook* (Palo Alto, CA: Information Publications, 1997), table 6.21, p. 231.

38. Michael Yates, *Why Unions Matter* (New York: Monthly Review Press, 1998), 117.

39. Frances Fox Piven and Richard A. Cloward, *Poor People's Movements: Why They*

Succeed, How They Fail (New York: Vintage, 1979), xxii.

40.   Guida West, *The National Welfare Rights Movement: The Social Protest of Poor Women* (New York: Praeger, 1981).

41.   For an analysis of ACORN's end, see Fred Brooks, "One Hypothesis about the Decline and Fall of ACORN," *Social Work* 58, no. 2 (April 2012): 177–80.

42.   The relationship of class, race, ethnicity, gender, and sexuality can usefully be seen a "matrix" of oppressions that don't merely coexist but interlock with and influence each other. While class is historically constructed and experienced in historically specific ways, it is also experienced by individual workers in racially and gender-specific ways. See, for instance, Evelyn Brooks Higginbotham, "African-American Women's History and the Metalanguage of Race," *Signs* 17, no. 2 (Winter 1992): 251–75; Ava Baron, "Gender and Labor History: Learning from the Past, Looking to the Future," in *Work Engendered: Toward a New History of American Labor*, ed. Ava Baron (Ithaca, NY: Cornell University Press, 1991), 1–46; and Patricia Hill Collins, *Black Feminist Thought: Knowledge, Consciousness, and the Politics of Empowerment* (Boston: Unwin-Hyman, 1990).

Chapter 1

1.   John Lewis, "Address at the March on Washington," in *A Documentary History of the Modern Civil Rights Movement*, ed. Peter Levy (New York: Greenwood, 1992), 120–21. Wage statistics from Victoria Bonnell and Michael Reich, *Workers and the American Economy: Data on the Labor Force* (Boston: New England Free Press, 1969), 15.

2.   Interview with Cleveland Robinson, in the Cleveland Robinson Papers, UAW District 65 Collection, Box 50, Folder 4, Wagner Labor Archives, New York University.

3.   August Meier and Elliott Rudwick, *CORE: A Study in the Civil Rights Movement, 1942–1968* (New York: Oxford University Press, 1973), 82.

4.   "Attack Launched on Jim Crow in Government and Unions," *Guardian*, February 27, 1961.

5.   *Proceedings of the Fourth Constitutional Convention of the AFL-CIO*, reprinted in *Black Workers: A Documentary History from Colonial Times to the Present*, ed. Philip Foner and Ronald Lewis (Philadelphia: Temple University Press, 1989), 554–65.

6.   Dorothy Sue Cobble, "'A Spontaneous Loss of Enthusiasm': Workplace Feminism and the Transformation of Women's Service Jobs in the 1970s," *International Labor and Working-Class History* 56 (Fall 1999), 26.

7.   Maxine Wolpinsky Jenkins, "Organizing the Unorganized," in *Women in the Labor Movement: Speeches from the California State Federation of Labor Women's Conference*, San Francisco, May 19–20, 1973.

8.   Meier and Rudwick, *CORE*, 232–46.

9.   Ralph Crowder, "'Don't Buy Where You Can't Work': An Investigation of the Political Forces and Social Conflict within the Harlem Boycott of 1934," *Afro-Americans in New York Life and History* 15, no. 2 (1991): 7–44.

10.   Larry Salomon, "The Movement for Jobs in Civil Rights-Era San Francisco,

1963–64" (MA thesis, San Francisco State University, 1994), 53–57, 60–62, 90.

11. Natalie Becker and Marjorie Myhill, *Power and Participation in the San Francisco Community Action Program, 1964–1967* (Berkeley: Institute of Urban and Regional Development, 1972), 7; "Hotel Picket Bedlam: 200 Jailed, Hundreds Jam Lobby," *News Call-Bulletin*, March 7, 1964; on the agreement, "The Hotel Hiring Agreement," *San Francisco Chronicle*, March 8, 1964.

12. "226 Sit-In Arrests," *San Francisco Chronicle*, April 12, 1964.

13. Salomon, "Movement for Jobs," 75–88; Meier and Rudwick, *CORE*, 238.

14. Jo Freeman, *At Berkeley in the Sixties: The Education of an Activist, 1961–1965* (Bloomington: Indiana University Press, 2004), 106.

15. Quote from ibid., 100; see also "At 18, a Civil Rights Veteran," *San Francisco Chronicle*, March 8, 1964.

16. See Salomon, "Movement for Jobs," 61–62, and Freeman, "At Berkeley in the Sixties," 100–105.

17. Meier and Rudwick, *CORE*, 187–90, 238.

18. "Shaw, Mississippi: New Sounds in the Delta" [1965?], vertical file (MFLU), Wisconsin Historical Society (WHS).

19. MFLU Draft Constitution, vertical file (MFLU); Shelton quotation from letter to friends of the MFLU [1965], Lise Vogel Papers, Box 1, Folder 1, WHS.

20. On membership, "Report on the Cotton-Choppers' Strike in Three Delta Counties," and "Mississippi Freedom Labor Union," in *SNCC Papers, 1959–1972*, Reel 59:51; and Clayborne Carson, *In Struggle: SNCC and the Black Awakening of the 1960s* (Cambridge, MA: Harvard University Press, 1981), 172. Quotes from "Shaw, Mississippi: New Sounds."

21. "Mississippi Freedom Labor Union Report from George Shelton," *SNCC Papers*, Reel 59:51. Oral accounts are in Stanford University's *Project South Oral History Collection*, no. 4, *Freedom Labor Union (F.L.U.)* (Glen Rock, NJ: Microfilming Corporation of America, 1975).

22. Meyer and Ruddick, *CORE*, 361. Mike Flug, *The Maryland Freedom Union: Workers Doing and Thinking* (Detroit: News and Letters, [1970?]).

23. Michael Flug, "Organized Labor and the Civil Rights Movement of the 1960s: The Case of the Maryland Freedom Union," *Labor History* 31, no. 3 (Summer 1990): 325.

24. Ibid., 327, 331; Flug, *Maryland Freedom Union*, 3.

25. Flug, "Organized Labor," 334–35.

26. Flug, *Maryland Freedom Union*, 3.

27. On Retail Clerks' remarks, see Flug, "Organized Labor," 336. On Reuther and the CLC, see "Organized Labor," 336–37.

28. Ibid., 340; Peter Levy, *New Left and Labor in the 1960s* (Urbana: University of Illinois Press, 1994), 64–65.

29. Jennifer Frost, *Interracial Movements of the Poor: Community Organizing and the New Left in the 1960s* (New York: New York University Press, 2001); Richie Rothstein, *ERAP and How It Grew* (Boston: New England Free Press, n.d.).

30. "Join Community Union, Program for 1966," February 27, 1966, Staughton Lynd Papers, Box 7, Folder 2, WHS. Quote from Rothstein, *ERAP and How It Grew*.

31. James O'Connor, "Toward a Theory of Community Unions," *Studies on the Left*, Spring 1964, 143–48. On union support, see Rothstein, *ERAP and How It Grew*, 4; Levy, *New Left and Labor*, 14–15.

32. Frost, *Interracial Movements*, 152.

33. Carson, *In Struggle*, 241–42.

34. Mike Higson, "Roosevelt Hotel Strike Draws Wide Support," *Southern Patriot* 26, no. 10 (December 1968).

35. Robert Analavage, "Laurel Struggle Continues: Workers Strike Back," *Southern Patriot* 26, no. 8 (October 1968).

36. Letter from Bob Zellner to Anne and Carl Braden, August 19, 1967, Southern Conference Education Fund (SCEF) Papers, Box 73, Folder 3, WHS; Memo on Masonite Boycott from Jane McManus, Ad Hoc Committee in Support of the Masonite Workers, February 4, 1969, SCEF Papers, Box 90, Folder 8, WHS.

37. Memo on Masonite from McManus.

38. "Who Are We Reaching in the South?" SCEF Papers, Box 90, Folder 8; *Rights of Man: A Working People's Newspaper* 1, no. 1.

39. "Description and list of officers of GPA," from Center for Community Change (CCC) Records, Box 34, Folder 27, Record Group 4 of the Rockefeller Brothers Fund, Rockefeller Archive Center, Sleepy Hollow, New York (RAC); William Lundberg, "Black and White Woodsmen Form New Union in the South," *New Leader*, March 6, 1972; "Politics of Paper," *Southern Patriot* 27, no. 8 (October 1969).

40. "Strike! The Great Mississippi Wood Strike of '71, a Report from the Gulfcoast Pulpwood Association" [1972], from vertical file, Tamiment Institute Library, New York University (NYU); "Woodcutters Win Strike," *Gulfcoast Pulpwood News* 2, no. 4 (December 1971), in Center for Community Change Records, Box 34, Folder 27, Archives of Labor and Urban Affairs, Wayne State University (WSU); "Woodcutters Strike Again in Deep South," *Southern Patriot* 31, no. 8 (October 1973). On material aid, press release in Jerry De Muth Papers, Box 1, Folder 1, WHS. On Maine woodcutters, see "Funding Request, the Maine Woodsman's Association," in Haymarket People's Fund, Western Massachusetts Records, University of Massachusetts, Amherst.

41. Tom Israel, "Organizing in the Woods: Timber Cutters Fell Paper Giants," *Dollars & Sense*, December 1982.

42. Bob Zellner, interview by author, March 24, 1999; "Poultry Workers Organize in Mississippi," *Southern Patriot* 30, no. 5 (May 1972); "New Poultry Union Wins," *Southern Patriot* 30, no. 10 (December 1972); "A Poultry Worker's Story: We Needed This Union," *Southern Patriot* 31, no. 5 (May 1973): 5.

43. Quote from "Women Face Oppression as Workers," *Guardian*, March 15, 1969; statistics from Bonnell and Reich, *Workers and the American Economy*, 10, 17.

44. "Nationwide Demonstration by Women," *Guardian*, September 5, 1970; "Program of the Liberation Women's Union," in *From the Movement toward Revolution*, ed. H. Bruce Franklin (New York: Van Nostrand Reinhold Co., 1971), 90–92.

45. "Witches Hex the Business World," *CWLU News: Newsletter of the Chicago Women's Liberation Union*, March 22, 1970 (Historical Pamphlet #74-3288 at

WHS). See also Margaret Strobel, "Consciousness and Action: Historical Agency in the Chicago Women's Liberation Union," in *Provoking Agents: Gender and Agency in Theory and Practice*, ed. Judith Kegan Gardiner (Chicago: University of Illinois Press, 1995), 52–68.

46. Wendy Edmon and Suzie Fleming, *All Work and No Pay: Women, Housework and the Wages Due* (Montpelier, UK: Falling Wall, 1975).

47. Entries by Patricia Alvarado and Marie Lamberti, respectively, in Babson-Bernays Competition Records, Schlesinger Library, Radcliffe College, Cambridge, MA; Cindy Felong, "Cleaning the Master's House," *Fifth Estate* 6, no. 2 (1971): 6–7.

48. See Evelyn Nakano Glenn, "Racial Ethnic Women's Labor: The Intersection of Race, Gender and Class Oppression," *Review of Radical Political Economics* 17, no. 3 (1985): 86–108; and Karen Brodkin Sacks, "Toward a Unified Theory of Class, Race, and Gender," *American Ethnologist* 16, no. 3 (August 1989): 534–50.

49. Mary Romero, *Maid in the U.S.A.* (New York: Routledge, 1992).

50. Piven and Cloward, *Poor People's Movements*, 273–75.

51. Piven and Cloward, *Poor People's Movements*; West, *National Welfare Rights Movement*; Jacqueline Pope, *Biting the Hand That Feeds Them: Organizing Women on Welfare at the Grass Roots Level* (New York: Praeger, 1989). "A Strategy to End Poverty" was initially a mimeographed essay passed between activists; it was later published in *The Nation*, May 2, 1966.

52. Piven and Cloward, *Poor People's Movements*, 277.

53. See Gwendolyn Mink, "Valuing Women's Work," in *From Poverty to Punishment: How Welfare Reform Punishes the Poor* (Oakland, CA: Applied Research Center, 2002), 139–46.

54. Johnnie Tillmon, "Insights of a Welfare Mother: A Conversation with Johnnie Tillman," *Journal of Social Issues*, January–February 1971, 23.

55. Eileen Boris, "When Work Is Slavery," *Social Justice* 25, no. 1 (Spring 1998): 28–46.

56. Piven and Cloward, *Poor People's Movements*, 287.

57. Dorothy Bolden, "Organizing Domestic Workers in Atlanta, Georgia," in *Black Women in White America: A Documentary History*, edited by Gerda Lerner (New York: Pantheon, 1972), 234–38. See Romero, *Maid in the U.S.A.*, on contemporary efforts by Latina domestic workers to control their working conditions.

58. Bolden, "Organizing Domestic Workers." Quote from Dorothy Cowser Yancy, "Dorothy Bolden, Organizer of Domestic Workers: She Was Born Poor but She Would Not Bow Down," *SAGE* 3, no. 1 (Spring 1986): 54. On the history of domestic worker organizing, see Premilla Nadasen, *Household Workers Unite: The Untold Story of African American Women Who Built a Movement* (Boston: Beacon Press, 2015).

59. Bolden, "Organizing Domestic Workers," 237.

60. On NCHE history, see Cobble, "Spontaneous Loss of Enthusiasm," 34; Phyllis Palmer, "Housework and Domestic Labor: Racial and Technological Change," in *My Troubles Are Going to Have Trouble with Me*, ed. Karen Brodkin Sacks and Dorothy Remy (New Brunswick, NJ: Rutgers University Press, 1984), 80–91.

61. "Domestics United for More Pay and Respect," *New York Times*, July 17, 1971;

"Household Workers Are Organizing, NCHE Is Forerunner of a Maid's Union," *Just Economics* 2, no. 9 (October 1974).

62. Palmer, "Housework and Domestic Labor," 86.

63. Friedan comment in "Domestics Try to Upgrade Jobs," *Detroit Free Press*, December 8, 1970); Giovanni quote in "The Silent Revolution of the Domestic Worker," in *Encore American and Worldwide News*, June 23, 1975, 36. McClendon quote from "Pay! Protection, Professionalism," McClendon Papers, Box 1, Folder 17, Archives of Labor and Urban Affairs, Wayne State University.

64. "Household Workers Organization," McClendon Papers, Box 1, Folder 3.

65. Speech by Mary McClendon, May 1, 1976, McClendon Papers, Box 1, Folder 3. On election loss, "A Milestone," McClendon Papers, Box 1, Folder 13.

66. Felong, "Cleaning the Master's House," 6–7.

67. Judy Edelman, "Unions on the Line: Myth vs. Reality," *Up from Under* 1, no. 1 (May/June 1970): 36. Criticism was common in feminist periodicals in the '70s; for instance, "Women and Unions: Help or Hindrance?" *Atlantis* 4 (Spring 1979): 48–70; "Are Unions Paying Their Dues?" *off our backs* 8 (November 1978).

68. Nancy MacLean, "The Hidden History of Affirmative Action: Working Women's Struggles in the 1970s and the Gender of Class," *Feminist Studies* 25, no. 1 (Spring 1999): 55.

69. Karen Nussbaum, "Women Clerical Workers and Trade Unionism," interview by David Plotke, *Socialist Review* 49 (January–February 1980): 151.

70. Joan Keller Burton, "Dilemmas of Organizing Women Office Workers," *Gender and Society* 1, no. 4 (December 1987): 432–46; Ann Curran, "Getting Organized," *Working Woman*, March 1979.

71. On membership, see Burton, "Dilemmas of Organizing Women Office Workers," 432. On activities, see "Working Women's Movement," Movement for Economic Justice Records, Box 32 Folder 5 (WHS); "Women Workers Organize for Justice," *Just Economics* 2, no. 1 (January 1974); "Angry Women Expose Employers; Announce Plan of Action," *Women Employed* 1, no. 2 (October/November 1973), in vertical file, WHS.

72. "Working Women Take Affirmative Actions," *Just Economics* 3, no. 1 (January 1975); "Tales of WOE," *Downtown Women's News* 1, no. 1 [1974]; Margie Albert, "Secretaries Unite!" *Downtown Women's News* 1, no. 3 (April 1974), in vertical file, WHS.

73. Quote in Curran, "Getting Organized," 56; Burton, "Dilemmas of Organizing Women Office Workers," 443–46.

74. Cobble, "Spontaneous Loss of Enthusiasm," 23.

75. Ibid., 28–30.

76. Ibid., 33.

77. On Poor People's Union Local 1, "Labor Shorts," *Southern Patriot* 31, no. 4 (April 1973); *BADWU Rag: The Newspaper of the Boston Area Daycare Workers Union*, Haymarket People's Fund Records, Carton 1, Folder 61, Special Collections, University of Massachusetts, Boston; "Reservation Indians Won the First Such Strike Ever," *Guardian*, February 22, 1969; "Union Organized for Gay Workers," *San Francisco Examiner*, October 22, 1976; "San Francisco Workers

Strike on Castro Street," *Union WAGE*, March–April 1979; Mark Dowie, "Unionizing Prison Labor," *Social Policy* 4, no. 3 (July/August 1973): 56–59. On the history of LGBTQ labor, see Miriam Frank, *Out in the Union: A Labor History of Queer America* (Philadelphia: Temple University, 2014).

78. Meyer and Ruddick, *CORE*, 6.

Chapter 2

1. Michael Yates, *Why Unions Matter* (New York: Monthly Review Press, 1998), 140.

2. Meany quote from Paul Buhle, *Taking Care of Business: Samuel Gompers, George Meany, Lane Kirkland and the Tragedy of American Labor* (New York: Monthly Review Press, 1999), 196.

3. Leon Fink and Brian Greenberg, *Upheaval in the Quiet Zone: A History of Hospital Workers' Union, Local 1199* (Urbana: University of Illinois Press, 1989); Sheila Michaels, interview with author, May 3–5, 1999.

4. Joan Turner Beifuss, *At the River I Stand: Memphis, the 1968 Strike, and Martin Luther King* (Brooklyn, NY: Carlson, 1989).

5. Brendan Sexton, "Unions and the Black Power Brokers," *Dissent*, February 1971, 41–49.

6. "Black Rank-and-File Steel Workers Meet," *Guardian*, August 2, 1969; Carl Bloice, "Black Power Is Black Labor," *Black Scholar*, October 1970, 29–31.

7. Union diversity statistics and quote from Dan Georgakas and Marvin Surkin's *Detroit: I Do Mind Dying—A Study in Urban Revolution*, updated ed. (Boston: South End, 1998), 32. Other accounts of DRUM include Charles Denby's *Indignant Heart: A Black Worker's Journal* (Boston: South End, 1978), James Geschwender's *Class, Race, and Worker Insurgency: The League of Revolutionary Black Workers* (Cambridge: Cambridge University Press, 1977), and Heather Ann Thompson's *Whose Detroit? Politics, Labor and Race in a Modern American City* (Ithaca, NY: ILR Press, 2001).

8. Herb Boyd, afterword to Georgakas and Surkin, *Detroit: I Do Mind Dying*, 220.

9. Thompson, *Whose Detroit?* 113.

10. Geschwender, *Class, Race, and Worker Insurgency*, 110–14; see also Peter Levy, *New Left and Labor in the 1960s* (Urbana: University of Illinois Press, 1994), 77.

11. Manning Marable, *Race, Reform, and Rebellion: The Second Reconstruction in Black America, 1945–1990* (Jackson: University Press of Mississippi, 1991), 116.

12. Robert Dudnick, "Black Storm Rages in Auto Plants," *Guardian*, March 8, 1969; Martin Glaberman, *Be His Payment High or Low: The American Working Class of the Sixties* (Detroit: Facing Reality Publishing Committee, 1966).

13. Letter to the editor, *Sepia*, August 1969, 6; statistics from Bonnell and Reich, *Workers and the American Economy*, 16, 17, 20.

14. Peter Henle, "Some Reflections on Organized Labor and the New Militants," *Monthly Labor Review*, July 1969, 21–25.

15. Madeleine Adamson and Seth Borgos, *This Mighty Dream: Social Protest Movements in the United States* (Boston: Routledge and Kegan Paul, 1984), 48.

16. Nelson Lichtenstein, *The Most Dangerous Man in Detroit: Walter Reuther and the Fate of American Labor* (New York: Basic Books, 1995): 389–90; Center for

Community Change, *25 Years of Community Change* (Washington, DC: Center for Community Change, 1992), 6–7.

17. Jack Barbash, *Trade Unions, the Low-Wage Worker, and Social Justice* (Madison: University of Wisconsin, Institute for Research on Poverty, 1973), 96.

18. Brendan Sexton, "Experimental Program to Assist Organization among Deprived Residents of Blighted Neighborhoods," vertical file (UAW), WHS.

19. South Central figures from Paul Bullock, *Hard-Core Unemployment and Poverty in Los Angeles* (Los Angeles: US Department of Commerce, 1964), 9. General statistics from Eva E. Jacobs, ed., *Handbook of US Labor Statistics*, 6th ed. (Lanham, MD: Bernan, 2003), 92.

20. Excerpts of taped interview with Watkins, March 1968, Center for Community Change (CCC) Records, Box 5, Folder 14, Archives of Labor and Urban Affairs, WSU; "Training for Hospital Jobs Begins," *WLCAC News*, December 1967, CCC Records, Box 5, Folder 16 (WSU).

21. "Watts Labor Community Action Committee," WCLAC files at California Library for Social Studies and Research, Los Angeles; "Meat Bargains in Watts," *Christian Science Monitor*, Eastern ed., September 26, 1973. On housing, "New Hope for Watts," *Sepia*, February 1971, 38.

22. "Community Based Watts Group to Expand Its Training Effort," *Manpower Information Service*, February 10, 1971, 250, CCC Records, Box 5, Folder 13 (WSU); "$2 Million for Saugus Center Job Training Program," *WLCAC News*, February 1969, in Rockefeller Foundation Record Group 1.2, Series 200, Box 105, Folder 930, Rockefeller Archive Center.

23. "Orientation Manual: Saugus Residential Job Center Program," Rockefeller Foundation Record Group 1.2, Series 200, Box 106, Folder 936 (RAC).

24. "EJS Diary re Senator Dymally, New York City," March 18, 1969, Rockefeller Foundation Record Group 1.2, Series 200, Box 105, Folder 930, Item 47 (RAC).

25. "Review of TELACU Organizational Activities," February 2, 1970, CCC Records, Box 8, Folder 13, Archives of Labor and Urban Affairs, WSU.

26. "Statement of Purpose and Objectives and Constitution," Alliance for Labor Action (ALA) Collection, Box 347, Folder 1, Southern Labor Archives, Georgia State University, Atlanta; Karl F. Treckel, *The Rise and Fall of the Alliance for Labor Action* (Kent, OH: Kent State University, 1975), 4–6.

27. Lichtenstein, *Most Dangerous Man in Detroit*, 431–32.

28. "Meany-Reuther Battle Escalating," *Atlanta Journal*, October 4, 1969.

29. "Statement of Purpose," ALA Collection.

30. Quote and demographics from "Teamsters Proposal for Implementing the Alliance for Labor Action," in ALA Collection, Box 347, Folder 1.

31. Treckel, *Rise and Fall of the Alliance*, 18.

32. Ibid., 53.

33. Leo J. Shapiro and Associates, "Atlanta: A Report Prepared for the Alliance for Labor Action," September 1970, ALA Collection, Box 347, Folder 8.

34. Treckel, *Rise and Fall of the Alliance*, 19–20. Lichtenstein cites a higher though still disappointing number (7,500) of workers organized in Atlanta (see *Most Dangerous Man in Detroit*, 431); William Genoese, "ALA Organizing Report,"

July 30, 1970, ALA Collection, Box 347, Folder 8.

35. Treckel, *Rise and Fall of the Alliance*, 23.

36. Ibid., 15; Lichtenstein, *Most Dangerous Man in Detroit*, 433.

37. Manpower Information Service, n.d., CCC Records, Box 5, Folder 9, Archives of Labor and Urban Affairs, WSU.

38. "Teamsters and UAW Unite," *Guardian*, June 7, 1969; Charles Denby, "Black Caucuses in Unions," in *Autocracy and Insurgency in Organized Labor*, ed. Burton Hall (New Brunswick, NJ: Transaction, 1972): 146; Lichtenstein, *Most Dangerous Man in Detroit*, 431.

39. Lichtenstein, *Most Dangerous Man in Detroit*, 429–33.

40. "Resolution of Disaffiliation from RWDSU, AFL-CIO," Cleveland Robinson Papers, UAW District 65 Collection, Box 24, RWDSU Correspondence, 1969, Wagner Labor Archives (WLA), New York City; "Interview with Cleveland Robinson," January 14, 1970, Robinson Papers, UAW District 65 Collection, Box 50, Folder 4, Wagner Labor Archives (WLA) New York City; "National Council Born at Suffolk Meeting," *Distributive Worker* 1, no. 1 (July 1969).

41. "Minutes of the Executive Board," October 4–5, 1969, UAW Counsel Files, Box 50, Folder 13, RWDSU Disaffiliation, Wagner Labor Archives (WLA), New York City.

42. "National Council Born."

43. Ibid.

44. Letter from Cleveland Robinson to Martin Luther King Jr., July 14, 1967, Robinson Papers, UAW District 65 Collection, Box 24, SCLC Correspondence, WLA.

45. "Campaign Starts for Negro Unions," *New York Times*, May 28, 1967.

46. Cleveland Robinson, "The War on Poverty Can Only Be Won by Organized Workers," *Distributive Worker* 1, no. 1 (July 1969); second quote in Gene Grove, "Something New in the House of Labor," *Tuesday Magazine*, March 1970.

47. "Breaks Ties with AFL-CIO; Charges Bias," *Jet*, June 1969, 19.

48. Numbers organized in "Organizing the Unorganized," *Distributive Worker* 2, no. 3 (May 1970); on MLK Day holiday, see "White Unions, Black Unions," *Sepia* 18 (July 1969): 9–15; on organizing, Frank Brown, "We're Organizing People, Not Just Cards or Books," *Distributive Worker* 1, no. 5 (November 1969).

49. Pete Gonzalez, "'65' Community Program Making Progress in Neighborhoods," *Distributive Worker* 1, no. 3 (September 1969); "Experts Call Administration Welfare Program Inadequate," *Distributive Worker* 1, no. 3 (September 1969).

50. "600 Hear Mrs. King Back New Union Chapter Here," *Atlanta Constitution*, May 13, 1970.

51. Cobble, "Spontaneous Loss of Enthusiasm," n37.

52. "At Columbia, Feminists Hope to Flex a Union's Muscles," *New York Times*, September 29, 1973; "Two Unions Step Up Organizing Drives at Book Publishers Here," *New York Times*, October 15, 1975; "*Village Voice* Employees to Join a Local of District 65," *New York Times*, July 1, 1977; "Barnard Clerks End Strike," *New York Times*, February 5, 1974; "Union Drive," *New York Times*, October 15, 1975; "If You Work in an Unorganized Office You Belong in '65,'" *Distributive Worker*, December 1976.

53. "UAW Affiliation Talks Are on the Right Track," *Distributive Worker* 10, no. 8

(October 1978). Merger date from US Department of Labor, "Labor Organization Annual Report Form LM-2," January 1, 1979–December 31, 1979. DWA membership from Bernard Rifkin and Susan Rifkin, *American Labor Sourcebook* (New York: McGraw-Hill, 1979), 2:27.

54. "Black Unionists Want Full Partnership with Labor Movement," *Distributive Worker*, July 1973.

55. Ann Withorn, "The Death of CLUW," *Radical America* 10, no. 2 [1976]: 47–51. For a history of CLUW, see Michele Hoyman, "Working Women: The Potential of Unionization and Collective Action in the United States," *Women's Studies International Forum* 12, no. 1 (1989): 51–58.

Chapter 3

1. "Welfare Rights Group Charts Course," *Guardian*, August 25, 1971.

2. "Boycott Schenley!" December 4, 1965, signed by George Wiley, CORE, and Elizabeth Sutherland, SNCC, George Wiley Papers, Box 4, Folder 9, WHS; letter of October 3, 1967 from Wiley to Alex Sarota, Wiley Papers, Box 24, Folder 7; Stephen Torgoff, "Yale Workers Win 7-Week Strike," *Guardian*, June 30, 1971.

3. Letters of December 30, 1969, and May 26, 1970, from Wurf to Wiley, and letter of April 8, 1970, from Walter Reuther to Wiley, Wiley Papers, Box 24, Folder 7. On union ties with NWRO, see Guida West, *The National Welfare Rights Movement: The Social Protest of Poor Women* (New York: Praeger, 1981), 145.

4. "Unemployment Rates, by Race, 1950–1985," in *A Documentary History of the Modern Civil Rights Movement*, ed. Peter Levy (New York: Greenwood, 1992), 251; "A Frightening Momentum," *New York Times*, February 9, 1975.

5. On debates within NWRO, see West, *National Welfare Rights Movement*, 76–141, and Nick Kotz and Mary Lynn Kotz, *A Passion for Equality: George A. Wiley and the Movement* (New York: W. W. Norton, 1977), 279–304.

6. On ACORN's early work, see Gary Delgado, *Organizing the Movement: The Roots and Growth of ACORN* (Philadelphia: Temple University Press, 1981).

7. Wade Rathke, interview by author, March 31, 1998, New Orleans.

8. "Unemployed Workers Meet," September 22, 1971, and petition to Dale Cline, Department of Labor, August 1971, ACORN Arkansas Project and Campaign Records, Box 5, Folder 18, WHS.

9. "Unemployment March in Rochester," *Guardian*, October 31, 1970; "Unemployment March in Seattle," *Guardian*, November 11, 1970; "Organizing among the Jobless," *Guardian*, August 23, 1972.

10. "A Union for the Unemployed—Will It Work?" *Providence Journal*, September 26, 1971.

11. "For the Unemployed, a New Rallying Point," *Providence Evening Journal*, September 16, 1971.

12. "Those Who Support the U.W.U. Proposals for Reform NOW," ACORN Arkansas Project and Campaign Records, Box 5, Folder 12, WHS.

13. "Judge Delays Ruling on New Union's Rights," *Providence Journal*, September 24, 1971; "Judge Allows Union Access to DES Offices," *Providence Journal*, October 21, 1971.

14. "RI Workers Association Organizes for Basic Justice," *Just Economics* 1, no. 3 (December 1973); George Nee, interview by author, June 5, 1997, Providence.

15. "RI Workers Association Organizes for Basic Justice."

16. "Licht Will Consider Changes in Jobless Pay," *Providence Evening Bulletin*, October 12, 1971; "Union of Unemployed Threatens Picket Action against Licht," *Providence Journal*, October 20, 1971.

17. Nee interview; see also "RI Workers Association Organizes for Basic Justice."

18. Numbers of locals and structure from Nee interview.

19. Nee interview.

20. "Unemployed Force Blue Cross Agreement," *Just Economics* 1, no. 5 (April 1975).

21. George Nee, "Chavez Was Right!," undated offprint in author's possession.

22. Nee interview.

23. "New Union with Community Ties Organized," *Just Economics* 4, no. 9 (December 1976).

24. Nee interview; "New Union with Community Ties Organized."

25. SEIU memo from James Manning to John Geagan, January 29, 1979, SEIU International Vice Presidents Collection, Box 5, Folder 16, Archives of Labor and Urban Affairs (WSU).

26. "New Union with Community Ties Organized."

27. SEIU memo from Manning.

28. Memo from Wiley to "Welfare Rights Leaders, Members, Friends and Supporters," December 15, 1972, Movement for Economic Justice (MEJ) Records, Box 1, Folder 3, WHS; see also "Welfare Activist Plans New Group; Will Leave Rights Post for Economic Justice Drive," *New York Times*, December 17, 1972.

29. "The Need for a Taxpayer's Uprising," transcription of Wiley's address to the National Council of Churches on March 5, 1973, Wiley Papers, Box 40, Folder 3.

30. Other rank-and-file NWRO activists were, by this point, at odds with Wiley's leadership. They sought to define NWRO as a women's organization focused on supporting caregiving work in the home. See West, *National Welfare Rights Movement*.

31. "Strategy to Counter the Nixon Budget Cut/Impoundments," memo from Wiley to Louis Stokes, chair of the Congressional Black Caucus, March 1, 1973, MEJ Records, Box 1, Folder 3; "Proposed Reorganization of the Poverty Rights Action Center," November 9, 1973, MEJ Records, Box 1, Folder 10; "Minutes of the Organizational Meeting of the Board of Directors," September 16, 1974, MEJ Records, Box 1, Folder 8; George Wiley, "Building a New Majority: The Movement for Economic Justice," *Social Policy* 4, no. 2 (September/October 1973): 33.

32. On plans for membership structure, see "Progress Report on the Planning Phase of MEJ," from Wiley, June 20, 1973, MEJ Records, Box 1, Folder 5. On first-year budget, see "Annual Report of the Movement for Economic Justice," February 1, 1974, MEJ Records, Box 1, Folder 2.

33. Wiley, "Need for a Taxpayer's Uprising," 7.

34. Ibid., 3.

35. Testimony by Wiley before the US House of Representatives, Committee on

Ways and Means, March 9, 1973, MEJ Records, Box 1, Folder 3.

36. Wiley, "Need for a Taxpayer's Uprising," 8. For a more recent critique of corporate welfare, see Mark Zepezauer's *Take the Rich off Welfare* (Boston: South End, 2004).

37. Kotz and Kotz, *Passion for Equality*, 300.

38. Madeleine Adamson, phone interview by author, April 14, 1998.

39. "New York City Welfare Jobs Rouse Controversy on Merits," *Christian Science Monitor*, August 10, 1971; "Work and Welfare," *Christian Science Monitor*, August 27, 1970.

40. "Why We Are Here," Wiley Papers, Box 31, Folder 8.

41. *WREP Workers Rights*, MEJ Records, Box 1, Folder 13.

42. "WREP Workers Organizing Project," MEJ Records, Box 10, Folder 3.

43. "Working Paper: WREP," MEJ Records, Box 10, Folder 3; *WREP Workers Organizing Project*, MEJ Records, Box 3, Folder 10.

44. "Progress Report: WREP Workers Organizing Project," MEJ Records, Box 10, Folder 3.

45. Gary Delgado, interviews by author, August 6 and 26, 1998, Oakland.

46. Letter to Hillary Palmer, New World Foundation, from Bert DeLeeuw, undated, and letter to Dale McCloud, MEJ, from Gary Delgado, November 5, 1973: MEJ Records, Box 10, Folder 3. On in-kind help, see "Progress Report: WREP Workers Organizing Project."

47. "UWW Organizers Manual," undated, in author's posession; "Jobs! Not Promises," *One by One* [1, no. 1], May 1974; quote from "WREP Workers Unite to Win Their Rights," *Just Economics* 2, no. 7 (July/August 1974).

48. "Who Are WREP Workers?" undated, in author's posession; workers quoted in WREP Workers Organizing Committee press release, in MEJ Records, Box 10, Folder 3.

49. "Full Employment," *New York Times*, June 15, 1974; "35 Nat'l Groups Endorse UWW," *One by One* 1, no. 3 (July 1974).

50. "Progress Report: WREP Workers Organizing Project."

51. "Local 371 Joins WREP Workers Fight," *Unionist: A Publication of SSEU Local 371* 6, no. 5 (July 12, 1974).

52. Delgado interviews.

53. Gotbaum's position is published in *One by One* 1, no. 3 (July 1974); Delgado interviews.

54. Delgado interviews.

55. Sandy Helling and Lillian Zerwick, "Workfare: The New York Experience," *Catalyst* 14 (1982).

56. "Organizations or Persons Involved in Unemployment Organizing" [1975], MEJ Records, Box 12, Folder 15; John Dodds, phone interview by author, July 29, 2003.

57. Letter to friends from DeLeeuw and Adamson, May 12, 1976, MEJ Records, Folder 13, Box 2; "Poor in 17 Cities Join in Welfare, Job Protests," *Washington Post*, May 13, 1978.

58. "Jobs and Justice," MEJ Records, Box 15, Folder 7.

Chapter 4

1. "Jobs and Justice Campaign Launched," *Just Economics* 6, no. 3 (May 1978); Mike Gallagher, interview by author, June 7, 1997, Boston.

2. "New World Foundation Fact Sheet," MEJ Records, Box 14, Folder 22.

3. Ibid.

4. Congressional Budget Office, *Report of Congressional Budget Office Conference on the Teenage Unemployment Problem* (Washington, DC: Congressional Budget Office, [1976]); Eva E. Jacobs, ed., *Handbook of US Labor Statistics*, 6th ed. (Lanham, MD: Bernan, 2003), 102–10.

5. "Jobs and Justice Campaign Launched," 4–5.

6. "Boston, Philadelphia Youth Win Jobs," *Just Economics* 6, no. 4 (July 1978).

7. Richard Kazis and Peter Sabonis, *Leveraging with a Toothpick: The Carter Administration's Private Sector Strategy for Job Creation* (Washington, DC: NCJJ, 1979); "New World Foundation Fact Sheet"; "Social Action Report: Jobs and Justice," *Social Policy* 9, no. 3 (November/December 1978).

8. Wade Rathke, interview by author, March 31, 1998, New Orleans; "Introduction and Background," MEJ Records, Box 14, Folder 22.

9. Gallagher interview; Richard Kazis, phone interview with author, January 4, 2000.

10. Letter from Bert DeLeeuw to Anne Peretz, Sherwood Forest Foundation, August 8, 1978, MEJ Records, Box 14, Folder 28.

11. National Center for Jobs and Justice Annual Report, 1978–1979, MEJ Records, Box 14, Folder 5.

12. Harold Meyerson, "A Second Chance: The New AFL-CIO and the Prospective Revival of American Labor," in *Not Your Father's Labor Movement: Inside the AFL-CIO*, ed. Jo-Ann Mort (London: Verso, 1998), 8, 10.

13. Kim Moody, *An Injury to All: The Decline of American Unionism* (London: Verso, 1988), 138; Jane Slaughter, *Concessions and How to Beat Them* (Detroit: Labor Education and Research Project, 1983), 5.

14. Jacobs, ed., *Handbook of US Labor Statistics*, 92.

15. William Tabb, "Urban Development and Regional Restructuring," in *Sunbelt, Snowbelt: Urban Development and Regional Restructuring*, ed. Larry Sawers and William Tabb (Oxford: Oxford University Press, 1984), 9.

16. See Martin Jay Levitt's *Confessions of a Union-Buster* (New York: Crown, 1993).

17. Thomas Geoghegan, *Which Side Are You On? Trying to Be for Labor When It's Flat on Its Back* (New York: Farrar Straus Giroux, 1991), 4.

18. "Service Work Gains against Production Jobs," *New York Times*, July 6, 1982; "'Big Mac' Supplants Big Steel as Manufacturing Jobs Lag," *New York Times*, May 31, 1982.

19. "Union Drive Wins First Fastfood Election," *Just Economics* 3, no. 2 (March/April 1980).

20. "Introduction and Background," 7.

21. "United Labor Unions, Constitution and By-Laws," Haymarket People's Fund Records, Carton 6, Folders 437–438, Archives and Special Collections, Healey Library, University of Massachusetts, Boston.

22. NCJJ Annual Report, 22.

23. Ibid.; Madeleine Adamson, phone interview by author, April 14, 1998; Rathke interview.
24. Louis Freedberg, "Behind the Counter: Teenage Workers Fuel Fast Food Assembly Line," SEIU 880 Records, Box 1, Folder 6, WHS; "Having It Their Way: Fast Food Union Wins Burger King Vote," *Detroit Free Press*, March 16, 1980.
25. *Fastfood Worker* 1, no. 1 (March 1, 1980), SEIU 880 Records, Box 1, Folder 6.
26. Daniel Cantor, phone interview by author, March 6, 1998.
27. "Having It Their Way." A previous, unsuccessful attempt to organize fast food in Detroit was made in 1972 by the National Black Independent Workers, a left group (Cantor interview). In 1998, workers at a McDonald's near Cleveland went on strike, winning a week's paid vacation and wage increases (Michael Colton, "Big Mac Attack: Did Somebody Say Strike? The Kids Who Took On McDonald's—and Won," *Washington Post*, April 26, 1998). Canadian unions also organized a McDonald's ("Drive to Unionize McDonald's a Success," *Kinesis*, September 1998, 7).
28. "Having It Their Way."
29. "Will Kelly Debate?" *Fastfood Worker* 1, no. 2 (March 15, 1980), and "Kelly: I Won't Debate the Union," *Fastfood Worker* 1, no. 4 (April 15, 1980), SEIU 880 Records, Box 1, Folder 6.
30. "Fast-Food Franchise Picketed," *Detroit Free Press*, February 23, 1980; "Burger King Workers Shut Store, Demand Recognition," *United Labor News* 2, no. 3 (June 1981).
31. "An Open Letter to Burger King and McDonald's Owners," SEIU 880 Records, Box 1, Folder 6; Keith Kelleher, interview by author, October 22, 1997, Chicago; Daniel Cantor, "ACORN, the UAW, and the Teamsters," *Social Policy* 13, no. 4 (Spring 1983), 21.
32. "Having It Our Way," *United Labor News* 1, no. 1 (October 1980).
33. "Business Gets Cold Feet on Subminimum Wage," *Washington Post*, March 20, 1981.
34. "Union Drive Wins First Fastfood Election," *Just Economics* 3, no. 2 (March/April 1980); Cantor interview.
35. US Court of Appeals, *Burger King Corp. v. National Labor Relations Board*, SEIU 880 Records, Box 3, Folder 11.
36. Cantor, "ACORN, the UAW, and the Teamsters," 20.
37. Cantor interview; Rathke interview.
38. Keith Kelleher, "ACORN Organizing and Chicago Homecare Workers," *Labor Research Review* 8 (Spring 1986): 40.
39. "Goldman Workers Get Tough, Win Big," *United Labor News* 2, no. 1 (January 1981).
40. "Tulane/P.F.M. Workers Win Contract," *United Labor News* 3, no. 2 (June/July 1982).
41. Rathke interview.
42. Rathke interview.
43. "HWOC on the Move," *United Labor News* 1, no. 1 (October 1980); "Fired Up! Hyatt Workers Lead the Way in New Orleans," *United Labor News* 2, no, 2

(April 1981).

44. Gallagher interview.

45. Gallagher interview.

46. Kelleher interview; see also "Schwartz Strike Victory Builds Union," *United Labor News* 2, no. 1 (January 1981).

47. "Pioneer Workers Sign 'Best Ever' Contract," *United Labor News* 2, no. 1 (January 1981).

48. Quote and subsequent description from Kelleher, "ACORN Organizing," 37.

49. For an overview, see Robert Fisher, ed., *The People Shall Rule: ACORN, Community Organizing and the Struggle for Economic Justice* (Nashville: Vanderbilt University Press, 2009).

50. See Robert Fisher, *Let the People Decide: Neighborhood Organizing in America* (New York: Twayne, 1994); Arlene Stein, "Between Organizing and Movement: ACORN and the Alinsky Model of Community Organizing," *Berkeley Journal of Sociology* 31 (1986): 93–115; see also Bardacke, *Trampling Out the Vintage*, 67–82, for a description of Alinsky's philosophy, especially as it related to unions.

51. Gary Delgado, *Organizing the Movement: The Roots and Growth of ACORN* (Philadelphia: Temple University Press, 1981), 184–85, 206–07; data on staff diversity in Fred Brooks, "Racial Diversity on ACORN's Organizing Staff: 1970–2003," *Administration in Social Work* 31, no. 1 (2007), 27–48; see also Stein, "Between Organizing and Movement."

52. Gwen Shaffer, "Dramatic Irony," *City Paper*, February 15–22, 2001; Decisions of the NLRB, 338–129, National Labor Relations Board, March 27, 2003.

53. Stein, "Between Organizing and Movement."

54. Peter Medoff and Holly Sklar, *Streets of Hope: The Fall and Rise of an Urban Neighborhood* (Boston: South End, 1994), 74–75.

55. Delgado, *Organizing the Movement*, 196, 206; Brooks, "Racial Diversity on ACORN's Organizing Staff"; Rathke, Kelleher, and Gallagher interviews.

56. Brooks, "Racial Diversity on ACORN's Organizing Staff."

57. "Health Care at Home: A Booming Market," *US News and World Report*, February 9, 1981, 68; "Homecare Workers Organize, Press for Changes in Law," *All Chicago City News*, May 8–June 1, 1984; Eileen Boris and Jennifer Klein, *Caring for America: Home Health Workers in the Shadow of the Welfare State* (New York: Oxford University Press, 2012), 6.

58. "Table 193, Employment in the Health Services Industries: 1980–1998," in *Statistical Abstract of the US: 1999* (Washington, DC: US Census Bureau, 1999), 131. Home health care was a $7.6 billion a year industry in 1987, and it grew to $19.2 billion by 1997 ("Table 1301, Service Industries: Annual Receipts of Taxable Firms, 1985–1997," in *Statistical Abstract of the US: 1999* [Washington, DC: US Census Bureau, 1999], 784).

59. Gallagher interview; numbers of workers in NCJJ/MEJ Education and Training Center, "Homemakers Organizing Project" (June 1981), Haymarket People's Fund Records, Carton 6, Folders 437–38, and "United Labor Unions Local 880 YE/YB Report," December 30, 1983, SEIU 880 Records, Box 1, Folder 1.

60. On the demographics of Boston's home healthcare workers, see "Health Care

Aides Strike," *Boston Herald American*, November 2, 1982, and "Haymarket Grant Application, United Labor Unions Local 1475, Homemakers Organizing Project," June 23, 1981, in Haymarket People's Fund Records, Carton 6, Folders 437–38. Race and gender characteristics of home healthcare workers nationally are not available, but results of a 1985 joint survey by Hunter College and Local 1199 found 99 percent of New York City's home healthcare workers were female, 70 percent were black, and 26 percent were Latina; 46 percent were immigrants, primarily from Jamaica, Puerto Rico, the Dominican Republic, and Haiti. The most common salary was less than $5,000 a year ("Poorly Paid Home Health Care Workers Subsidize an Industry," *New York Times*, June 2, 1987).

61. On organizing methods, "Homemakers Organizing Project Report," June 1982, Haymarket People's Fund Records, Carton 6, Folders 437–38; quote from "Homemakers Organizing Project," December 15, 1981, SEIU 880 Records, Box 1, Folder 22.

62. "Homemakers Organizing Project."

63. Melissa Everett, "Homemakers Fight for Economic Justice," *Equal Times: Boston's Newspaper for Working Women* 6, no. 119 (September 6, 1981).

64. "Homemakers Organizing Project," June 1981, 34.

65. Letter to clients from the Suburban Homemaker Organizing Committee, August 27, 1981, SEIU 880 Records, Box 1, Folder 22.

66. Everett, "Homemakers Fight for Economic Justice."

67. Sheryl Katz, "Paying Their Dues: Homemakers Struggle to Unionize," *Brookline*, September 9, 1981.

68. "Major Union Victory," *Bay State Banner*, December 2, 1981.

69. "Home Care Workers on Strike," *Boston Globe*, November 2, 1982; "Homemakers Organize New Union," *Labor Page: A Publication of City Life* 6 (December 1982–January 1983).

70. "Homemakers Organize New Union," 4; on homemakers' visits to clients see "Health Care Aides Strike; Union Members Don't Neglect Aged Patients," *Boston Herald American*, November 2, 1982; Gallagher interview.

71. "United Labor Unions Local 880 YE/YB Report," December 30, 1983, SEIU 880 Records; Kelleher interview.

72. Chicago Homecare Organizing Project, "Introduction," SEIU 880 Records, Box 2, Folder 20.

73. Ibid.

74. "United Labor Unions Local 880 YE/YB Report"; "Progress and Plans to Date," July 9, 1985, SEIU 880 Records, Box 2, Folder 20.

75. United Home and Health Care Workers, SEIU Local 1475, [1985], SEIU 880 Records, Box 2, Folder 20.

76. "Homecare Workers Organize, Press for Changes in Law;" "Aged Poor Cheated under Home-Care Plan, Says Union," *Chicago Sun-Times*, May 15, 1984; King's comments in "Homemakers Speak against Exploitation," *Bay State Banner*, March 22, 1984.

77. Steve Early, "Business Forum: Revival Is Possible and Necessary," *New York Times*, January 20, 1985.

78. "Four Years Back, Five Years Forward," August 1983, Box 2, Folder 20, SEIU Local 880 Records.

79. United Domestic Workers of America, "A Brief Look at Our History," SEIU 880 Records, Box 2, Folder 41. The affiliation ended a few years later over financial disputes (see "Politics—and Money, Too—Makes Strange Bedfellows," *Sacramento Bee*, January 15, 1988). The group later affiliated with AFSCME.

80. "Affiliation Fact Sheet," SEIU 880 Records, Box 2, Folder 20; Rathke interview.

81. "Unions Regroup amid US Smokestack Shift," *Christian Science Monitor*, July 9, 1984; Kelleher interview.

82. "United Labor Unions Affiliates with SEIU," *Organizer* 10, no. 3 (Fall 1984): 25. Membership numbers from author's correspondence with Rathke, November 2, 2000.

83. Richard W. Hurd and William Rouse, "Progressive Union Organizing: The SEIU Justice for Janitors Campaign," *Review of Radical Political Economics* 21, no. 3 (1989): 70–75.

84. "Organizing Effort by Union Targets Home Health Aides," *Los Angeles Times*, April 19, 1988.

85. Kelleher interview.

86. Lisa Ranghelli, *The Monetary Impact of ACORN Campaigns: A Ten-Year Retrospective, 1995–2004* (New York: ACORN, 2005).

87. Gary Delgado, "Reflections on Movement Building and Community Organizing," *Social Policy* 39 (2009): 6–14.

88. Fred Brooks, "One Hypothesis about the Decline and Fall of ACORN," *Social Work* 58, no. 2 (April 2012): 177–80.

Chapter 5

1. Janice Fine, *Worker Centers: Organizing Communities at the Edge of the Dream* (Ithaca, NY: ILR Press, 2006), 23.

2. This account relies on Peter Kwong, *The New Chinatown* (New York: Hill and Wang, 1987), 140–47, as well as "Securing Justice and Dignity for New York's Chinese Workers: Celebrating CSWA's First Decade" (New York: CSWA, 1990) and "CSWA: 12 Years of Empowering Chinese Immigrants" (n.p., n.d.), both in Chinese Staff and Workers' Association Records [unprocessed], Wagner Labor Archives, New York University.

3. Kwong, *New Chinatown*, 143.

4. "Chinese Staff and Workers Association," in *The New Rank and File*, ed. Staughton Lynd and Alice Lynd (Ithaca, NY: ILR Press, 2000), 243–54.

5. Kwong, *New Chinatown*, 144–45.

6. Xiaolan Bao, *Holding Up More Than Half the Sky: Chinese Women Garment Workers in New York City, 1948–92* (Urbana: University of Illinois Press, 2001), 217, 239–40. See also Miriam Ching Yoon Louie's *Sweatshop Warriors: Immigrant Women Workers Take On the Global Factory* (Boston: South End, 2001), 201.

7. Kwong, *New Chinatown*, 149–57.

8. "Asian Investors Battle for Footholds in Chinatown," *New York Times*, December 29, 1981.

9. Louie, *Sweatshop Warriors*, 43–44.

10. Dana Frank, *Buy American: The Untold Story of Economic Nationalism* (Boston: Beacon, 1999), 148.

11. Statistics from Los Angeles garment industry and cited in Louie, *Sweatshop Warriors*, 5.

12. JoAnn Wypijewski, "Profits of Pain," *The Nation*, April 11, 1994, 471–72.

13. Demographics and wage rates from Louie, *Sweatshop Warriors*, 33.

14. Peter Kwong, "Chinese Staff and Workers' Association: A Model for Organizing in the Changing Economy?" *Social Policy* 25, no. 2 (Winter 1994): 30–38; on 1991 settlement, letter from Edward Dun and Wing Lam to supporters, January 3, 1992, CSWA Records.

15. Louie, *Sweatshop Warriors*, 19–20.

16. Immanuel Ness, "Organizing Immigrant Communities: UNITE's Workers Center Strategy," in *Organizing to Win: New Research on Union Strategies*, ed. Kate Bronfenbrenner et al. (Ithaca, NY: ILR Press, 1998), 87–101.

17. Kwong Hui, interview by author, May 30, 1997, New York City.

18. "CSWA: 12 Years of Empowering Chinese Immigrants."

19. Kwong, *New Chinatown*, 132.

20. B. J. Kowalski, "Protesting 'Coolie Labor': Chinatown Agency Targeted by Workers," *Village Voice*, March 13, 1990; CSWA Press Conference Notes, October 8, 1991, "In Re Chinatown Planning Council vs. Independent Workers Union," CSWA Records (WLA); "Uproar Erupts over City-Financed Job Training Program," *New York Observer*, January 23, 1989.

21. CSWA Press Conference Notes, October 8, 1991, "In Re Chinatown"; "Chinese-American Planning Council and Its Anti-labor Record," n.d., in CSWA Records (WLA).

22. "Immigrant Workers Sue City," *New York Newsday*, September 13, 1990.

23. "Workers Due Back Wages," *New York Newsday*, February, 26, 1991.

24. "Union Fights for Older Workers," *CSWA News* 3, no. 1 (Winter 1992).

25. "1,500 Dine, and Back Restaurant in Battle with Union," *New York Times*, April 2, 1995; "Why Is This Bowl of Noodles So Cheap? Answer: Low Wages and Fierce Competition in Chinatown," *New York Times*, April 23, 1995; "Suit Charges Slave Labor; Eatery Stole 1.5M from Workers," *New York Daily News*, January 24, 1997; "NYC Waiters Settle $1.1 Million Suit with Chinatown Restaurant," *New York Times*, October 30, 1997.

26. "Chinese Construction Workers Demand Jobs," *CSWA News* 3, no. 1 (Winter 1992).

27. "CSWA Battles for Economic Justice at Foley Square," *CSWA News* 3, no. 2 (Fall 1992). On wages, see "Chinese Construction Workers Demand Jobs."

28. *The Economic Impact of the Hispanic Population of Long Island*, New York (Port Washington, NY: Horace Hagedorn Foundation, n.d.), 5.

29. Omar Henriquez and Jennifer Gordon, interviews by author, June 12, 1997, Hempstead.

30. Jennifer Gordon, "We Make the Road by Walking: Immigrant Workers, the Workplace Project, and the Struggle for Social Change." *Harvard Civil Rights–*

Civil Liberties Law Review 30, no. 2 (Summer 1995): 439.

31. Ibid., 429–30.

32. Other immigrant workers also pursued this tactic. See Yvonne Martínez, "Workers on the Corner, Organizing for Power," *Labor Notes* 225 (December 1997); J. Pozzi, "Street Corner Labor," *City Limits* 21, no. 1 (January 1996): 8–9; David Bacon, "L.A.'s Newest Union: Street Corner Workers Join the Labor Movement," *El Andar* 10, no. 2 (Summer 1999): 50–52.

33. Gordon interview.

34. Case cited in Gordon, "We Make the Road by Walking," 432; similar cases recounted in Henriquez interview.

35. "Organizing Low-Wage Immigrants: The Workplace Project," *WorkingUSA*, Summer 2001, 90.

36. Anna Gorman, "Burbank Hiring Site Draws Ire," *Los Angeles Times*, January 10, 2006.

37. Fine, *Worker Centers: Organizing at the Edge of the Dream*, 197. On settlements, see Janice Fine and Ruth Milkman, *U.S. Country Inventory of Informal Worker Organizing* (Los Angeles: UCLA Institute for Research on Labor and Employment), October 2013, 8, www.irle.ucla.edu/research/documents/US.pdf.

38. Janice Fine, "Workers Centers: Entering a New Stage of Growth and Development," *New Labor Forum* 20, no. 3 (Fall 2011), 48.

39. National Domestic Workers Alliance, University of Illinois at Chicago, and DataCenter, *Home Economics: The Invisible and Unregulated World of Domestic Work*, n.d., www.domesticworkers.org/homeeconomics/.

40. Hector L. Delgado, *New Immigrants, Old Unions: Organizing Undocumented Workers in Los Angeles* (Philadelphia: Temple, 1993), 134.

41. Ibid., 22.

42. Ibid., 17.

43. Marta Jimenez, Mexican American Legal Defense and Educational Fund attorney, interview by author, March 23, 1997, San Francisco.

44. "At Work, at Risk: Undocumented Latinos, Especially, Fear INS Visit," *Newsday: The Long Island Paper*, June 8, 1997; "The Big Payback: Area Advocacy Centers Help Latino Workers," *Newsday: The Long Island Paper*, January 7, 1996.

45. David Bacon, "Employer Sanctions," *Z Magazine*, July 2001, 13.

46. Gordon, "We Make the Road by Walking," 427.

47. "Organizing Low-Wage Immigrants," 100.

48. Letter from Brian McLaughlin, *New York Times*, September 29, 2000.

49. Steven Greenhouse, "A Union in Spirit," *New York Times*, August 11, 2013.

50. Carlos Pérez de Alejo, "Building a Better Austin from Below: Immigrant Workers Confront the Construction Industry in Texas' State Capital," *Dollars and Sense*, September/October 2009, 26–29.

51. Steven Greenhouse, "In Florida Tomato Fields, a Penny Buys Progress," *New York Times*, April 24, 2014. On the history of the CIW, see Silvia Giagnoni, *Fields of Resistance: The Struggle of Florida's Farmworkers for Justice* (Chicago: Haymarket Books, 2011).

52. Steven Greenhouse, "Farm Labor Groups Make Progress on Wages and Working

Conditions," *New York Times*, July 3, 2015.

53. Sara Jayaraman, *Behind the Kitchen Door* (Ithaca, NY: Cornell University Press, 2013).

54. Quotations from "Organize the South!" *Justice Speaks* 6, no. 11 (July 1989).

55. Jennie Bauduy, "New Groups Galvanise Communities for Workers' Rights," InterPress Service, November 19, 1995.

56. On activity within trade unions, see "NC AFL-CIO Convention Report," *Justice Speaks* 7, no. 3 (November 1989). On black leadership in unions, see "Organize the South!"

57. "International Unions Begin to Look South," *Justice Speaks* 9, no. 3 (December 1991); "CWA Organizing Raleigh City Workers," *Justice Speaks* 9, no. 4 (January/February 1992); "Organize Southern Public Service Workers," *Justice Speaks* 8, no. 7 (March 1991).

58. Gordon Dillahunt, "Workers' School in the Black Belt," *Southern Exposure* 13, no. 5 (September/October 1985): 10.

59. Myles Horton and Paulo Freire, *We Make the Road by Walking: Conversations on Education and Social Change*, ed. Brenda Bell, John Gaventa, and John Peters (Philadelphia: Temple University Press, 1990).

60. "Worker Labor Organizations: Unions from the Bottom Up!" *Justice Speaks* 11, no. 10 (June 1994).

61. "BWFJ Wins against Shoney's," *Justice Speaks* 5, no. 4 (January/February 1988).

62. Peter Perl, "Unionization Wins a Round in South: Unusual Coalition at Catfish Plant Overcomes Opposition," *Washington Post*, October 12, 1986.

63. "Shame on Delta Pride: Catfish Workers Strike," *Justice Speaks* 8, no. 3 (November 1990); Mary Hollens, "Catfish Workers Win Strike," *Labor Notes* 143 (February 1991).

64. "K-mart Workers Fight Back," *Justice Speaks* 13, no. 8 (April 1996). See also Robin D. G. Kelley, "Building Bridges: The Challenge of Organized Labor in Communities of Color," *New Labor Forum* 5 (Fall/Winter 1999): 42–58.

65. "African American Workers in NC Begin Nationwide Kmart Boycott," *Justice Speaks* 13, no. 6/7 (February/March 1996); "Kmart Workers Declare Victory!" *Justice Speaks* 14, no. 1 (September 1996).

66. "Radioactive Waste Site: Economic Blackmail," *Justice Speaks* 5, no. 8 (June 1988).

67. "Housekeepers' Organizing Pushes Minimum State Salary to $14,549," *Justice Speaks* 11, no. 6 (February 1994).

68. Saladin Muhammad, phone interview by author, September 16, 2003; Bob Kingsley, phone interview by author, September 8, 2003; quote from "UE Local 150 Demands Justice on UNC Campuses," *UE News*, February 1999.

69. Muhammad interview; Steve Bader, "'Pre-majority' Public Workers Union Makes Gains in North Carolina," *Labor Notes*, September 2002; "Service Workers: We Won't Run from This Attack," *UNC Prism*, n.d.

70. Muhammad interview; Dani McClain, "How the Moral Monday's 'Fusion Coalition' Is Taking North Carolina Back," *The Nation* (July 21, 2014), 23–25.

71. On community support, see letter from Dun and Lam of CSWA to supporters; "Shinwa Workers Fight against Racism," *CSWA News* 3, no. 1 (Winter 1992).

72. Anuradha Advani, "Against the Tide: Reflections on Organizing New York City's South Asian Taxicab Drivers," in *Making More Waves: New Writing by Asian American Women*, ed. Elaine H. Kim et al. (Boston: Beacon, 1997), 215–22; Somini Sengupta, "Deploring Giuliani Proposals, Cabbies Shun Fares for a Day," *New York Times*, May 14, 1998; Vijay Prashad, "Taxi Workers Strike Back," *Frontline* (Chennai, India) 15, no. 12 (June 6–19, 1998).

73. "Workers' Center Opens in Loisaida," *CSWA News* 3, no. 1 (Winter 1992).

74. "LWC Proposal to the Tides Foundation, 5/97," in author's possession; Mónica Santana and Pam Galpern, interviews by author, June 13, 1997, New York City.

75. See Nahar Alam, "Domestic Workers Do Their Homework," *SAMAR: South Asian Magazine for Action and Reflection* 8 (Summer/Fall 1997); Anannya Bhattacharjee, "Yellow Cabs, Brown People," *SAMAR*, Summer 1993; and Fine, "Workers Centers: Entering a New Stage of Growth," 48.

76. Louie, *Sweatshop Warriors*, 244 n15. See also Richard Sullivan and Kimi Lee, "Organizing Immigrant Women in America's Sweatshops: Lessons from the Los Angeles Garment Worker Center," *Signs* 33, no. 3 (Spring 2008): 527–32. On funding, see Matthew Blake, "U.S. Chamber of Commerce 'Exposes' Union Backing of Worker Centers," *In These Times* (February 27, 2014).

77. Fine, *Worker Centers: Organizing Communities at the Edge of the Dream*, 202, 232–33.

78. Sebastian Quinac, interview by author, June 13, 1997, New York City.

79. See "Former Slave and Sweatshop Laborers Demand Retailer Accountability," *KIWA News* 5 (Spring 1996), and KIWA's bilingual *Update / LA Noticia*.

80. Elizabeth Martínez, "Case Study: African American / Latino Alliance Born in North Carolina," *Z Magazine*, October 2000; Kim Diehl, "Black Belt Justice," *ColorLines* 3, no. 4 (Winter 2000–01); 2011 statistics are from the Pew Research Center's "Hispanic Trends," www.pewhispanic.org/states/state/nc/.

81. Louie, *Sweatshop Warriors*, 14–15.

82. Fine and Milkman, *U.S. Country Inventory of Informal Worker Organizing*; Janice Fine, "Non-union, Low-Wage Workers Are Finding a Voice as Immigrant Workers' Centers Grow," *Labor Notes*, August 2003.

83. Leah Wise, phone interview by author, October 30, 1996; "National Federation for Industrial Retention Formed," *Federation for Industrial Retention and Renewal News* 1, no. 1 (January 1989); SouthWest Organizing Project, *1981–1991: A Decade of Struggle for Justice* (Albuquerque, NM: Southwest Community Resources, n.d.).

84. "AFL-CIO and NDLON, Largest Organization of Worker Centers, Enter Watershed Agreement to Improve Conditions for Working Families," press release, August 9, 2006, www.aflcio.org/Press-Room/Press-Releases/AFL-CIO-and-NDLON-Largest-Organization-of-Worker. On NDWA, see Fine and Milkman, *U.S. Country Inventory of Informal Worker Organizing*, 8.

85. Goldberg Harmony and Randy Jackson, "The Excluded Workers Congress: Reimagining the Right to Organize," *New Labor Forum* 20, no. 3 (Fall 2011): 54–59; Eduardo Soriano-Castillo, "Excluded Workers, AFL-CIO Build Addition to the House of Labor," *Labor Notes*, May 11, 2011.

86. United Workers Congress, Background and Vision, www.unitedworkerscongress.org/

background--vision.html.

87. Jennifer Gordon, "The Campaign for the Unpaid Wages Prohibition Act: Latino Immigrants Change New York Wage Law," Carnegie Endowment for International Peace Working Papers (Washington, DC: Carnegie, 1999).

88. Jennifer Gordon, "Immigrants Fight the Power," *The Nation*, January 3, 2000, 16.

Chapter 6

1.   I attended the Jobs with Justice convention in Chicago (October 24–25, 1997) and the California Labor/Welfare Summit in San Francisco (September 26–27, 1997). Please note: Jobs *with* Justice (founded in 1986) is a different organization from Jobs *and* Justice (begun in 1978 and discussed in chapter 4).

2.   AFL-CIO Executive Council, "Welfare Reform and Union Representation," February 17, 1997.

3.   Frances Fox Piven, "The New Reserve Army of Labor," in *Audacious Democracy: Labor, Intellectuals, and the Social Reconstruction of America*, ed. Steven Fraser and Joshua B. Freeman (Boston: Houghton Mifflin, 1997), 114.

4.   Gwendolyn Mink, *Welfare's End* (Ithaca, NY: Cornell University Press, 1998).

5.   Aurelio Rojas, "Lifeline or Dead End? Debate Rages over Workfare Compensation," *San Francisco Chronicle*, February 16, 1998.

6.   "Employers Lapping Up Welfare Hiring Incentives," *Wall Street Journal*, April 23, 1997.

7.   Steven Greenhouse, "Many Workfare Participants Are Taking the Place of City Workers," *New York Times*, April 13, 1998; Annette Fuentes, "Slaves of New York," *In These Times*, December 23, 1996, 14–17.

8.   City of New York, "Mayor's Management Report," February 13, 1997, in author's possession; David Firestone, "New York Braces for Surge in Workfare Effort," *New York Times*, August 13, 1996.

9.   Edriss Anderson, interview by author, June 3, 1997, New York City.

10. "Ex-welfare Workers in Georgia Replaced with Prison Slaves," *Prison Legal News*, November 1999.

11. "Post-welfare Jobs No Cure for Poverty, Study Finds," *Los Angeles Times*, September 7, 2000; "Evidence Is Scant That Workfare Leads to Full-Time Jobs," *New York Times*, April 12, 1998. On job rates nationally, see Christopher Cook, "Turning Welfare Workers into City Employees," *Christian Science Monitor*, February 11, 1999.

12. Liz Krueger, Liz Accles, and Laura Wernick, *Workfare: The Real Deal II* (New York: Community Food Resource Center, 1997); Charles Tilly, *Workfare's Impact on the New York City Labor Market: Lower Wages and Worker Displacement* (New York: Russell Sage Foundation, 1996).

13. Melissa Healy, "N.Y. 'Workfare' Not So Fair after All, Some Say," *Los Angeles Times*, July 5, 1997.

14. Joe Sexton, "Discontented Workfare Laborers Murmur 'Union,'" *New York Times*, September 27, 1996.

15. Brenda Stewart, presentation at WEP Forum, New York City, May 28, 1997.

16. "Workfare Recipients Win Equal Protection," *New York Times*, February 17, 2004.

17. "Non-English Speakers Denied Welfare-to-Work Services, Suit Says," *Los Angeles*

Times, December 16, 1999.

18. "County Takes Steps to Avert Massive Foodstamp Cuts; Aid: Expanded 'Workfare' Program Will Help 63,000 Poor Adults," *Los Angeles Times*, November 28, 1996; "Wisconsin's Workfare Plan Establishes US Precedent," *Toronto Star*, April 26, 1996; "Brown Rebuffs Welfare Recipients' Union Proposal," *San Francisco Chronicle*, June 12, 1997.

19. Benjamin Dulchin and Sharryn Kasmir, "Organizing and Identity in the New York City Workfare Program," *Regional Labor Review*, Fall 2004.

20. Arthur Cheliotes, presentation at WEP Forum, New York City, May 28, 1997; Dominic Chan, interview by author, June 2, 1997, New York City; quote from Chan in "Union Friends Unite to Bash Foes," *New York Times*, November 22, 1996.

21. On Hill's reversal, see Steven Greenhouse, "Layoffs Rupture Tie between Giuliani and Labor Leader," *New York Times*, April 25, 1998. See also "Labor Leader Drops Demand on Workfare," *New York Times*, September 28, 1996; Joy Purnick, "On Workfare, Fig Leaves and Silence," *New York Times*, September 30, 1996; E. Assata Wright, "The Fight to Unionize Workfare Workers: Divided They Fall?" *Village Voice*, January 28, 1997; Steven Greenhouse, "Union Head Is Assailed on Workfare Concessions," *New York Times*, October 1, 1996.

22. Heidi Dorow and Arthur Poland, interviews by author, June 9, 1997, New York City; Milagros Silva, interview by author, August 6, 1997, New York City.

23. "Marchers Call on Giuliani to Support Workfare Union," *New York Times*, December 11, 1997; "Bronx up Close: Anger in Workfare Ranks," *New York Times*, June 1, 1997.

24. "Workfare Rights: Laborers Seek Union Benefits," *Newsday*, April 20, 1997; Silva interview.

25. Dorow and Silva interviews; phone conversation with Silva, August 6, 1998. WWT phased out its organizing less than a year later. A third, much smaller group, Workfareness, also briefly attempted to organize workfare workers in New York City.

26. "United Stance / Workfare Employees Vote Overwhelmingly to Unionize," *New York Newsday*, October 24, 1997; Amanda Ream, "New York Workfare Workers Vote Union," *Labor Notes* 225 (December 1997).

27. Stanley Hill, interview by author, June 2, 1997, New York City; quote from Steven Greenhouse, "Petitions Seek Vote on Union for Workfare: Organizing Group Says It Has 13,000 Signatures," *New York Times*, July 3, 1997.

28. This official, interviewed in 1998, requested anonymity.

29. "Top Court Says New York Can Continue Minimum Wage for Workfare," *New York Times*, February 23, 2000. More recently, the US Court of Appeals for the Second Circuit ruled that the Fair Labor Standards Act *does* apply to workfare participants. Bureau of National Affairs, "New York Public Assistance Recipient Is 'Employee' under FLSA, Court Says," *Government Employee Relations* 2051, no. 42 (March 23, 2004): 282; Kest quote from "He Fights, Patiently, for Workfare Laborers," *New York Times*, January 16, 1998.

30. Hill interview.

31. See n. 28 above.

32. Silva interview.
33. Steve Williams, phone interview by author, August 14, 1998; Emma Harris and Ilana Berger, interviews by author, December 10, 1997, San Francisco.
34. Williams interview.
35. Mooney quoted in Cook, "Turning Welfare Workers into City Employees."
36. Bale Butler, phone interview by author, August 20, 1998.
37. Richard A. Cloward and Francis Fox Piven, "Workers and Welfare: The Poor against Themselves," *The Nation*, November 25, 1968, 558–62.
38. Garth Ferguson, interview by author, July 11, 1998, San Francisco.
39. Butler interview.
40. David Turner, phone interview by author, August 30, 1998.
41. "Slaves of New York," *Wall Street Journal*, July 31, 1997.
42. Elly Leary, e-mail interview by author, August 8, 1998.
43. Nancy E. Rose, *Workfare or Fair Work: Women, Welfare and Government Work Programs* (New Brunswick, NJ: Rutgers University Press, 1995).
44. "Clinton Will Seek Tax Break to Ease Path off Welfare," *New York Times*, January 28, 1997; "Workfare," *Forbes*, November 4, 1996.
45. Michael B. Katz, *The Undeserving Poor: From the War on Poverty to the War on Welfare* (New York: Pantheon, 1989), 8.
46. Krueger, Accles, and Wernick, *Workfare*, 1–8.
47. "Nonprofit and Religious Groups Vow to Fight Workfare Program," *New York Times*, July 24, 1997.
48. Committee on Ways and Means, US House of Representatives, Table 8-25: Historical Trends in AFDC Enrollments and Average Payments, 1970–2001, in *1996 Green Book* (Washington, DC: Government Printing Office, 1996), 467.
49. "Maryland Shields Jobs from Welfare Law," *Washington Post*, May 4, 1997; "Workfare Must Pay Minimum Wage, White House Says," *Washington Post*, May 17, 1997; Cynthia Cheski, "Reforming Welfare," *Human Rights* 21, no. 4 (Fall 1994): 10–11, 42.
50. "Federal Suit Accuses City of Not Acting on Harassment Complaints in Workfare Jobs," *New York Times*, July 15, 2001.
51. Healy, "N.Y. 'Workfare' Not So Fair."
52. Leary interview.
53. David Weiner, phone interview by author, August 15, 1998; "ACORN and CWA: Combining Self-Interest around Welfare Reform," *Organizing* (Center for Community Change), June–July 1998.
54. Ed Sabol, phone interview by author, August 15, 1998.
55. *Workfare to Wages: A Bridge to Living Wage Jobs* (Oakland, CA: Applied Research Center, 1999).
56. Ellen Reese, *They Say Cutback, We Say Fight Back!* (New York: Russell Sage Foundation, 2011).
57. "L.A. Establishes First Workfare Grievance Process," *Colorlines Magazine*, Summer 2001; Jon Kest, phone interview by author, September 15, 2003.
58. Stewart, WEP Forum.
59. Welfare mothers at Montana's Working for Equality and Economic Liberation

organized in 2002 to get the state to pay low-income parents to care for their children at home. See "Safety Net Gains: Advocates Seek Creative Options for Welfare Reform," *Missoula Independent* 13, no. 28 (July 18, 2002): 9, and Vanessa Tait, "Expanding Labor's Vision: The Challenges of Workfare and Welfare Organizing," in *The Sex of Class: Women Transforming American Labor* (Ithaca, NY: ILR Press, 2007), 194–210.

60. Vijay Prashad, *Keeping Up with the Dow Joneses: Debt Prison, Workfare* (Boston: South End, 2003), 150.

61. Gary Delgado and Rebecca Gordon, "From Social Contract to Social Control: Welfare Policy and Race," in *From Poverty to Punishment: How Welfare Reform Punishes the Poor* (Oakland, CA: Applied Research Center, 2002), 38.

62. Kest interview.

63. Williams interview.

Chapter 7

1. Kim Moody, "Building a Labor Movement for the 1990s," in *Building Bridges: The Emerging Grassroots Coalition of Labor and Community*, ed. Jeremy Brecher and Tim Costello (New York: Monthly Review, 1990), 216–28.

2. Zach Nauth, "Cleaning House: Justice for Janitors Is Bringing Fresh Ideas—and New Members—to America's Labor Movement," *In These Times*, May 1, 1995, 18–21.

3. Camille Colatosti, "Police Give Janitors No Justice," *Labor Notes* 136 (July 1990): 1, 14.

4. Stephen Lerner, "Strategic Labor Organizing: How to Win against the Odds," *Dollars and Sense* 205 (May–June 1996): 32–38.

5. Richard W. Hurd and William Rouse, "Progressive Union Organizing: The SEIU Justice for Janitors Campaign," *Review of Radical Political Economics* 21, no. 3 (1989): 70–75.

6. "Roosevelt Bridge Blocked in Protest of DC Budget," *Washington Post*, September 21, 1995. Republican US representative Thomas M. Davis III later called the action "traffic terrorism" and increased financial penalties for such demonstrations (see "Rush-Hour Protests Assailed," *Washington Post*, October 7, 1995).

7. Stephen Lerner, "Reviving Unions: A Call to Action," *Boston Review* 21, no. 2 (April/May 1996) and 22, nos. 3/4 (Summer 1996). A photo of activists chained to the developer's headquarters is in the *Washington Post*, November 9, 1990; on tax cut, see "Janitors Union Expands Its Campaign," *Washington Post*, March 23, 1995.

8. Nauth, "Cleaning House," 21.

9. Michele Hoyman, "Working Women: The Potential of Unionization and Collective Action in the United States," *Women's Studies International Forum* 12, no. 1 (1989): 55; "Union, Women's Group Join to Gain Clerical Jobs," *Washington Post*, March 4, 1981.

10. Patricia Lee, "Sisters at the Borders: Asian Immigrant Women and HERE Local 2," in *Building Bridges: The Emerging Grassroots Coalition of Labor and Community*, ed. Jeremy Brecher and Tim Costello (New York: Monthly Review, 1990), 38–46.

11. Simon Greer, "Labor-Community Alliance Unionizes Carolina Resort," *Labor Notes* 189 (December 1994); Laura McClure, "Will the AFL-CIO Apply Grass-roots Wisdom?" *Z Magazine*, July/August 1996.

12. On UNITE and HERE, see Hector Figueroa, "The Growing Force of Latino Labor," *NACLA Report on the Americas* 30, no. 3 (November–December 1996): 19–25. On CWA, see Steve Early and Larry Cohen, "Jobs with Justice: Building a Broad-Based Movement for Workers' Rights," *Social Policy* 25, no. 2 (Winter 1994): 7–18.

13. "Mine Workers Say They'll Devote Half Their Resources to Organizing," *Labor Notes* 141 (December 1990).

14. Figueroa, "Growing Force of Latino Labor." For a longer view of the UFW's history, see also Bardacke, *Trampling Out the Vintage*.

15. Peter Olney, interview by author, January 13, 1996, Berkeley; "Stoppage by Truck-ers Shrivels Activity at California Ports," *Wall Street Journal*, May 2, 1996; Hector Delgado, "The Los Angeles Manufacturing Action Project: Lessons Learned, an Opportunity Squandered?" in *Organizing Immigrants: The Challenge for Unions in Contemporary California*, ed. Ruth Milkman (Ithaca, NY: ILR Press, 2000).

16. Tom Juravich and Jeff Hilgert, "UNITE's Victory at Richmark: Community-Based Union Organizing in Communities of Color," *Labor Studies Journal* 24, no. 1 (Spring 1999): 27–41.

17. See Rachel Sherman and Kim Voss, "'Organize or Die': Labor's New Tactics," in *Organizing Immigrants: The Challenge for Unions in Contemporary California*, ed. Ruth Milkman (Ithaca, NY: ILR Press, 2000), 103–05.

18. Richard Bensinger, "When We Try More, We Win More: Organizing the New Workforce," in *Not Your Father's Labor Movement: Inside the AFL-CIO*, ed. Jo-Ann Mort (London: Verso, 1998), 28.

19. Survey "Being Heard" by the firm of Greer, Margolis, Mitchell, Burns & Associ-ates, quoted in Harry Kelber, "Labortalk: AFL-CIO Shocked by Survey It Com-missioned," *Labor Educator*, December 18, 1994.

20. Barry Hirsch and David Macpherson, table 1a, in *Union Membership and Earn-ings Databook* (Washington, DC: Bureau of National Affairs, 2004), 11. On Great Depression unemployment, see *Historical Statistics of the United States, Colonial Times to 1970* (White Plains, NY: US Department of Commerce, Bureau of the Census, 1989).

21. Hirsch and Macpherson, tables 1b and 1f, in *Union Membership and Earnings Data Book*, 12, 16.

22. See William Tabb, "Urban Development and Regional Restructuring," in *Sunbelt, Snowbelt: Urban Development and Regional Restructuring*, ed. Larry Sawers and William Tabb (Oxford: Oxford University Press, 1984), 9. For an analysis of this phenomenon during the '70s, see Barry Bluestone, Bennett Harrison, and Lawrence Baker, *Corporate Flight: The Causes and Consequences of Economic Dis-location* (Washington, DC: Progressive Alliance, 1981), 26.

23. Hirsch and Macpherson, tables 1d and 1e, in *Union Membership and Earnings Data Book*, 14, 15.

24. John J. Sweeney, Richard Trumka, and Linda Chavez-Thompson, "Rebuilding

the American Labor Movement: A New Voice for American Workers," June 28, 1995, in author's possession.

25. "Union Push Shows Scant Payoff for American Labor Work," *Los Angeles Times*, November 8, 1997.

26. Sweeney, Trunka, and Chavez-Thompson, "Rebuilding the American Labor Movement."

27. Ibid.

28. Paul Buhle, *Taking Care of Business: Samuel Gompers, George Meany, Lane Kirkland and the Tragedy of American Labor* (New York: Monthly Review, 1999), 205.

29. "Organizing Program Seeks Innovation," *AFL-CIO News*, March 8, 1996.

30. Kim Moody, "Up against the Polyester Ceiling: The 'New' AFL-CIO Organizes—*Itself!*" *New Politics* 6, n.s. no. 4, whole no. 24 (Winter 1998): 12.

31. AFL-CIO Elected Leadership Task Force on Organizing, "Organizing for Change, Changing to Organize!" (1996), in author's possession.

32. McClure, "Will the AFL-CIO Apply Grassroots Wisdom?"

33. Ibid.

34. Jeremy Brecher and Tim Costello, "A New Labor Movement in the Shell of the Old? Part 2, The Future of the Reform Agenda," *Z Magazine*, May 1996.

35. "AFL-CIO to Step Up Efforts," *Boston Globe*, December 17, 1996; Russ Davis, "AFL-CIO Unveils Program to Revitalize Labor Movement," *Labor Notes* 216 (March 1997).

36. Moody, "Up against the Polyester Ceiling," 6.

37. Fernando Gapasin and Michael Yates, "Organizing the Unorganized: Will Promises Become Practices?" *Monthly Review* 49, no. 3 (July–August 1997): 48.

38. JoAnn Wypijewski, "Subject: Union Time," *The Nation*, October 3, 1997; Moody, "Up against the Polyester Ceiling," 6; Robert Fitch, "Labor Pain," *The Nation*, November 25, 1996, 27.

39. Wypijewski, "Subject: Union Time."

40. Gapasin and Yates, "Organizing the Unorganized," 58.

41. Ibid., 47. Fitch, "Labor Pain," 26, quotes a source at SEIU who says the union organized only 200,000 new members between 1985 and 1996, even though its membership nearly doubled during those years; Fitch claims the balance was made up by affiliations of independent unions.

42. Janice Fine, "Non-union, Low-Wage Workers Are Finding a Voice as Immigrant Workers Centers Grow," *Labor Notes*, August 2003.

43. Steve Early, "New Organizing Should Be Membership-Based," *Labor Notes* 205 (April 1996). See also Early's "Thoughts on the 'Worker-Student Alliance'— Then and Now," *Labor History* 44, no. 1 (February 2003): 5–13.

44. Dan Clawson, *The Next Upsurge: Labor and the New Social Movements* (Ithaca, NY: ILR Press, 2003), 22–23.

45. Early, "New Organizing."

46. Kate Bronfenbrenner and Tom Juravich, "It Takes More Than House Calls: Organizing to Win with a Comprehensive Union-Building Strategy," in *Organizing to Win: New Research on Union Strategies*, ed. Kate Bronfenbrenner et al. (Ithaca, NY: ILR Press, 1998), 19–36.

47. Moody, "Up against the Polyester Ceiling," 10.

48. See Steve Early, *The Civil Wars in U.S. Labor* (Chicago, IL: Haymarket, 2011), and Cal Winslow, *Labor's Civil War in California: The NUHW Healthcare Workers' Rebellion* (Oakland, CA: PM Press, 2010).

49. Nauth, "Cleaning House," 21.

50. Roger Waldinger et al., "Helots No More: A Case Study of the Justice for Janitors Campaign in Los Angeles," in *Organizing to Win: New Research on Union Strategies*, ed. Kate Bronfenbrenner et al. (Ithaca, NY: ILR Press, 1998), 112–13.

51. "Organizing in the South: A New Day, or a Replay?" *Justice Speaks*, October 1996.

52. On democracy movements in the '70s and '80s, see Kim Moody, *An Injury to All: The Decline of American Unionism* (London: Verso, 1988), 221–47. On SEIU, see Martha Gruelle, "Service Employees Open Debate on Their Union," *Labor Notes* 204 (March 1996); Bob Fitch, "Sweeney among the Warlords," *New Politics* 6, no. 2 (Winter 1997): 152–58; and Michael Hirsch, "Job Selling at the Janitor's Local," *New Politics* 6, no. 2 (Winter 1997): 159–61.

53. Harry Kelber, "How to Democratize the AFL-CIO," *Labor Notes* 196 (July 1995).

54. For instance, see Sal Rosselli, "One Member, One Vote: Let's Have Direct Elections for AFL-CIO Officers," *Labor Notes* 197 (August 1995).

55. Martha Gruelle, "Black Unionists Demand Meat on 'Diversity' Bones," *Labor Notes* 199 (October 1995).

56. Susan Stanton, "'No Money, No Suits': New Clerical Union Ousts AFSCME at University of California," *Labor Notes* 225 (December 1997): 3. On UPTE, see Steve Early, "Membership-Based Organizing," in *A New Labor Movement for the New Century*, ed. Gregory Mantsios (New York: Monthly Review Press, 1998), 93–94. I am a member and staffer in UPTE-CWA and was previously an elected official in AFSCME and a founding member of CUE.

57. "Coalition of University Employees," in *The New Rank and File*, ed. Staughton Lynd and Alice Lynd (Ithaca, NY: ILR Press, 2000), 230–42; Stanton, "'No Money, No Suits'."

58. Michael-David Sasson and Margy Wilkinson, "Cross-Union Solidarity Boosts Clerical Workers on Strike," *Labor Notes*, September 30, 2002.

59. Teamsters for a Democratic Union, "Hoffa Moves toward Trusteeship in Newest Teamster Local" (March 15, 2012), www.tdu.org/hoffa-moves-toward-trusteeship-newest-teamster-local.

60. David Bacon, "Los Angeles Janitors Leave Local 399" (February 18, 2002), http://dbacon.igc.org/Unions/29LAJanitors.htm.

61. "What? The Members Want to Run the Union?" *Labor Notes* 197 (August 1995).

62. Quote in Jane Williams, "Restructuring Labor's Identity: The Justice for Janitors Campaign in Washington, DC," in *The Transformation of US Unions: Voices, Visions and Strategies from the Grassroots*, ed. Ray M. Tillman and Michael S. Cummings (Boulder, CO: Lynne Rienner, 1999).

63. Michael Baratz, phone interview by author, May 21, 2004.

64. Trusteeship statistics courtesy of Steve Early, who obtained them directly from SEIU.

65. Richard Leung, phone interview by author, September 19, 2003.

66. Ibid.; Williams, "Restructuring Labor's Identity," 213–15.

67. Olga Miranda, interviews by author, September 19, 2003, and August 30, 2004, Berkeley; Bureau of National Affairs, "San Francisco Janitors Reject SEIU in Favor of United Service Workers for Democracy," *Labor Relations Weekly* 18 (2004): 118.

68. Stephen Lerner, "Three Steps to Reorganizing and Rebuilding the Labor Movement: Building New Strength and Unity for All Working Families," *Labor Notes*, December 2002.

69. Sweeney, Trumka, and Chavez-Thompson, "Rebuilding the American Labor Movement."

70. *There Once Was a Rally in Miami*, Jobs with Justice pamphlet; Steve Early and Larry Cohen, "Jobs with Justice: Mobilizing Labor-Community Coalitions, *WorkingUSA*, November/December 1997, 49–57; Eric Larson, ed., *Jobs with Justice: 25 Years, 25 Voices* (Oakland, CA: PM Press, 2013).

71. Steve Early and Larry Cohen, "Jobs with Justice: Building a Broad-Based Movement for Workers' Rights; "Welfare Day of Action," editorial, *The Nation*, December 15, 1997, 7–8; Fred Azcarate, interview by author, Chicago, October 25, 1997, and phone interview by author, December 9, 1997.

72. Russ Davis, "Activists Plan Workfare Day of Action, Discuss Relationship with AFL-CIO," *Labor Notes* 225 (December 1997). Quote and financial figures from Suzanne Gordon, "New AFL-CIO Offers Praise—and Pennies—for Jobs with Justice," *Labor Notes* 216 (March 1997).

73. Jeremy Smith, "Jobs with Justice Activists Hope for Warming Relationship with AFL-CIO," *Labor Notes* 209 (August 1996); see also Early, "Membership-Based Organizing," n. 16.

74. Carol Zabin and Isaac Martin, *Living Wage Campaigns in the Economic Policy Arena: Four Case Studies from California* (New York: New World Foundation, 1999); Peter Dreier, "Why the Housing Movement and Organized Labor Need Each Other," *Shelterforce*, May/June 2000, 8–11, 29.

75. Angela Glover Blackwell and Kalima Rose, "Overcoming the Obstacles: Forging Effective Labor-Community Alliances," *New Labor Forum* 5 (Fall/Winter 1999): 59–67.

76. Janice Fine, "Community Unionism in Baltimore and Stamford," *WorkingUSA*, Winter 2000–01, 59–85.

77. Daniel HoSang, "All the Issues in Workers' Lives: Labor Confronts Race in Stamford," *Shelterforce*, May/June 2000.

78. Clawson, *Next Upsurge*.

79. "Union Welcomes 75,000 in Largest Addition Ever," *Chicago Tribune*, February 26, 1999; "A New Union Wave Gathers Momentum in California," *Christian Science Monitor*, March 15, 1999.

80. *The American Work Force: 1992–2005* (Washington, DC: Department of Labor, Bureau of Labor Statistics, 1994), 47.

81. Linda Delp and Katie Quan, "Homecare Worker Organizing in California: An Analysis of a Successful Strategy," *Labor Studies Journal* 27, no. 1 (Spring 2002): 1–23; Fred P. Brooks, "New Turf for Organizing Family Child Care Providers," *Labor Studies Journal* 29, no. 4 (Winter 2005): 45–64. On membership numbers,

see Michelle Chen, "Shouldn't Home Care Workers Earn a Living Wage?" *The Nation*, June 29, 2015.

82. Early, "Thoughts on the 'Worker-Student Alliance,'" 8.

83. Bensinger, "When We Try More, We Win More," 27.

84. Union growth in Hirsch and Macpherson, "AFL-CIO Membership Data," in *Union Membership and Earnings Data Book*. For membership rates, Hirsch and Macpherson, table 1a, in *Union Membership and Earnings Data Book*, 11.

85. Steve Early, "AFL-CIO's Organizing Summit Looks at 'Best Practices'—But Leaves Much Unexamined," *Labor Notes*, February 2003.

86. Andrew Stern, "United We Win," internal memo, in author's possession, and second revised memo dated January 8, 2003; Aaron Bernstein, "Breaking Ranks with the AFL-CIO," *Business Week*, September 15, 2003.

87. JoAnn Wypijewski, "The New Unity Partnership: A Manifest Destiny for Labor," *Counterpunch*, October 6, 2003, www.counterpunch.org/2003/10/06/the-new -unity-partnership-a-manifest-destiny-for-labor/.

88. Larry Cohen, "Collective Bargaining Is the Priority," *New Labor Forum* 14, no. 1 (Spring 2005): 68–71.

89. Open letter signed by twelve AFL-CIO Central Labor Council presidents, undated flyer in author's possession.

90. William Johnson, "The UNITE-HERE Merger: Is It a Step Forward . . . or Business as Usual?" *Labor Notes*, April 2004.

91. Bill Fletcher Jr. and Fernando Gapasin, *Solidarity Divided: The Crisis in Organized Labor and a New Path toward Social Jusice* (Berkeley: University of California Press, 2008), 152.

92. "United We Win" internal memo; see also Harold Meyerson, "Organize or Die," *American Prospect*, September 2003, 42; and William Johnson and Chris Kutalik, "New Unity Partnership: Five Union Presidents Launch Big to 'Revolutionize' AFL-CIO," *Labor Notes*, October 2003.

93. Harold Meyerson, "Time's Up for the NUP," *American Prospect*, January 18, 2005.

94. Herman Benson, "Sweeney Critics Would Bureaucratize to Organize," *Union Democracy Review*, no. 149 (December 2003/January 2004).

95. Mark Brenner, "Longshore Union Quits the AFL-CIO," *Labor Notes*, August 31, 2013. On union disputes, see Early, *The Civil Wars in U.S. Labor*.

96. Wypijewski, "New Unity Partnership."

97. "Union Member Summary," Bureau of Labor Statistics, January 2015. In 2015 union membership increased nationwide by 219,000 workers, but after accounting for job growth, the unionization rate remained at 11.1 percent." (See Bureau of Labor Statistics, News Release: Union Members – 2015, http://www.bls.gov /news.release/pdf/union2.pdf).

98. Fletcher and Gapasin, *Solidarity Divided*, 168.

99. "AFL-CIO and NDLON, Largest Organization of Worker Centers, Enter Watershed Agreement to Improve Conditions for Working Families," press release, August 9, 2006, www.aflcio.org/Press-Room/Press-Releases/AFL-CIO-and -NDLON-Largest-Organization-of-Worker.

100. Richard Trumka, remarks to National Press Club, January 11, 2010,

www.aflcio.org/Press-Room/Speeches/Remarks-by-Richard-L.-Trumka
-President-of-the-AFL-CIO-National-Press-Club-Washington-D.C.

101. Josh Eidelson, "A Reboot for the AFL-CIO?" *The Nation*, September 23, 2013.

102. Jeff Crosby and Bill Fletcher Jr., "Viewpoint: AFL-CIO Convention Repositions Unions to Speak for All Workers," *Labor Notes*, October 17, 2013.

103. Steve Early, "House of Labor Needs Repairs, Not Just New Roommates," *Labor Notes*, September 16, 2013; Peter Olney, "AFL-CIO Follows Path of Least Resistance," *Labor Notes*, October 23, 2013.

104. Harold Meyerson, "At AFL-CIO Convention, Labor Embraces the New America," *Washington Post*, September 10, 2013.

105. Mari Jo Buhle and Paul Buhle, eds., *It Started in Wisconsin: Dispatches from the Front Lines of the New Labor Protest* (London: Verso, 2011).

106. Bureau of Labor Statistics, "Economic News Release." For historical statistics, see Hirsch and Macpherson, "Union Membership, Coverage, Density, and Employment Among Public Sector Workers, 1973–2014," in *Union Membership and Coverage Database from the CPS*, www.unionstats.com.

107. Micah Uetricht, *Strike for America: Chicago Teachers against Austerity* (London: Verso, 2015).

108. Joe Berry, *Reclaiming the Ivory Tower* (New York: Monthly Review Press and North American Alliance for Fair Employment, 2005); Lance Compa, "Labor at a Crossroads: How Unions Can Thrive in the 21st Century," *American Prospect*, January 27, 2015.

109. Steve Greenhouse, "The Rapid Success of Fight for $15: 'This Is a Trend That Cannot Be Stopped,'" *Guardian*, July 24, 2015.

110. Jenny Brown, "Fast Food Strikes: What's Cooking?" *Labor Notes*, June 23, 2013.

111. Trish Kahle, "Betting on Militancy," *Jacobin*, October 2013, www.jacobinmag.com/2013/10/beyond-fast-food-strikes/.

112. Steven Greenhouse, "Strong Voice in the Fast-Food Fight for $15 an Hour," *New York Times*, December 5, 2014; Jim Young, "15 versus the Five-O," *The Nation*, September 29, 2014.

113. Steven Greenhouse and Jana Kasperkevic, "Fight for $15 Swells into Largest Protest by Low-Wage Workers in US History," *Guardian*, April 15, 2015.

114. Nolan Feeney, "Burger King Founder Says Higher Wages Could Kill Off 'Dollar Menus,'" *Time*, April 20, 2015; David Card and Alan B. Drueger, "Minimum Wages and Employment: A Case Study of the Fast-Food Industry in New Jersey and Pennsylvania," *American Economic Review* 84, no. 4 (September 2014), 772–93.

115. Patrick McGeehan, "New York Plans $15-an-Hour Wage for Fast Food Workers," *New York Times*, July 22, 2015.

116. Tianyi Dong, "UC Minimum Wage Will Rise to $15 per Hour in 2017," *Daily Californian*, July 22, 2015.

117. Arun Gupta, "Fight for 15 Confidential: How Did the Biggest-Ever Mobilization of Fast-Food Workers Come About, and What Is Its Endgame?" *In These Times*, December 2013; see also Micah Uetricht, "Is the Fight for 15 Real?" *In These Times*, September 19, 2013.

118. Kahle, "Betting on Militancy."

119. Eidelson, "Reboot for the AFL-CIO?"

Conclusion

1. Julie Quiroz-Martínez, "Let Freedom Roll: Immigrants Hit the Road for Civil Rights," *The Nation*, October 27, 2003, 13.

2. James Parks, "The Immigrant Workers Freedom Ride: What Made It Work?" *America@Work*, April 2004.

3. See, for instance, Jeremy Brecher and Tim Costello, *Global Village or Global Pillage: Economic Reconstruction from the Bottom Up* (Boston: South End, 1994); Immanuel Ness, ed., *New Forms of Worker Organization* (Oakland, CA: PM Press, 2014); Peter Evans, "Is It Labor's Turn to Globalize? Twenty-First Century Opportunities and Strategic Responses," *Global Labour Journal* 1, no. 3 (2010): 352–79.

4. On economic justice movements around the world, see Sheila Rowbotham and Swasti Mitter, *Dignity and Daily Bread: New Forms of Economic Organizing among Poor Women in the Third World and the First* (London: Routledge, 1994); Jeremy Brecher, John Brown Childs, and Jill Cutler, eds., *Global Visions: Beyond the New World Order* (Boston: South End, 1993). On the Brazilian Workers' Party, see Jorge Castañeda, *Utopia Unarmed: The Latin American Left after the Cold War* (New York: Alfred A. Knopf, 1993). On workers' opposition to ecological destruction, see Arundhati Roy, *The Cost of Living* (New York: Modern Library, 1999). On SEWA, see Kalima Rose, *Where Women Are Leaders: The SEWA Movement in India* (London: Zed, 1992).

5. For more on this concept, see Robin D. G. Kelley, *Race Rebels: Culture, Politics, and the Black Working Class* (New York: Free Press, 1994); James C. Scott, *Domination and the Arts of Resistance: Hidden Transcripts* (New Haven, CT: Yale University Press, 1990).

6. Michael E. Gordon and Lowell Turner, eds., *Transnational Cooperation among Labor Unions* (Ithaca, NY: ILR Press, 2000).

7. Victor Narro, "Impacting Next Wave Organizing: Creative Campaign Strategies of the Los Angeles Worker Centers," *New York Law School Law Review*, no. 2 (2005–06), 465–514; on United Workers Congress, see www.unitedworkerscongress.org; on POWER, Steve Williams, phone interview by author, September 5, 2003.

8. Evans, "Is It Labor's Turn to Globalize?"

9. See laborrights.org/labor-rights-defender-communications-workers-america.

10. Peter Evans, "National Labor Movements and Transnational Connections: Global Labor's Evolving Architecture under Neoliberalism," IRLE Working Paper 116-14 (September 2014); Jamie K. McCallum, *Global Unions, Local Power: The New Spirit of Transnational Labor Organizing* (Ithaca, NY: ILR Press, 2013).

11. Manning Marable, *Race, Reform, and Rebellion: The Second Reconstruction in Black America, 1945–1990* (Jackson: University Press of Mississippi, 1991), 114.

12. Michael Honey, *Southern Labor and Black Civil Rights: Organizing Memphis Workers* (Chicago: University of Illinois Press, 1993); Robert Korstad and Nelson Lichtenstein, "Opportunities Found and Lost: Labor, Radicals, and the Early

Civil Rights Movement," *Journal of American History*, December 1988, 786–811.

13. See, for instance, John Brown Childs, *Transcommunality: From the Politics of Conversation to the Ethics of Respect* (Philadelphia: Temple University Press, 2003), and George Katsiaficas, *The Imagination of the New Left* (Boston: South End, 1987).

14. Aldon D. Morris, *The Origins of the Civil Rights Movement: Black Communities Organizing for Change* (New York: Free Press, 1984).

15. For analysis of some current campaigns, see Lee H. Adler, Maite Tapia, and Lowell Turner, eds., *Mobilizing against Inequality: Unions, Immigrant Workers and the Crisis of Capitalism* (Ithaca, NY: Cornell University Press, 2014).

16. See, for instance, Els de Graauw's account of coalitional work in San Francisco on living and minimum wage laws, "Nonprofits and Organizational Collaborations to Promote Local Labor Rights Policies," *WorkingUSA* 18 (March 2015): 103–26.

17. Howard Wial, "The Emerging Organizational Structure of Unionism in Low-Wage Services," *Rutgers Law Review* 45, no. 671 (Spring 1993): 671–738.

18. Bill Fletcher Jr. and Richard W. Hurd, "Is Organizing Enough? Race, Gender and Union Culture," *New Labor Forum*, Spring/Summer 2000.

19. For a concise how-to manual on democratic unionism, see Mike Parker and Martha Gruelle, *Democracy Is Power* (Detroit: Labor Education and Research Project, 1999).

Afterword

1. Emily Timm and Amy Price, *Build a Better Texas: Construction Working Conditions in the Lone Star State* (Austin: University of Texas at Austin, Division of Diversity and Community Engagement, 2013).

2. Ibid.

3. "Union Member Summary," Bureau of Labor Statistics, January 2015.

4. Organisation for Economic Co-operation and Development, "Employment Outlook Report," 2014, www.keepeek.com/Digital-Asset-Management/oecd/employment/oecd-employment-outlook-2014_empl_outlook-2014-en#page289.

5. Texas is one of only two states that don't require employers to carry workers' compensation coverage for workers. There is no state law that guarantees workers the right to rest breaks, and state law preempts local governments from creating their own living-wage regulations.

Index

289

--

About the Authors

Journalist and labor activist Vanessa Tait received her PhD in sociology from the University of California, Santa Cruz. Her writings have appeared in *New Labor Forum, Critical Sociology*, the *Boston Phoenix*, and the *Guardian*. Her radio work appears regularly on KPFA/Pacifica.

Bill Fletcher Jr. has been an activist since his teen years. Upon graduating from college he went to work as a welder in a shipyard, thereby entering the labor movement. Over the years he has been active in workplace and community struggles as well as electoral campaigns. He has worked for several labor unions in addition to serving as a senior staffperson in the national AFL-CIO. Fletcher is the coauthor (with Peter Agard) of *The Indispensable Ally: Black Workers and the Formation of the Congress of Industrial Organizations, 1934–1941*; the coauthor (with Dr. Fernando Gapasin) of *Solidarity Divided: The Crisis in Organized Labor and a New Path toward Social Justice*; and the author of *"They're Bankrupting Us!" and 20 Other Myths about Unions*. Fletcher is a syndicated columnist and a regular media commentator on television, radio, and the Web.

Cristina Tzintzún is the founder of Workers Defense Project (WDP), a statewide, membership-based workers' rights organization that is winning better working conditions for Texans. At WDP, Tzintzún has spearheaded efforts to ensure safe and dignified jobs for the nearly 900,000 construction workers that labor in the state. She also coedited *Presente!: Latin@ Immigrant Voices in the Struggle for Racial Justice / Voces Inmigrantes Latin@s en la Lucha por la Justicia Racial*.